The Arc of Spirituality

The Arc of Spirituality

The Western Love Affair with God

Robert P. Vande Kappelle

WIPF & STOCK · Eugene, Oregon

THE ARC OF SPIRITUALITY
The Western Love Affair with God

Copyright © 2021 Robert P. Vande Kappelle. All rights reserved. Except for brief quotations in critical publications or reviews, no part of this book may be reproduced in any manner without prior written permission from the publisher. Write: Permissions, Wipf and Stock Publishers, 199 W. 8th Ave., Suite 3, Eugene, OR 97401.

Wipf & Stock
An Imprint of Wipf and Stock Publishers
199 W. 8th Ave., Suite 3
Eugene, OR 97401

www.wipfandstock.com

PAPERBACK ISBN: 978-1-6667-3177-4
HARDCOVER ISBN: 978-1-6667-2466-0
EBOOK ISBN: 978-1-6667-2467-7

09/14/21

Unless otherwise indicated, all Scripture quotations are taken from the New Revised Standard Version Bible, copyright © 1989 the Division of Christian Education of the National Council of the Churches of Christ in the United States of America. Used by permission. All rights reserved.

Contents

1 Introduction | 1
2 Covenant Spirituality: Ancient Israelite Piety | 11
3 Wisdom Spirituality: Postexilic Jewish Piety | 28
4 Apocalyptic Spirituality: Early Christian Piety | 43
5 Mystic Spirituality: Early Medieval Christian Piety | 60
6 Penitential Spirituality: Late Medieval and Renaissance Christian Piety | 76
7 Faith Spirituality: Reformation Piety | 89
8 Pietist Spirituality: Romantic Piety | 105
9 Existentialist and Neo-Orthodox Spirituality: Nineteenth- and Twentieth-Century Piety | 121
10 Ethical Spirituality: Enlightenment, Liberal, and Late Neo-Orthodox Piety | 139
11 Fundamentalist Spirituality: Late Nineteenth- and Twentieth-Century Piety | 155
12 Ecumenical, Pluralist, and Eco–Spirituality | 171
13 Secular Spirituality: Late Twentieth- and Twenty-First-Century Piety | 187

Epilogue | 204
Bibliography | 207
Index | 213

1

Introduction

HUMAN EXISTENCE IS FILLED with mental and emotional tension, much of it caused by conflict and polarity. In fact, one cannot live without conflict, and the secret of life is learning to embrace and somehow reconcile one's polarities. To do so successfully requires spirituality. Without spirituality, human beings find themselves trapped in cycles of boredom, irritation, and discontent. By spirituality, I don't mean religion, though they are related.

In the past, people of faith rarely distinguished between being religious and being spiritual. Actually, they rarely used the terms "spiritual" or "spirituality," collapsing them under the broader category of religion. What we call spirituality today they might have called "piety," analogous to "being religious." Today, the terms "spiritual" and "spirituality" are in vogue, as opposed to the term" religious," which, like "piety," is often used negatively or pejoratively as a synonym for "religiosity."

In recent studies, religious pollsters in a number of countries have begun asking people whether they consider themselves "spiritual but *not* religious; religious but *not* spiritual; religious *and* spiritual; or *not* spiritual and *not* religious." The most surprising result is to the first option. In the United States, 30 percent of adults declared they were "spiritual but not religious." In Canada, 40 percent selected this choice, and in England, as many as 51 percent understand themselves in this way. In 2009, Princeton Survey Research Associates found that only 9 percent of Americans considered themselves "religious but not spiritual," while some 48 percent viewed themselves as "religious and spiritual." The World Values Survey, associated with the University of Michigan, found that in many developed nations, as high as 70 percent of the population self-defined as "generalized spirituality in contrast to traditional religions."[1] As these polls demonstrate, the word "spiritual" is far more appealing in post-Christian societies than the term "religious."

In her seminars across the United States, American church historian Diana Bass discovered that only 6 percent of the attendees self-identify as "religious only," 20 percent say they are "spiritual but not religious," while 72 percent of those who claim affiliation with a religious denomination consider themselves "spiritual and religious."[2]

While most Americans see themselves as both religious and spiritual, this has not always been the case. As recently as 1999, Gallup polled Americans asking whether they considered themselves to be spiritual or religious. At that time, 54 percent of the respondents answered "religious only," while only 6 percent answered "both spiritual and religious." Only ten years later, a *Newsweek* poll showed 9 percent answering "religious only," while 48 percent answered "both spiritual and religious." In both cases, the figures for "spiritual only" (30 percent) and "neither spiritual nor religious" (9 percent) remained the same.

In *Christianity After Religion*, Bass notes that for much of Western history, the words "religious" and "spiritual" meant roughly the same thing, namely, how humans relate with God through rituals, practices, and communal worship. However, the popular meaning of the words diverged during the twentieth century. The word "spiritual" gradually came to be associated with the private realm of thought and experience, while the word "religious" came to be connected with the public realm of membership in religious institutions, participation in formal ritual, and adherence to official denominational doctrines. In general, "spirituality" came to take a positive and attractive meaning, as somehow authentic, whereas "religious" took on a more negative connotation.

For traditionalists, the term "spirituality" suggests something vague or vacuous, lacking substance and consistency. Spirituality, however, is neither vague nor meaningless. While it lacks precision, the word "spiritual" is both a critique of institutional religion and a longing for meaningful correction. The following partial list helps distinguish these categories.

---

1. Bass, *Christianity After Religion*, 66.
2. Bass, *Christianity After Religion*, 92.

Religion	Spirituality
institution	experience
order	searching
dogma	intuition
defined	open
principles	wisdom
boundaries	inclusive
certainty	doubt

Based on these distinctions, we can begin treating the terms "religion/religious" and "spirituality/spiritual" as polarities, and we can analyze the topic of spirituality, as it developed historically, through the prism or lens of polarities. In other words, we can best describe a historical phase of spirituality by understanding the polarities emphasized by its practitioners. The following partial list helps distinguish these polarities.

Religion	Spirituality
realism	idealism
communalism	individualism
conformity	nonconformity
rationalism/reason	mysticism/intuition
clarity	ambiguity
dualism	nondualism
conservatism	liberalism

Speaking of polarities, we need to distinguish this mindset from dualistic thinking, a feature in human consciousness manifested in conventional religious thought. Unlike polarities evident in logic and morality, dualistic thinking refers to a mindset that perceives reality as divided into opposing metaphysical entities such as good versus evil, spirit versus matter, and God versus Satan. Nondualist or holistic thinking does accept the existence of opposites or distinctions in nature, such as maleness and femaleness, lightness and darkness, active and passive, but they are viewed on a continuum and thus, as interrelated.

This ultimate relatedness of all things in the universe is best exemplified by the striking Eastern concept called the Tao (pronounced dhow), which speaks of "the way" of reality, the orderly movement of the natural world according to the principle of yin and yang. This is best depicted by the famous Chinese symbol of a circle divided by a backward or reverse S into light and dark (or red and yellow) areas. According to Taoist teaching, yin is the negative force in nature. Understood as passive, it is seen in darkness, coolness, dampness, and femaleness, and is represented by earth, specifically by the moon. Yang is the positive force in nature. Understood as active, it is seen in lightness, warmth, dryness, maleness, and is represented by heaven, specifically by the sun.

All things are on a continuum between yin and yang. For instance, all males have some yin, and all females some yang. These forces are not confined to humans, nor are they static. A rotting tree is said to be losing yang and becoming damp and therefore more yin. No value judgment is given to yin and yang, for neither is better than the other, and neither is solely good or solely evil. Except for a few objects, such as the sun and the earth, which in their totality are yin or yang, the rest of nature, and even events, are a combination. When the two forces work together in harmony, life is as it should be.

Because human brains are hardwired to think in binary or dualistic ways, religious scholar Cantwell Smith distinguished between "conflict dualism" and "complementary dualism." In ancient Mesopotamia, as evident in Zoroastrianism and Manicheism, we find the ideology of conflict dualism, where opposites such as good and evil or God and Satan are locked in constant war. Such ideas influenced Judaism, Christianity, and Islam, based on Greek and Western logic, in which opposites cannot be reconciled. Eastern logic, as exemplified in Taoism and certain forms of Hinduism and Buddhism, emphasizes complementary dualism (nondualist thinking).

The brilliant word, nonduality (*advaita* in Sanskrit), is used by many different traditions, both Eastern and Western, to distinguish from monism, a perspective that erases all diversity and difference, reducing all things to one sameness. Nondualism celebrates difference and affirms diversity. It simply refuses to see this diversity as anything other than the greater unity of a singular Reality.

When referring to nondualism, Cantwell Smith spoke of complementary dualism, but the underlying reality is the same. In nature, things appear as opposites, not to conflict with one another but rather to complement each other. In everything they see, think, and experience, nondualists find the dimension of the other.

C. S. Lewis seems to have had this in mind when he identified universal truths in concepts such as the Tao (the Way) in ancient China and *rita* (divine Law or Truth) in early Hinduism.³ In Hinduism, *rita* is the principle of natural order that regulates and coordinates the operation of the universe and everything in it. Likewise the Chinese speak of the Tao as the essence of reality or the Way of the universe. The ancient Jews conceived of Torah as way, truth, and life. The author of the gospel of John seems to allude to this notion of a universal principle of natural order when he speaks of Jesus as the Logos (the divine Word) in John 1:1, 14 and as the Way, the Truth, and the Life in 14:6.

Spirituality: The Journey of Life

While we can define religion or theology with some degree of meaning and specificity, the word "spirituality" is often used traditionally with little or no clear meaning, or in a broad and vague manner. In antiquity, the word was not used, and when first introduced in the English-speaking world, it referred to the clergy, specifically to the ecclesiastical vocation, as distinct from secular or temporal vocations. From this sixteenth-century usage, the term came to describe spiritual as distinct from material things, including spirits, ghosts, or souls.

The meaning of a religious way of life, notably one's piety or acts of religious devotion, came still later, although its use in Ignatius Loyola's *Spiritual Exercises* referred to the practice of piety and more specifically, techniques of devotion. When first used in the French-speaking world, the term "spirituality" was a term of reproach, associated with mystical or

---

3. Lewis, *Abolition of Man*, 27–29. In an appendix, "Illustrations of the Tao," Lewis examines eight examples of the Natural Law found in legal and religious texts across cultures of antiquity, 95–121.

ascetic devotion such as used by pietists and related sects and movements not in the religious mainstream. In this respect, spirituality represented an excess of striving after the purely immaterial.

By the nineteenth century, the term was no longer one of reproach but simply a description of prayerful piety, with a view toward the practice of ascetics and mystics. At times spirituality came to be associated with the "inner" or "interior life" of humans in general. In the first half of the twentieth century, the terms spirituality and spiritual theology were applied to ascetic and mystical theology, as opposed to dogmatic and moral theology.

In nineteenth- and twentieth-century Protestant liberalism, with the advance of biblical criticism and widespread skepticism on matters of faith, pious people focused on religious practice (*lex orandi*) over against the vicissitudes of historical belief (*lex credenti*), and "spirituality" expressed what was sought. In the late twentieth century, the word "spirituality" found wide usage yet went undefined, having a vague association with living holistically, contemplatively, fully, and harmoniously with nature, others, and all of life. This latter perspective, that all life has a spiritual aspect, is associated widely with spirituality, and the term has become disengaged from theology in general or religion in particular.

Such lack of specificity, however, makes the concept so universal as to lack value. For our purposes, I reconnect the term with its root meaning, that is, with Spirit, or as the ancient Hebrews did, with the "wind" or "breath" of God. To be spiritual is to breathe deeply and harmoniously with Reality (Infinity). Spirituality, then, is a hopeful, creative, life-filled path, a Spirit-filled way of living. In using the term "path," Taking a path is a different way of living from driving down a highway. Unlike highways, paths seem more personal. Unlike a highway, paths are not goal-oriented, for spirituality implies choice, uncertainty, and risk-taking. To quote Matthew Fox, spirituality is

> the way itself, and every moment on the way is a holy moment; a sacred seeing takes place there. All who embark on a spiritual path need to be willing to learn and to let go; to know that none of us has all the answers, and yet that none of us is apart from deity ... What is common to all paths that are spiritual is, of course, the Spirit—breath, life, energy. That is why all true paths are essentially one path—because there is only one Spirit, one breath, one life, one energy in the universe. It belongs to none of us and all of us. We all share it. Spirituality does not make us otherworldly;

it renders us more fully alive. The path that spirituality takes is a path away from the superficial into the depths; away from the "outer person" into the "inner person"; away from the privatized and individualistic into the deeply communitarian.[4]

Spirituality, traditionally defined by Christians as "life in the Spirit," encompasses the journey of life from a distinct perspective. Spirituality is the journey of life "from God, to God, and with God." As a result, it is also a journey toward Self. In other words, the process of coming to know or to experience God is also the process of knowing oneself. Through this process, one comes to differentiate between one's temporary or false self, which we call the ego, and one's permanent or True Self, that part of us made in the image of God and made for ongoing or everlasting relationship with God. In the end, we discover that we know God by being known, much like one loves by being loved.

In his public lecture "The Seven Spiritual Laws of Success," the prominent Indian-American physician and philosopher Deepak Chopra defines success as "the progressive realization of worthy goals." Humans are goal-seeking organisms. Because worthy goals involve the ability to love and be compassionate, harmful addictive behavior qualifies as unworthy. From this perspective, a requisite quality for goal-seeking is the ability to hear one's inner voice, to be in touch with the Spirit within, one's true self and creative center. Living out of one's core, one's innermost being, Chopra believes, is what humans mean by "spirituality." Spirituality, simply defined, is "Self-awareness." You will notice I capitalize the word "Self," for this is both intentional and essential to a proper understanding of the concept.

Because it is easy to fall into a simplistic or merely humanistic view of spirituality, let me clarify what I mean. When I think of spirituality, I have in mind the account of Jesus healing a victim of blindness in Mark's gospel. According to Mark 8:22–26, when Jesus healed a blind man in the town of Bethsaida, the healing occurred in three stages. First, the man was blind. Next, Jesus laid hands on him, using saliva to anoint the man's eyes. At this stage, the man's vision was blurry and indistinct. Lastly, Jesus again laid hands upon the blind man's eyes, whereupon his sight was fully restored, enabling him to see everything clearly.

The same pattern can be applied to spirituality (its three stages also understood as three distinct types of spirituality):

---

4. Fox, *Creation Spirituality*, 12.

1. *self-consciousness.* This stage of awareness—the first-half-of-life-phase—denotes "self-awareness," a self-centered, egocentric state. In this stage, an immature and dream-like state, humans are in the dark, unaware, and self-deceived.

2. *God-consciousness.* This phase, a transitional phase, constitutes institutional allegiance, attachment to ethical and man-made religious belief systems. This phase of spirituality, evident historically in salvation-by-effort approaches, can be likened to sleepwalking. In this stage participants strive to make progress, yet are still in the dark. They are serving external requirements, pleasing an authoritarian deity.

3. *Self-consciousness.* This stage of awareness—the second-half-of-life phase—is entered through realization, by awakening. Those thus connected to their soul or core being are now "in the light," connected finally to their higher power. Such awareness—such living and thinking—is a gift of grace. This state of awareness cannot be earned, but, like the biblical Pearl of Great Price (see Matt 13:45–46), it can be found through love and by letting go, more by subtraction than by addition.

These stages represent the journey from darkness to light, illustrated in nature by the three phases of the twenty-four-hour day: night, twilight/dawn, and day.

The central defining characteristic of spirituality is an individual's sense of connection to a greater whole. At its heart, spirituality involves an emotional experience of awe and reverence. Such experience is highly desired, fervently sought, endlessly disagreed upon, and thoroughly fascinating. Why did our ancestors have such a wonderful idea of God? Because they lived in an awesome world. They wondered at the magnificence of whatever it was that brought the world into being. This led to a sense of adoration. This adoration, this gratitude, we call religion. Now, as the outer world is diminished, our inner world is drying up. The task of spirituality is to help us regain our sense of awe and reverence, beginning with a profound commitment to nature and continuing with an equal commitment to the whole of humanity and every living creature. If we do not love what is visible around us, how can we love God, whom we cannot see? (1 John 4:19–20).

Introduction

Overview

Despite new chapters and themes, this book has many things in common with my earlier books, *The Second Journey* and *The Church Alumni Association*. While these works are companion volumes, *Arc* is best read as a sequel, for it borrows freely from *Second Journey* while following a broader and less nuanced understanding of spirituality. In *Ark*, I think of spirituality as a "love affair with God," a relationship that, while described religiously and theologically, can also be described holistically and naturally, for in my estimation, how one relates to God is how one relates to others, nature, and oneself.

The Arc of Spirituality examines Western Christian spirituality as it developed historically through twelve phases, beginning with the spirituality of ancient Israel and postexilic Judaism and culminating in the present with "secular" spirituality. While these phases are not necessarily progressive in nature, they can be seen to summarize or typify particular eras or epochs of Western history. In presenting twelve phases of spirituality, my intent is not to provide detailed analysis on ways of being spiritual, but rather to offer historical and literary perspective on the distinct spiritual ethos of a cultural or historical period, often by examining the life and thought of representative personalities. As readers will notice, my approach is more evocative than analytical, suggestive rather than descriptive. My goal in this project is to present each phase of spirituality as a stage in a journey, with the understanding that somehow the journey is the goal.

This book is not a handbook on spirituality, not a step-by-step instruction manual on how to be more spiritual. Spirituality is the journey of a lifetime. While spirituality requires effort, it is also effortless, in that it requires letting go. In the journey of spirituality, progress is expected; there are steps forward, certainly, but also many more backward. The goal of spirituality is always God, and while God makes the journey interesting, it is never easy. Orthodox or traditional spirituality—called first-half-of-life spirituality—is formulaic and instructional; in other words, it can be taught. Second-half-of-life spirituality is more caught than taught, for there are no clear steps to follow or learn.

Questions for Discussion and Reflection

1. What are some polarities in your life that cause you tension and conflict, and how does spirituality help you reconcile your polarities?
2. Using Diana Bass's analysis, describe the difference between the terms "religious" and "spiritual." If you were asked to choose between them, which would you select? Why?
3. Explain the difference between dualistic and nondualistic thinking. Do nondualists accept polarities? If so, how do they do so differently from dualist thinkers? How do the Eastern concept of the Tao and the principle of yin and yang contribute to your understanding of holistic living?
4. In one sentence, define spirituality.
5. Explain and assess Matthew Fox's idea that spirituality does not make us otherworldly but rather "renders us more fully alive."
6. Assess Deepak Chopra's definition of spirituality as "Self awareness." Explain the three stages of spiritual awareness described in this chapter. What, for you, is the difference between "self-consciousness" and "Self-consciousness"? In your estimation, is "God-consciousness" a transitional or a terminal phase in spirituality? Explain your answer.
7. In your own words, explain the meaning of the statement, "While spirituality requires effort, it is also effortless."

2

Covenant Spirituality

Ancient Israelite Piety

IF BY SPIRITUALITY WE mean the spiritual life of individuals, rather than the corporate expression of religious practice better classified as "liturgy," then we find that much of our study of spirituality in the Old Testament is extremely limited. While the Bible introduces numerous noteworthy individuals, the emphasis is not on individualism but on "corporate personality." The Bible portrays Israel as God's people, not simply as a collection of individuals but as a divine company ("a priestly kingdom and a holy nation"; Exod 19:6; 1 Pet 2:9). Out of families, clans, and tribes God forms a nation, with a corporate personality: When one person suffers, everyone suffers; when one person is blessed, the people enjoy the benefits; when one person sins, the whole nation participates in the judgment; when one person receives a promise, he or she does so on behalf of the nation.

Americans today live in a pluralistic society, with diverse cultures, religions, and societal values, and we are taught to be tolerant. Ancient societies were quite the opposite; they were homogeneous, with little tolerance or diversity, and with no such thing as freedom of religion. The concept of corporate personality provided Israel with stability, solidarity, and unity during the period of its ascendency. These qualities enabled Israelites to maintain social and religious cohesion in a sea of paganism. Their laws, rituals, and values provided them with a distinctive way of life, which has preserved them to this day.

God's Love for All Humanity: The Call of Abraham

To understand the biblical concept of community, we must go back to the story of Abraham: God started with one family, declaring a promise so wondrous yet absurd as to engender laughter, creating something in Sarah's womb when she was unable to conceive: "Is anything too wonderful for the Lord?" (Gen 18:14). From Isaac came Jacob, and from him the twelve tribes of Israel. They took his name, his personality, his style of life, and the covenant he had with God. They called themselves *"bene Israel,"* sons of Israel. The doctrine of election reminded them that they were beloved, God's intentional creation. They were not one nation *out of* many, but one nation *for* many. In such unity there is resolve, resilience, and strength.

In the Bible, the prototypical model for the journey of faith is found in the patriarchal stories of Genesis 12–50, starting with the story of Abraham. For Jewish readers and listeners gathered for worship in synagogues to hear these accounts, the underlying significance of chapters 12–50 is not the accounts of the individual patriarchs and matriarchs but the story of Israel's self-understanding. At the time this material is put into writing, the main question is not, "Who are Abraham, Isaac, Jacob, and Joseph?" but "Who is Israel?" Israel is grappling with her identity, her self-understanding as a people called by God. The theological answer is found in the doctrine of election, the notion that the people of Israel are chosen by God.

But what does election mean? Is God racist, favoring some people over others? The Bible answers this question with a resounding "No." The covenant God establishes with Israel should not be regarded as an expression of divine preference for Jews over others, or as divine commission for one group to rule others, or as reward for good conduct on Israel's part. As the history of Israel demonstrates, the establishment of the covenant is not followed by good conduct. Moreover, the Bible portrays the covenant people as sinful, stiff-necked, stubborn, and singularly inept at learning from their experiences. In fact, in the Bible the Israelites are punished repeatedly, and more severely than others are. Nevertheless, God does not nullify the contract or make it void. The biblical answer to election is given in the portrayal of Abraham, Isaac, and Jacob, patriarchs whose lives are characterized by the following traits:

1. They *live by faith in God*. In Abraham, Israel understands something about herself, that she has been called into existence by God himself, that she has been created by God's initiative and preserved by God's grace.

2. They are *called to be a servant people*. Election does not mean that some people are chosen because they are better than others, but rather that they are called to spread God's grace. God's purpose is seen in Genesis 12:3 ("in you all the families of the earth shall be blessed"); it is a universal purpose, one that moves from particulars to universals, from individuals to communities and nations. In Abraham, God brings one person of faith into existence in order that God's blessing might be extended to all humanity. This is the Bible's stress on election, that when God calls a people, they are called to service, and the rest of the Old Testament, and then the gospels and epistles, show what it means to be a servant people. In the Bible, the election of a people becomes the basis for good news, what the New Testament calls "gospel." This is the message of Genesis 12–50, and it is transported to a higher key in the New Testament.

3. They are *called to a life of pilgrimage*—a life of mobility, movement, and change. Biblical faith is a calling faith, a calling to go forth, to be on the way, to be moving in God's direction, to be pioneers of faith. Abraham is told to break his ties with his land and his former security, a way of life that up to that point had been deeply rooted to the land. Like Abraham, God's people are called to a nomadic consciousness. We see this clearly in the prophetic consciousness, a stance that could be counter-cultural in the sense that one could be both an agent of change and a critic of the established order. The prophetic message is that God is doing a new thing. As we see in Abraham, faith is not so much consent or agreement as something dynamic, manifested in movement. The story of Abraham and the patriarchs is the story of God on the move with his people.

Covenant Theology

Biblical theology begins with the doctrine of creation, a belief central to all biblical faith traditions. The doctrine affirms that God created all things, meaning that the world and everything in it depends on God for its existence. Whereas prominent thinkers in antiquity, including philosophers such as Plato and Aristotle, virtually ignored origins, accepting the explanation that matter, and therefore the world, was eternal, the Bible presents an external force that creates and continually sustains the cosmos.

In the Bible, however, the doctrine of creation does not stand alone, for it depends upon and elaborates on the redemptive activity of God in history. In the Old Testament, creation is viewed in the light of Israel's covenant faith; in the New Testament, creation is viewed in the light of Jesus Christ and the "new creation" that through him became a historical reality. In both testaments, the doctrine emphasizes the sovereignty of God, the goodness of creation (that the cosmos and everything in it is characterized by divinely decreed order), the supreme position of honor and responsibility that God has given to human beings, and the divine purpose that undergirds and controls history from its beginning to its consummation.

Creation faith, particularly as affirmed in the historic creeds of Christianity, represents a repudiation of metaphysical dualism, which might suggest that the created world is evil, and a repudiation of metaphysical randomness, which might suggest that life is essentially meaningless. Creation faith is what Christians affirm when they profess: "I believe in God the Father almighty, maker of heaven and earth."

In sharp contrast to humanist thought, where human beings are the center of life and social relationships, the Bible presents God not only as creator but also as the focal point of all cultural activities. Whereas secular morality emphasizes human efforts to build a society that embodies goodness and justice, biblical theology argues that God's nature and will should direct social development.

The basis of all societal views in the Bible is the covenant treaty God established with Israel through individuals such as Abraham, Moses, and David. The covenant relationship serves to reveal God's nature, purpose and, more importantly, how God's people are to live. The covenant is the means by which God regulates biblical society, establishing statutes, laws, and principles. Biblical stories about Adam, Noah, Abraham, Moses, David, as about judges, priests, kings, prophets, and sages, are accounts about community writ large.

In 1933 Walther Eichrodt published in Germany a groundbreaking polemical work in which he took aim against the entire nineteenth-century historical-critical movement. Published in English decades later under the title *Theology of the Old Testament*, Eichrodt sought to articulate what was constant and therefore normative in the Old Testament, and he determined that all of the variations and developments of Israel's religion could be seen to be in the service of a single conceptual notion: Covenant (commonly expressed by the Hebrew word *berith*). To subsume all of the Old Testament under one idea seemed risky, but to Eichrodt's credit he made an excellent choice in noting that what most characterizes Israel's vision of reality is that all things—God, Israel, humanity, the world—partake of relatedness. The implications of this insight are enormous, not only for divine-human interaction, but for the relation of God and the world. Eichrodt's readiness to relate "cosmology and creation" to covenant suggests that even "the world" is to be understood not as an independent system, but as a creature and partner to God.

This is an enormous claim when viewed in the context of Enlightenment thinking about the autonomy of the scientific world. To subsume creation under the rubric of covenant directly nullifies any attempt to understand the world either autonomously or pantheistically. Thus, Eichrodt's capacity to treat creation in this way was an extraordinary insight in his time and place. Moreover, as interest grows in the relation between ecology and biblical faith, this covenantal interpretation of world reality is likely to continue to be important.

Because of the centrality of the concept of covenant, not only in the Pentateuch but also throughout all scripture, we need to define the concept and place it in its historical and literary setting. As in a marriage or a business contract, a covenant describes a binding relationship between two parties (nations, individuals, or a person and God), based on commitment. The Old Testament speaks of covenants established by God with Noah (Gen 6), Abraham (Gen 15 and 17), Moses (Exod 20 and Deut 5), David (2 Sam 7 and Ps 89), and Israel (Jer 31:31–34 and Ez 36:22–38). In reality, these are differing views of the covenant between God and Israel.

In antiquity, secular covenants could be divided into two main types: (a) *parity treaties* governed relationships between equal parties, and (b) *suzerainty treaties* governed relationships between unequal parties. In the second type of covenant, the superior was known as the suzerain and the inferior as the vassal. In the Bible, God is the suzerain and humans are the vassal. This covenant agreement involves certain obligations, with sanctions (blessings or curses) to follow, depending upon the carrying out of the obligations. Often a solemn oath gives force to the covenant.

Two forms of the suzerain-vassal treaty are found in the Old Testament, depending on whether the text emphasizes God as being bound to Israel unconditionally or Israel being bound to God conditionally: (1) In a *promise covenant*, God swears an oath of unconditional loyalty to Israel. In this case God assumes the responsibility and obligations set down in the agreement. A prime example is Genesis 15, where God promises to give posterity and land to Abraham. In the account Abraham prepares the ritual of the covenant, dividing sacrificial animals into two pieces with the intention of walking through them to seal the treaty. A deep sleep, however, overcomes Abraham and God alone passes between the parts, thereby assuming full responsibility for the covenant and its promises.

(2) In a *law covenant*, both parties swear to uphold the terms of the treaty. God establishes the laws (stipulations) by which Israel is to live. Because both God and Israel are required to fulfill certain covenantal demands, both stand under what is known as the "sanction," which describes the results of obedience or disobedience to the stipulations. In conditional covenants with Israel, such as the Mosaic covenant at Sinai, God enacts the sanctions, which can be either positive (a reward or blessing) or negative (a punishment or curse).

A seal or ritual sign of blood confirmed the agreement. The significance of using blood in the ritual is important, for the Israelites believed that blood was the key to life. To seal a covenant with blood expressed the primacy of the commitment between God and Israel: it implied blessing and curse, life and death. In fact, the terminology used in the Old Testament for sealing a covenant agreement is "to cut a covenant," implying blood. The best examples are the "cutting" of the animals by Abraham in Genesis 15:10 and the "cutting" of circumcision in Genesis 17:9–14. Exodus 24 portrays the ceremony of covenant making where the entire assembly of Israel ratifies the covenant by participating in a sacrifice. Half the blood is dashed against the altar as a symbol of God's participation in the rite, while the other half is poured into basins. Acting as covenant mediator, Moses then reads to the people "the book of the covenant" (Exod 24:7), which the people pledged to accept and obey. Moses then dashes the blood upon them as a symbol of their participation in the rite.

The two understandings of the covenant—conditional (law) and unconditional (promise)—stand in tension with one another throughout Israelite history.

The Covenant at Sinai

The Exodus account is firmly embedded into the story of Israel's theological history. It is part of the narrative that runs from Genesis 12 to 2 Kings 25. The first nineteen chapters of Exodus tell the story of the Israelites' bondage in Egypt and their deliverance by Yahweh. It describes the call of Moses and his powerful encounters with Pharaoh. It presents the story of the plagues on Egypt, culminating in the visit by the angel of death and the institution of the festival of the Passover. Next, Moses leads the Israelites out of Egypt and through the sea. The book of Exodus then describes their journey in the wilderness until, in chapter 19, the Israelites arrive at Mount Sinai, where God calls them into covenant relationship. The Ten Commandments in Exodus 20 and the laws that follow are part of this story.

History in the Old Testament is the history of a covenant relationship. This relationship is initiated and established by God, the sovereign Lord (suzerain); as vassals, humans respond to it and bind themselves in obedience. The covenant involves not only obligations toward God but also obligations toward the other members of the community. The legal stipulations are binding, yet not static. They can be adaptable to new cultural circumstances, but the basic principle remains constant: persons are absolutely responsible to one another (Second Table of the Law, commandments 5–10) because they are absolutely responsible to God (First Table of the Law, commandments 1–4).

Ethical responsibility is motivated by gratitude for what God has done. Nevertheless, the Mosaic covenant contains a conditional element: "*If* you will obey my voice and keep my covenant . . ." (Exod 19:5). Faithfulness to the covenant yields blessing, betrayal brings judgment. This element of the covenant would become central to the great prophets of Israel, for despite God's faithfulness, Israel would be unfaithful. While there are consequences for betrayal, the biblical story places the accent on divine grace. The following biblical pattern unfolds: God establishes the covenant; humans break the covenant; God restores the covenant. Hence the covenant is re-enacted and re-established.

The most fully developed law covenant in the Old Testament is the Mosaic covenant described in Exodus 19–23. This covenant provided the laws and ordinances by which Hebraic society was to function. It governed the relationship between God and the Hebrews and determined the code of conduct with the Israelite society. Although covenant law at times was altered, the basic principles upon which it rested did not. In the Old Testament, covenant statutes were based upon justice, righteousness, and steadfast love.

In the Old Testament, the term "justice" (*mishpat*) denotes the rights and duties of each party to fulfill their obligations under the covenantal law. These laws, however, refer not only to the vertical relationship with God, but also to the horizontal relationship between humans, that is, to society as a whole. The Old Testament articulated the administration of legal justice under the concept of Lex Talionis, meaning that punishment or restitution should be in proportion to what a person deserves. This law of retribution, known popularly as "life for life, eye for eye, tooth for tooth" (see Deut 19:19–21), means that the community would not tolerate retaliation greater than the actual injury done.

Whereas the Hebrew word for justice refers to the rights and duties of covenant participants, the Hebrew word for righteousness (*zedek*) pertains to the conduct or attitude of the covenant people. It is often used of God and man having the right and consistent conduct in all matters of life, social and religious. Ultimately, righteousness is an attribute of God, namely, God's perfection in all areas of covenantal conduct. Because humans are not perfect or consistent in their conduct, the Old Testament understands human righteousness not as a human attribute but as a human response. Noah "found favor in the sight of the Lord" (Gen 6:8) and Job was "blameless and upright" (Job 2:3) not because they were perfect but because their lives largely reflected the righteousness of God.

If justice and righteousness were the only covenant principles, the relationship between God and humanity would remain strictly legal. The divine-human relationship, however, transcends impersonal legal and moral codes of conduct, for it is based on the concept of *hesed*, a Hebrew word usually translated as "loving-kindness" but better understood as steadfast love or loyalty, a covenant love that presupposes the mutuality of relationship: "For I desire steadfast love and not sacrifice, the knowledge of God rather than burnt offerings" (Hos 6:6). The covenant love of Yahweh is a faithful love, a steadfast unshakeable maintenance of the covenantal relationship. Both parties must have a deep love and loyalty for the other. As with the other principles discussed, human beings are to build a *hesed* relationship not only with God but with each other as well.

These principles, and their accompanying laws and application, provide the basis for Israelite society. The Hebrews, both individually and communally, were to abide by these principles and regulations in order to maintain a proper relationship with God and with one another. The Israelites' failure to live by these basic principles, however, led to injustice at all levels of society, a state of heart and mind that resulted in prophetic condemnation.

Despite this emphasis on corporate personality, the God Israelites worshipped was concerned for the needs of the individual as well as the group; powerful enough to grant their requests; angry with sin yet willing to forgive it; amenable to reasoned argument; glorious yet terrible, deserving of praise but dangerous to behold; reliable, yet not predictable; merciful but just. The Israelites clearly portrayed and worshiped God as a person, though as a larger-than-life person, whose absence was acutely painful even if his presence could be far from comfortable.

The Prophetic Task: The Call to Covenant Loyalty

The task and vocation of biblical prophets are today greatly misunderstood. Popularly viewed, the role of the prophet is to predict future events. Modern scholarship downplays this understanding of the role of prophets. Biblical scholars now understand the prophetic role as having involved three distinct yet related tasks, each with a different temporal focus: (a) they were predictors of the future (*foretelling*); (b) they were reformers who kept alive the Mosaic past through continuous appeal to the theocratic ideals expressed in the covenants (*retelling*); and (c) they were social critics who spoke out boldly and without compromise against current disobedience and disbelief within the social, religious, and political establishment (*forthtelling*). Of the three tasks, the most significant was forthtelling and the least significant was foretelling. Biblical prophets rarely, if ever, made open predictions about the future, and when they did so, the predictions were linked to their role as social critics, which focused on the consequences for unrepentance. The prophet's futuristic role was associated primarily with the certainty of the coming of the Lord, a coming to make things right through judgment and reward.

The key to understanding the Old Testament prophets is their relationship to the covenant. Of special importance in understanding the prophets is what can be called the "covenant lawsuit," a concept related to the ancient Hittite suzerainty treaties. There we find a provision related to covenant disloyalty. In cases where a vassal failed to fulfill the stipulations of a sworn treaty, the suzerain would institute a lawsuit, a procedure carried out through messengers and consisting of two distinct stages: The first stage consisted of *warnings*, delivered by the messenger, reminding the vassal of the suzerain's benefits and of the stipulations agreed upon. In addition, the vassal would be reminded of the curses or sanctions of the covenant. Using interrogation, the messenger would require an explanation of the vassal's offenses against the suzerain, charging the vassal with a change in behavior and warning of the vanity of appealing to alien help as a means of escaping the consequences. Finally, the messenger would issue an *ultimatum*: "if you continue, the curses will go into effect." If the messenger of the suzerain was rejected, the legal process moved into the second distinct stage: *declaration of war* as an execution of the sanctions of the treaty.

Like messengers of the Hittite suzerain, the mission of the Old Testament prophets was to serve as Yahweh's messengers to enforce the covenant mediated to Israel through Moses. Amos, the first of the classical writing prophets, was a vigorous upholder of the Mosaic tradition. The keynote of Amos's prophecy is struck in Amos 3:1–8, a passage that begins by recalling the crucial event of Israel's history: the exodus from Egypt. Through God's action in this event, Israel had become a "family" bound together by religious loyalty. Through this event God had entered into a covenant relationship with Israel: "You only have I known of all the families of the earth; therefore I will punish you for all your iniquities" (Amos 3:2).

This passage, marked by solemnity, raises immediate questions: In what sense is it true that Yahweh has known only Israel, and why the "therefore"? What is the logical connection between God's knowledge of Israel and her fate? The passage makes little sense unless we know that we have here a usage of "know" borrowed from international relations. Hittite and other ancient Near Eastern texts reveal that "to know" in this technical legal sense means to recognize treaty stipulations as binding. In this context the term could be translated "recognize" or "be loyal to" a suzerain.[1] This clarification makes Amos's terminology understandable. Yahweh had recognized only Israel as legitimate servants, "therefore," since this sort of covenant involves obligations that were not fulfilled, "I will punish you for all your iniquities."

Other prophets speak in the same way. Jeremiah uses "know" in this way when describing a future repentance of the people: "I will give

---

1. Hillers, *Covenant*, 121–22.

Covenant Spirituality

them a heart to know that I am the Lord; and they shall be my people and I will be their God, for they shall return to me with their whole heart" (Jer 24:7). That this kind of knowledge is closely related to the people's conduct is evident from another passage in Jeremiah, where the prophet indicts the reigning monarch for thinking that being king is a matter of privilege rather than of justice: "Are you a king because you compete in cedar? Did not your father eat and drink and do justice and righteousness? . . . He judged the cause of the poor and needy . . . Is not this to know me?" (Jer 22:15–16).

Hosea, best known for his extended use of the marriage metaphor to describe the relationship between Yahweh and Israel, makes the same connection. "Hear the word of the Lord, O people of Israel; for the Lord has an indictment [lawsuit] against the inhabitants of the land. There is no faithfulness or loyalty, and no knowledge of God in the land. Swearing, lying, and murder, and stealing and adultery break out; bloodshed follows bloodshed. Therefore the land mourns . . ." (Hos 4:1–3a). In addition to using the technical Hebrew term meaning "covenant lawsuit" (*rîb*), Hosea provides a list of specific words very much like the Ten Commandments.

Along with Hosea 4, various additional texts in the prophetic literature contain references to the covenant lawsuit literary form, including Isaiah 1 and Jeremiah 2, but the classic passage is Micah 6:1–8, often cited as the sum and substance of Old Testament ethics. Like the book's opening oracle, this passage employs the imagery of a controversy in a law court. Notice the dramatic structure of the lawsuit pattern:[2]

1. *Summons* (Mic 6:1–2): the trial opens with a summons by the prophet, who acts as God's prosecuting attorney. As we find in Hittite and other ancient international treaty patterns, the mountains serve as witnesses, before which Israel must present its case.

2. *The Plaintiff's Charge* (Mic 6:3–5): Here God, through the prophetic attorney, interrogates the people, appealing to Israel's historical traditions rather than to specific laws recorded in a treaty. The appeal is based on events that displayed *hesed* or covenant love toward the people, beginning with the exodus from Egypt and culminating in the occupation of the Promised Land. The prophet is appalled at the incongruity between God's benevolent deeds and Israel's disloyalty.

---

2. Anderson, *Understanding the Old Testament*, 311–12.

3. *The Defendant's Plea* (Mic 6:6–7): Finally Israel speaks, but finds no case to plead save to confess betrayal of the covenant. Empty religious ritual does not satisfy the covenant demands, but seemingly adds to the offense.

4. *The Indictment* (Mic 6:8): The passage reaches a climax as the prophet proclaims the essence of the covenant stipulations: "to do justice (*mishpa*t), to love kindness (*hesed*), and to walk humbly with God." This simple statement expresses the prophetic demand for justice, righteousness, and steadfast love. Is this not to know God?

The prophets predict that in the end there will only be a remnant who will be faithful, hence only a portion of the people will experience covenant blessing. The prophets are often considered to have been messengers of doom, because they proclaimed a message of judgment. The truth is that before there can be good news, there must be truthtelling. Like God's *opus alienum* ("strange deed") in Isaiah 28:21, where God judges by fire his own people as a means to judge their enemies, the redemptive work of God is alien, more like the work of a surgeon—who uses a scalpel to cut living tissue, even stuffing gauze into the wound to keep the incision open until the blood flows red and the poison is gone—than like a parent, who uses "tough love" to discipline a child. The analogy applies to John 3:16, which can be revised to read: For God so loved the world that he bled—until his blood flowed red—that whosoever accepts this love may live in God's presence eternally.

The story of the Old Testament is the record of Israel's failure to live by covenant principles. Because God's people broke their covenant with God, they were eventually conquered by an invading nation, Babylon, and were taken into exile. But all hope is not lost. In the latter years of Israel's history the prophet Jeremiah promised that God would do something new in the future, once again restoring the people to proper relationship with God and one another.

God's Presence with Humanity: Moses and the Exodus

The presence of God is one of the central themes of the Old Testament. The Torah (the first five books of the Bible) sets out the terms on which God will be with the people of Israel; the historical writings show from concrete examples how God's presence can be forfeited, and how gracious God is, who never allows absence from an unworthy people become permanent; the prophetic writings look forward to the day when God will never seem absent again; and the psalms reflect on all aspects of presence and absence as they affect both the worshipping community and the individual at prayer.

The earliest global civilizations, whether Asian, Indian, or Middle Eastern, are religious, and their religions precede and give rise to their cultures. This principle particularly exemplifies the Egyptians and the ancient Semitic empires of the Middle East. From the first, these cultures conceive of the problem of life on earth as dependent on the larger reality of the cosmos and the transcendent. We know of no time when humans in this region are conscious of themselves but not yet of the divine. As early as the fourteenth century BCE there is an Egyptian monarch (Akhenaton; also known as Amenhotep IV) who conceives of a god who is the creator of the world and of all humankind.

About a century later, an Israelite named Moses leads a captive people out of slavery toward a new land of settlement. This event, known as the exodus, is marked by a wilderness encounter with deity that results in a new self-understanding and identity for the people. Moses and his Israelite followers define their religion in terms of that experience. Their God is the one "who brought them out of the land of Egypt, out of the house of bondage" (see Exod 20:2). This becomes the first statement of belief in the Judeo-Christian tradition; like all those that follow, it is an affirmation that something significant happened in the past.

When we seek to understand the meaning of our individual life stories, we do not actually begin with birth or infancy, even though written autobiographies might start there. Rather, we view early childhood in the light of later experiences that are formative or pivotal. Likewise, Israel's life story does not begin with the time of Abraham or even the Creation, although the Old Testament starts there. Rather, Israel's history has its true beginning in a crucial historical experience that creates a self-conscious historical community—an event so decisive that earlier happenings and subsequent experiences are seen in its light. That decisive event—the great watershed of Israel's history—is the exodus from Egypt. Through the ages, the story of the deliverance of slaves from bondage, and their march through the wilderness toward a Promised Land, has had a powerful appeal to the religious imagination of many oppressed groups and individuals. It is the paradigmatic biblical story of salvation and deliverance.

Exodus 1–24, a passage that speaks of the exodus and the birth of the nation of Israel, is less concerned with what happened historically and more concerned with the meaning behind these events. This is not to say that the narrative does not describe actual events, but to emphasize that it describes them theologically. While providing interesting stories about Moses and the Israelites, the exodus account focuses not so much on Moses as liberator of the people but on God's redemptive role. God, not Moses, is the primary actor. Hence the exodus story, the paradigmatic pattern of deliverance from Egyptian slavery, including the covenant enacted on Mount Sinai and the subsequent wilderness experience that led to the conquest of the Promised Land, is not recorded for its own sake, but rather as a clue to who God is and how God acts toward humanity, particularly toward those who are downtrodden and oppressed.

Despite his upbringing in Pharaoh's court, Moses identified with the Hebrew slaves, an impulse that led to his slaying an Egyptian taskmaster. Forced to flee, Moses took refuge in "the land of Midian," an area of the Sinai Peninsula occupied by shepherds. There he married the daughter of a Midianite priest. While tending the flocks of his father-in-law, Moses came upon "the mountain of God." Moses's encounter with the God of the ancestors (Exod 3:13) in that sacred place and his role in the ensuing encounter with the Pharaoh is one of the masterpieces of religious literature. It was in the Midianite wilderness that God disclosed essential aspects of the divine nature, including (1) God's personal name (Yahweh), which, literally untranslatable, has come to be associated with *God's creative activity* ("I am", "I cause to be") and (2) *God's redemptive activity* ("I will be with you"; see Exod. 3:12) on behalf of Israel.

Yahweh appeared to Moses with memorable words: "I have observed the misery of my people . . . I have heard their cry . . . I know their sufferings, and I have come down to deliver them . . . and to bring them to a good and broad land, a land flowing with milk and honey . . ." (Exod 3:7–8). In a fundamental declaration of faith, the ancient Israelites affirmed that their history originated in a marvelous liberation from oppression, declaring climactically the mighty deeds of God on their behalf. The verbs of the narrative sweep to a climax: God heard, God saw, God rescued.

The primary purpose of the exodus narrative is to glorify the God of Israel, the "divine warrior" whose strong hand and outstretched arm wins the victory over Pharaoh and his armies. The text heralds five interlocking biblical themes: (1) *divine love* (when things on earth get bad, God's love is greater still); (2) *divine mercy* (God's is always "for us," never "against us"); (3) *divine initiative* (God always takes the initiative in restoring that which is broken, forgotten, or lost); (4) *divine sovereignty* (God is completely in control, even to the point of hardening Pharaoh's heart); and (5) *divine freedom* (while disclosing the divine name, God nevertheless retains the divine freedom that eludes human control: "I will be gracious to whom I will be gracious, and will show mercy on whom I will show mercy. But you cannot see my face; for no one shall see me and live"; Exod 33:19–20).

As we learn from the third commandment, God's name is not to be taken in vain (Exod 20:7), meaning that God cannot be manipulated or influenced magically. This commandment, read contextually, is less a prohibition against using God's name as a curse and more against attempting to use worship or religious ritual to manipulate or control God in a possessive sense. The God who speaks to Moses is the Lord, not the servant of the people. From this time forward, the question "what is God like?" would be answered in concrete historical events. That is precisely the point of the conquest with Pharaoh, the plagues against Egypt, the crossing of the sea, the guidance through the wilderness, and the conquest of the Promised Land. Because God is sovereign, God controls history, the powers of nature, and on occasion, even the human heart. In describing the Pharaoh, the text states repeatedly that God hardened Pharaoh's heart, but also that Pharaoh hardens his own heart. The narrator tells the story in a way that allows for human obstinacy while ultimately glorifying the God of Israel. Pharaoh is given freedom, but not so much that he can exceed the bounds of God's sovereign control (see Rom 9:17–18).

The Hiddenness of God: Moses and Elijah

Biblical talk about God is paradoxical. Because God is a person who is alive and active and yet has an awesome, even overwhelming personality, friendship with God is both a privilege and yet elusive. While it is difficult to live with God, it is impossible to live without God. Yet the hiddenness of God—perhaps even God's absence—seems the dominant reality for many seekers throughout history.

A helpful place to examine this conundrum is 1 Kings 19, a passage that records a memorable experience of the prophet Elijah on Mount Sinai. Elijah (his name means "Yahweh is my God"), persecuted by Jezebel (King Ahab's Phoenician wife) for his faithfulness to Yahweh, flees to

Mount Sinai, where he prepares for an encounter with the divine: "Now there was a great wind, so strong that it was splitting mountains and breaking rocks in pieces before Yahweh, but Yahweh was not in the wind; and after the wind an earthquake, but Yahweh was not in the earthquake; and after the earthquake a fire, but Yahweh was not in the fire; and after the fire a sound of sheer silence" (1 Kgs 19:11–12; these last few words are traditionally translated "a still small voice").

Elijah's experience on Mount Sinai reminds us of the climactic experience of Moses with God at the same location, the vision of God in darkness described at Exodus 33:17–23. If even Moses sees only God's back, is there any hope that anyone else can see God's "face" and live? For practical purposes, the God of the Old Testament is a hidden God, hidden yet everywhere present. Yet, according to the prophet Isaiah, the God who is hidden can be known by the person who does not seek to "see" God, but rather to obey God's will: "I dwell in the high and holy place," says the Lord, "and also with those who are contrite and humble in spirit" (57:15).

In the book of Jeremiah, the prophet speaks of two epochs: the time of the Mosaic covenant, which ends in human failure, and the time of the new covenant, when the divine Torah (law, teaching) is written on the heart, resulting in such personal knowledge of God that religious teaching would no longer be necessary. This vision of the restored community of Israel is profoundly expressed in Jeremiah's prophecy of the new covenant (Jer 31:31–34), a prophecy that eventually gives the name to the canon of Christian writings ("New Testament" means "New Covenant"). In the New Testament, God is said to be fully with us in Jesus. As we read in John 1:18, "No one has ever seen God. It is God the only Son, who is close to the Father's heart, who has made him known."

Questions for Discussion and Reflection

1. In your estimation, does the modern emphasis on individualism distort the intended biblical message? Why or why not?

2. What significance did Abraham's story have for ancient Israel? What significance does it have for modern Christians?

3. Assess the biblical emphasis on election; what did it mean then, and what does it mean for us today?

Covenant Spirituality

4. In your estimation, does "creation faith" represent repudiation of metaphysical dualism? If so, how?

5. Explain the role of the covenant in Israel's history, in the New Testament, and in biblical theology as a whole. In your estimation, what is the relevance and significance of covenant theology for Christians today? Explain your answer.

6. In your estimation, what is the role of the Ten Commandments for Christians today? Do you tend to think about the Ten Commandments solely as law, or do they contain an element of promise as well? Explain your answer.

7. If, according to the text, Old Testament covenant statues are based upon justice (*mishpat*), righteousness (*zedek*), and steadfast love (*hesed*), how are these three principles related to one another? In your estimation, does one of these have priority over the others? Explain your answer.

8. Explain the relation between Israel's prophets and the concept of covenant.

9. Does this chapter's discussion of God's presence in the Old Testament clarify or confuse your understanding of God's presence in your life? Explain your answer.

3

Wisdom Spirituality
Postexilic Jewish Piety

LOOKING BACK FROM THE postexilic period, namely, from the Restoration period following the Babylonian exile, Israel understood its history to be a life of coexistence with God. In times of nationhood and even in the most catastrophic event, the end of Israel as a nation, Israel viewed history as the dramatic narrative of God's presence in the midst of the people. Though Israel felt called to be a partner with God in this historical drama, the accent fell on the "mighty acts" of God. As a covenant partner, Israel did not remain silent. Not only did the Israelites recall God's actions in narrative and written traditions, but they also addressed God in personal ways. The finest examples of Israel's relationship with God are found in the book of Psalms.

The Role of Worship in Israel's Spirituality

Throughout the biblical period, Israel's primary bond of unity was worship of God. According to the Bible, the enslaved Israelites were liberated from Egyptian bondage so that they might worship God at Sinai (Exod 3:12). During the period of the tribal confederacy, instituted by Joshua, the Israelites gathered at cultic centers such as Shechem and Shiloh to celebrate the great annual festivals and to renew the covenant tradition. During the time of David, Jerusalem became the cultic center of the nation, to which Solomon added the impressive temple. During the period of the divided monarchy, when the northern kingdom became independent from Judah and Jerusalem, the kings of Israel gathered at pilgrimage shrines in their own territory, especially at Bethel. When the exiles returned from Babylon, their first thought was to rebuild the Jerusalem temple. Throughout its history, Israel was a worshipping community, recalling God's actions in narrative and written traditions but also addressing God in bold, honest, and deeply personal ways. For this reason the book of Psalms represents the very heart and center of the Hebrew Bible, Israel's "conversation" with Yahweh.

About one third of the Hebrew Bible is poetry. Awareness of this feature of Israel's liturgical and literary expression is invaluable for reading and interpreting scripture. Poetry is a personal way of expressing faith, both individually and communally. Poetry appeals to our human nature, making us realize the importance of emotion and signifying that we are more than intellect. Worship, like other interpersonal communication, involves both head and heart.

The book of Psalms in its present form is the product of postexilic Judaism. Insofar as the Psalter reflects the liturgical practice of this period, one can speak of it as the Hymnbook of the Second Temple, though this material continues to be chanted in Jewish synagogues. The collected psalms were intended to be sung, generally as a kind of chant and often accompanied by instrumental music. Some psalms provide hints of the original musical setting in the titles, headings, and opening words, largely added later but still preserving ancient tradition. In addition to their use as hymns, the psalms also function as prayers, recited corporately and privately.

There are, of course, numerous psalms that are expressions of community celebration, and these doubtless served as liturgies for such occasions as the various festivals and holy days described in the Pentateuch. But there are others of a more individual character, psalms that evoke states of distress such as illness or personal intrigue, or that offer thanks for God's having "heard my cry" in times of need. Yet these psalms lack detail. The identity of the psalmist's "enemies" or the precise nature of the predicament involved is glossed over. They are alluded to starkly as "Sheol" or "the Pit," but they remain ambiguous. Apparently, this lack of specifics was intentional, a way of tailoring the individual's plea or praise to his or her circumstances, but in such a way as to permit the reuse of a particular text repeatedly by different worshipers.

Classification of the psalms by literary type, such as whether its intent is principally praise or lament, or whether a psalm is apparently intended for the individual or the community, may well lessen its impact and meaning. There is clear evidence that within the biblical period, psalmody had already developed something of an independent existence. The singing or speaking of the words of existing psalms, as well as the creation of new ones inspired by existing models, became a form of individual and group devotion outside of the temple setting. Under such new circumstances, the very words of the psalms sometimes took on new meanings. Because the book of Psalms reflects many aspects of the religious experience of Israel, its intrinsic spiritual depth and beauty have made it from earliest times a treasury of resources for public and private devotion in both Judaism and Christianity.

An important connection can be made between the book of Psalms and God's Torah ("teaching"), the revelation of God's will as found in the Pentateuch. Significantly, the first psalm emphasizes the benefits of meditating on God's Torah (see also Ps 19:7–14). Furthermore, the book of Psalms seems to reach its climax with Psalm 119, the longest of the psalms and the most formal in its structure. This psalm consists of twenty-two stanzas, each corresponding to one letter of the Hebrew alphabet. In addition, each stanza contains eight verses, every line in the stanza beginning with the same letter of the alphabet. Psalm 119 is a celebration of love for God's gift of Torah. The chapter has been titled, "The Love of God's Law," based on the exclamation in verse 97: "Oh, how I love your law!" The reference to "love" in this psalm should not be taken as an emotional outburst of support or delight at specific commandments. The psalmist is not displaying a feeling but a commitment, a commitment to God and to Torah as God's greatest gift. In a larger sense, Psalm 119 is a prayer for wisdom.

The psalm opens by saying, "Happy are those whose way is blameless, who walk in the law of the Lord" (119:1). The wording and sentiment are similar to the opening of Psalm 1; in both cases, the focus is on the delight of pondering Torah day and night, much as does someone who enjoys chemistry, computer science, history, literature, mathematics, music, or some other academic discipline. As scholars love their subject, so people are exhorted to love and study Torah. There is a difference, however, for the psalmist is speaking of a cultivated devotion to God that results from committing oneself to study of Torah. The desired result is to be transformed by study and thereby inspired to live the life that the study of Torah requires. It is possible that at one stage of editing the Psalter ended with Psalm 119, in which case the book concluded on the same note as it began: God's revelation in the Torah.

The Role of Wisdom in Israel's Spirituality

While Israel's poetic literature was adaptable to both private devotion and corporate worship, Israel's wisdom spirituality focused on the individual. Through stirring teachings, the sages of the biblical wisdom tradition offer time-honored advice about some of life's most difficult questions, including the problem of pain, the suffering of the innocent, the nature of evil, the justice of God, and dealing with death. They also address such themes as friendship, virtue and vice, marriage and spousal choice, decision-making, life priorities, child rearing, illness, and death. The insights offered in the biblical tradition and the efforts of the biblical sages to integrate faith, reason, revelation, and human wisdom rival those of the renowned philosophical schools of ancient Greece.

In Israel there were probably three separate settings for wisdom teaching: the clan, the court of the king, and the school. In the clan, the father and mother were the sages. In the royal court, the kings were associated with sages who advised them (see 2 Sam 16:23; 17:14). Later wisdom writings give evidence of a house of learning, that is, a school in which sages instructed the young. The primary purpose of the book of Proverbs is to instruct youth in the life of wisdom, principally the children of wealthy elite connected to the royal court. It is likely that Ecclesiastes also emerged from school instruction, its author a scribe or teacher who lived in Jerusalem. The reference to "those who are wise" in Daniel 12:3 points to a group of trained scholars who served as exemplars in society, praised and viewed in tandem with "those who lead many to righteousness."

Biblical wisdom literature includes not only Proverbs, Job, and Ecclesiastes, but the deuterocanonical books of Sirach and the Wisdom of Solomon. While these books have provided perspective, guidance, and consolation to generations of believers, they can also be of significance for unbelievers, precisely because this literature provides perspective to some of humanity's greatest concerns, including suffering, educating our young, governing wisely, avoiding temptation and vice, growing in virtue, choosing better vocations, selecting friends, and choosing marriage partners.

While the Torah and the prophets agreed in placing the nation at the center, during the period of the Restoration, the individual gradually came to the fore. Personal happiness and success, together with individual fears and hopes, had been recognized in the Torah and by the prophets, but after the exile, the problem of individual suffering became central to Jewish thought. Increasingly, too, the prophets, concerned with the ideal future of the nation, focused on the happiness of the individual. "It was the decline of faith in the fortunes of the nation, coupled with the growth of interest in the individual and with individual destiny, that stimulated the development of wisdom. Wisdom was not concerned with the group, but with the individual, with the realistic present rather than with a longed-for future."[1]

In ancient Israel there were three principal intellectual and spiritual currents, found in the three sections of the Hebrew Bible: Torah (the Law), Nebiim (the Prophets), and Ketubim (the Writings). The Septuagint, the Greek version of the Hebrew scriptures, expanded the Writings to include a fourth category: Wisdom Literature, adding to that literature the books of Sirach and the Wisdom of Solomon. A tripartite division of scripture appears in Sirach: "How different the one who devotes himself to the study of the law of the Most High! He seeks out the wisdom of all the ancients and is concerned with prophecies" (38:34b—39:1). What is unusual about this division is that "wisdom" is placed second, after "law" but before "prophecy." The passage extols the activity of the scribe as one who preserves the sayings of the famous and penetrates the subtleties of parables; he seeks out the hidden meanings of proverbs and is at home with the obscurities of parables" (34:2–3).

It is clear that Hebrew wisdom was not an isolated creation in Israel. On the contrary, it was part of a vast intellectual activity that had been cultivated for centuries in the Fertile Crescent, especially in Egypt and Babylonia. Situated at the cultural crossroads of the ancient world, the Israelites were influenced from an early time by Eastern wisdom writings. These writings, which circulated far beyond the land of their origin, dated back to the Egyptian Pyramid Age (about 2600–2175 BCE) and to the Sumerian era in Mesopotamia. However, wisdom had a timeless quality, transcending time and culture. Though ancient sages reflected on problems of society as they knew them, these were human problems

---

1. Gordis, *God and Man*, 40.

found in varying forms in every society. Thus, the wisdom movement was fundamentally international.

According to the historian Charles A. Beard, one of the lessons of history can be summarized by the proverb, "The bee fertilizes the flower it robs."[2] This is particularly true of the Jews during the exile and the Restoration. Although the experience seemed bitter to many at the time, the people came to realize that God was working for good. While the surrounding culture was regarded as a threat to Israel's faith, the exile also awakened a new world-consciousness, enlarging Israel's faith to an extent never before seen, not even in the cosmopolitan age of Solomon. The exiles realized that they must look beyond their own community to the whole civilized world, if they would behold the glory and majesty of God's purpose in history. The time was ripe for a deeper understanding of the conviction that Israel was called to be God's agent in bringing blessings to all the nations of the earth.

The view that world-shaking events may have a double and seemingly contradictory effect on people's lives characterized a small but highly literate and influential group of Palestinian Jews living in Judah under Persian rule during the fourth and fifth centuries BCE. These sages flourished during this "Golden Age of Wisdom," a peaceful era of two hundred years aided by a common lingua franca (Aramaic) across the Persian empire, a new sense of Jewish identity, and a new internationalism. During this period the books of Job and Ecclesiastes were written and the wisdom material found in the book of Proverbs was collected and finalized.

The wisdom of the biblical sages, unlike the regulations of the priests or the oracles of the prophets, usually made no claim to being divine revelation. It was, of course, self-evident that God was the source of Hebrew wisdom, as of every creative aspect of human nature. Thus, when Isaiah described the ideal Davidic king who would govern in justice and wisdom, he envisioned the spirit of the Lord resting upon him, "the spirit of wisdom and understanding, the spirit of counsel and might, the spirit of knowledge and the fear of the Lord" (Isa 11:2). Some of wisdom's most fervent advocates went further. By endowing wisdom with a cosmic role, they sought to win for wisdom a status almost equal to that of Torah and prophecy. In their most lavish praise of wisdom, the Hebrew sages attributed her with great antiquity, declaring her to have been established

---

2. Cited in Anderson, *Understanding the Old Testament*, 425.

"at the first, before the beginning of the earth" (Prov 8:23). In Job's magnificent "Hymn to Wisdom" (Job 28), wisdom is endowed with cosmic significance and is virtually personified (28:20–28).

In Palestinian Judaism, where the study and interpretation of the Torah ultimately produced the Mishnah, wisdom was equated with the Mosaic law. In the Diaspora, outside of Palestine, where Greek ideas were more influential, wisdom received a more philosophic interpretation. In the case of Philo, the celebrated Alexandrian Jew of the first-century CE, wisdom assumed the doctrine of the Logos or the Divine Word, which became the instrument by which God creates and governs the universe. It is only a further step to conceive of the Divine Word as the intermediary between God and the world, even as a distinct "person" or "aspect" of the divine nature (cf. the Logos Hymn in John 1:1–5).

Ultimately, however, biblical wisdom's claim to authority rested on its pragmatic truth. The Hebrew sages insisted that the application of wisdom "worked," meaning that when coupled with human reason and careful observation, it brought human beings success and happiness. Its origin might be in heaven, but its justification was to be sought in society and nature: "keep sound wisdom and prudence, and they will be life for your soul and adornment for your neck. Then you will walk on your way securely and your foot will not stumble. If you sit down, you will not be afraid; when you lie down, your sleep will be sweet. Do not be afraid of sudden panic, or of the storm that strikes the wicked; for the Lord will be your confidence and will keep your foot from being caught" (Prov 3:19–26).

The Underlying Principle for Israel's Sages

What was the goal of Israel's sages? What did they hope to achieve by coining proverbs and formulating observations about the meaning of life? One means of discovering the self-consciousness of Israel's sages as a distinct group within society is to examine the carefully worded introduction to the book of Proverbs, where we find listed a cluster of words and phrases that characterize those who master the proverbial tradition: wisdom, instruction, understanding, intelligence, righteousness, justice, equity, discretion, knowledge, prudence, learning, and skill. Taken together, they constitute individual facets of the quest for "Life," what philosophers call "the good life." The canonical sages pursued the good life in all its manifestations: health, wealth, honor, progeny, longevity, and remembrance.

A study of four books central to the Jewish wisdom spirituality reveals different results in describing the object of the sapiential search:[3]

1. The book of Proverbs represents a quest for *practical knowledge*, an understanding about nature and human beings that enable people to live wisely and well. For the authors of Proverbs, finding "life" means not so much biologically but relationally, life with another. For the sage, "to live" means to live with wisdom, to banquet with her in her house. According to Proverbs 9:4, living with wisdom is the opposite of living in ignorance. To live with wisdom requires "pondering," meaning that one must live with discernment. Living with the proverbs is like living in a house or a school of wisdom, where wise sayings are examined deeply. Hence the proverbial material is often couched in parables, allegories, riddles, and other enigmatic sayings, with emphasis on subtlety, paradox, and wordplay. Proverbial themes may appear simplistic or repetitive, but careful study reveals that details are important and vital to the meaning of the text.

2. The book of Job is not primarily a search for knowledge about how to cope with the enigmas of ordinary existence, but rather represents a quest for *God's presence*. The author, like the character of Job, acknowledges God's gracious presence in the past, and therefore cannot endure a God who is hidden in the present. Job searches the darkest depths of despair in pursuit of his God, and eventually risks death and even damnation to achieve restored communion. To Job, God is "Life," the highest good, and compared to that *summum bonum*, biological life pales.

3. The book of Ecclesiastes represents the quest for *meaning in a silent universe*. Like Job, Qoheleth (the author of Ecclesiastes) cannot affirm biological life as the supreme good, but unlike Job, Qoheleth does not enter into dialogue with the living God. Lacking confidence in life's goodness, he searches in vain for some meaning that can enable him to endure his empty existence.

4. The book of Sirach represents the quest for Jewish *identity and continuity* in a Hellenistic world that esteemed quite different cultural and religious values. His intention is to convince Jewish youth that Greeks are not the only ones with a magnificent intellectual

---

3. The following analysis is adapted from Crenshaw, *Old Testament Wisdom*, 62–65.

heritage. Highlighting the role of tradition for oneself and for one's community, his goal is tantamount to survival of the Jewish religion and way of life.

Each book, in addition to representing a different object of search, also provides a different temporal focus. The book of Proverbs looks to the distant past, when God established a pattern for the cosmos and for life. The book of Job, focusing on suffering, is concerned wholly with the present. Qoheleth is unable to discern any future worth living for, since death is the great leveler and silencer of hope. Sirach looks to Israel's glorious past in order to provide his generation the ability to resist cultural compromise in the present and thereby give a future to Diaspora Jews. Invariably, Israel's sages, whatever their goals, arrive at a closed door called Mystery, and none except God hold the key to this room. This understanding is what Proverbs 25:2 affirms when it declares that God's glory lies in the tendency to conceal essential reality.

There is a fundamental paradox in the Jewish sapiential tradition, for wisdom is both an object of search but also a gift from God. A relentless search oscillates between two extremes, trusting in one's ability to secure existence and dependence upon God's mercy. The latter, however, represents the final word, for the ultimate quest is that of a gracious God in search of humanity. For humans, the bottom line seems clear: self-discipline, coupled with trust, leads to joy: "When you get hold of [wisdom], do not let her go. For at last you will find the rest she gives, and she will be changed into joy for you" (Sir 6:27–28).

In one sense wisdom authors are highly conservative, for they revere tradition. Yet in another sense they are highly innovative and progressive, for they also revere their own experience and value their own insights. In the biblical tradition, the understanding and insight that constitute "wisdom" ultimately come from God, but are accessible in three primary forms: wisdom taught by God, wisdom taught by nature, and wisdom that arises from reflection on human experience. In these writings, wisdom is the rare attainment of intelligence, sound judgment, ethical conduct, humility, and the distinctive piety identified in the motto of the book of Proverbs: "The fear of the Lord is the beginning of wisdom" (Prov. 9:10). Within the biblical wisdom tradition, certain themes take on increasing significance: the fear of the Lord, God's self-manifestation through personified wisdom, the problem of innocent suffering, the meaning of life, the justification of God's ways, the limits of human knowledge, and the inevitability of death. Given the range of this literature, we may conclude that Israel's sages struggled with life's fundamental questions. Their way of addressing these, and the solutions they reached, point to a remarkable group of people.

Wisdom's practical goals for temporal success appealed primarily to those groups in society that benefitted from the status quo—government officials, rich merchants, great landowners, even high-priestly families. The goal of upper-class education was the training of youth for successful careers. These needs were admirably met by the wisdom teachers who arose, primarily in Jerusalem, the capital city.

The upper-class orientation reflected in the book of Job emerges in the treatment of the book's basic theme—the problem of suffering. While wisdom writers could not ignore the inequities of the present order. at the same time, as representatives of affluent social groups, they did not find the status quo intolerable. The lower classes, oppressed by poverty and marginalized at the hands of domestic and foreign masters, were deeply afflicted by the prosperity of the wicked and the suffering of the righteous. Holding resolutely to their faith in God, they were nevertheless unable to see divine justice operating in the world. Their solution to this problem was the espousal of the doctrine of the afterlife, a future world where the inequalities of the present order would be rectified. Thus, the idea of life after death became an integral feature of Pharisaic Judaism and of Christianity.

Jewish wisdom spirituality profoundly influenced the New Testament community. Wisdom images and ideas appear in every layer of the New Testament, from the letter of James, an early document attributed to the brother of Jesus, to the gospels, which portray Jesus as a wisdom teacher, to the letters of Paul, where Christ is called the wisdom of God (1 Cor 1:24). Early christological hymns, embedded in the New Testament, utilize wisdom motifs to express Christian belief in the incarnation of Jesus (John 1:1–18) and in his cosmic rule (Col 1:15–20; Heb 1:1–4). Among the various influences on the New Testament was the identification of wisdom (Jesus) with divine spirit (2 Cor 3:16–18), word (John 1:1), and law (Matt 5:17–20; 7:24–29). The study of Jewish wisdom literature as found in the Hebrew Bible provides readers of the New Testament with an entirely new and intriguing perspective on Jesus and early Christianity. Following the resurrection of Jesus, when early Christians were looking for language and concepts to express their experience and understanding of Jesus, one of the most helpful resources was the wisdom literature. Of course, other parts of the Hebrew Bible were valuable, such as the prophets, the psalms, and the historical traditions of Israel, but the authors of the New Testament and the leaders of the early Christian communities found in wisdom spirituality an important resource for understanding Jesus and their new life in Christ.

Wisdom and Spirituality

A strong correlation can be found between the wisdom tradition and spirituality, particularly if spirituality represents the ability to live life authentically, for wisdom thinkers found ordinary human existence fascinating. Kathleen O'Connor, a Roman Catholic religious educator, views wisdom as a form of spirituality for the market place. Such spirituality represents the arena "where humans struggle to cope with the chaos of daily life, where Wisdom and Folly compete for human loyalties, and where the divine and the human meet."[4] A spirituality for the market place points equally to two aspects of the natural world; (a) a realm or sphere of life wherein humans might expect to meet God, and (b) a way of living in the world. Popular thinking often limits divine-human exchange to specifically religious activities and places, claiming that God is to be found primarily in the privacy of the individual soul. Wisdom literature provides a resource for a more holistic spirituality, one that perceives outer and inner life, individual and community life, and God and the world as inextricably intertwined. Understanding the realm of divine-human encounter to be ordinary human life, wisdom promotes the pathway of relationship.

The implications for such an understanding of spirituality are enormous. Wisdom spirituality leaves little room for dualistic thinking or living. Ordinary life and the life of faith are not separate or antithetical spheres, for all life exists in the presence of its Creator. From wisdom's perspective, the struggles and conflicts of daily life should not to be shunned or avoided as though they are evil, but rather embraced in full consciousness of their revelatory and healing potential. When Israel's wisdom literature focuses on mundane concerns, it is not ignoring but assuming faith.

Wisdom's focus on human concerns has caused some biblical interpreters to question the presence of this literature in the Bible, but

---

4. O'Connor, *Wisdom Literature*, 14.

these books should not be viewed as secular orphans next to their more theological siblings, the law, the prophets, the gospels, or the epistles. In defending wisdom's viewpoint by referring to it as "theological anthropology," Roland Murphy makes the point that by starting with the realm of human experience, wisdom writers were not excluding God from their world, but rather focusing on what it means to be human in the presence of God. Murphy maintains that the modern distinction between the realms of the secular and the sacred never existed in Israel. Wisdom does not impose God on life but assumes God's presence and activity in every facet of its existence. The various wisdom books all agree that to be wise is to live harmoniously with one's community, the earth, and the creator.

Wisdom literature appreciates the ambiguity of human experience. It finds in ambiguity and confusion the opportunity for breakthrough into mystery. It struggles against rote religious answers to human problems. According to wisdom, life is not a simple set of truths to be followed indiscriminately, but a continual encounter with conflicting truths, each making competing claims upon the seeker. The subject matter of Proverbs, Job, Ecclesiastes, and the Song of Solomon is profoundly ambiguous and paradoxical. Opposing truths are set side by side and in some instances left unresolved. This is evident in the basic literary genre of wisdom, the *mashal*, a pithy saying, proverb, or riddle (see Prov 30:4, a riddle whose answer seems to be "God"; cf. Job 38:5–11). For the sages, life itself is a *mashal*, a world of ambiguity, a series of puzzles small and great. However, the point of ambiguity or paradox is not to bring the individual to an intellectual impasse or a spiritual angst, but to lead one beyond the obvious into deeper understanding. Offering a spirituality of discovery, wisdom requires openness, discernment, and choice. Because wisdom views life as paradoxical, it also calls for patience, trust, and a glad heart.

According to Israel's sages, humans live in a moral universe. Discovering this "rational rule" enabled the sages to protect their existence by acting in harmony with the fundamental order that sustains the cosmos. One's conduct either strengthens the existing order or contributes to the forces of chaos that threaten survival itself. Once the sages discovered this moral or rational principle, it became their task to transfer it from the realm of nature to the human sphere. They accomplished this goal through analogy. Close observation of nature and the animal kingdom convinced Israel's sages that the world was truly a harmonious entity (see

Prov 30:19). The search for proper analogies had as its goal the securing of life. Those who successfully achieved correct knowledge purchased longevity for themselves, together with other indications of divine favor. Knowledge was therefore a means to an end, never an end itself.

While Israel's wisdom literature stands by itself in the Jewish corpus, from a very early period the wisdom movement exerted a pervasive influence on Israel's historical, prophetic, and poetic literature. Certain passages in Isaiah (9:6; 11:2, 9; 28:23–29; 31:2) emphasize wisdom and understanding, so much so that some scholars consider Isaiah to have been a sage before he became a prophet. Similar conclusions have been reached concerning Amos, whose home town of Tekoa is said to have been a center of wisdom. By way of support, scholars point to his universalistic message (whereby all nations are subjected to God's judgment), his use of special vocabulary such as the word "right," his use of unusual rhetorical devices (such as the "woe" sayings), and linguistic phenomena such as numerical sayings, all of which place Amos squarely within clan wisdom. Similar arguments have led to the claim that Micah and Jonah wrote under the influence of the wisdom tradition. Within the historical literature, the Succession Narrative (2 Samuel 9–20 and 1 Kings 1–2) has been attributed to a wisdom writer who sought to illustrate the teachings of certain parables (see Nathan's rebuke of David in 2 Samuel 12) into his narrative, telling stories that embody eternal truths. The same goes for the Joseph Narrative in Genesis, which may have been written by a sage in the royal court to serve as a model for professional courtiers. The association of court stories and wisdom in the book of Esther has led some interpreters to conclude that the author was a sage who wished to emphasize the rewards that come to those who combine wisdom with integrity. The primeval history in Genesis 1–11 has been found to exhibit wisdom influence, particularly in references to a tree of knowledge and to the concept of the knowledge of good and evil. The entire book of Deuteronomy, which emphasizes retribution, life and death (see 30:15–20), and the importance of observing God's commandments, has been attributed to sapiential authorship. Some scholars argue that wisdom gave birth to apocalyptic, pointing to Daniel's association with the legacy of the sages, both Babylonian (1:4) and Israelite (12:3). Eventually, Israel's wisdom literature was fully integrated into Israel's historical faith, as evidenced by the identification of Torah and wisdom in a group of "wisdom psalms" and by the combining of familiar personalities and the events of Israel's history with the wisdom tradition in the later books of Sirach and the Wisdom of Solomon.

Although most people today do not turn to the wisdom literature for prophetic inspiration, the wisdom method of reflection on life experience is gaining prominence. People are again recognizing that God is encountered *through* human experience, not despite it. In their quest for wisdom, students of biblical wisdom literature will be encouraged to know that sacred learning—including study and intellectual questioning—is and always has been at the heart of true spirituality. Those who read this literature will be exposed to a set of core values necessary for vital citizenship and effective leadership at all levels of life. They will also obtain time-honored advice about how to deal with life's uncertainties in a holistic and pragmatic manner, because biblical wisdom is based upon theological tenets such as monotheism, God's providential care for humanity, the moral nature of the universe, and the notion of covenant. Such tenets promote the perspective that people who belong to communities of faith are related to God in patterns of worship, trust, love, obedience, service, protection, and grace.

Questions for Discussion and Reflection

1. What does Israel's history teach about God's nature, purpose, and motivation?
2. In your estimation, what is the primary insight regarding the psalms gained from this chapter? Explain your answer.
3. In your estimation, what do the psalms teach us about the role of community in spirituality?
4. In your estimation, what do the psalms teach us about private and individual spirituality?
5. What lessons did the Jews learn during the Babylonian exile, and how did this experience impact postexilic Judaism?
6. In your estimation, what does wisdom literature teach us about the role of community in spirituality?
7. In your estimation, what does wisdom literature teach us about private and individual spirituality?

8. Of Israel's three canonical books of wisdom (Proverbs, Job, Ecclesiastes), which do you find most relevant to your life today? Explain your answer.

9. In your estimation, what is the primary insight you gained from the segment "Wisdom and Spirituality." Explain your answer.

4

Apocalyptic Spirituality
Early Christian Piety

FOR CHRISTIANS, THE RELATIONSHIP between the Old and New Testaments is one of continuity and discontinuity. Like two partners joined in marriage, neither is a substitute for the other, nor are they independent of one another. Rather there is relative independence, whereby they complement one another. For Christians, the gulf between the testaments is bridged by Jesus Christ, whose person and work establishes deep discontinuity with Israel's scripture and, at the same time, deep continuity in the purpose of God.

Until the emergence of the historical and critical study of the Bible in the eighteenth and nineteenth centuries, the Bible was revered as sole authority for Christian practice and belief. For a time, Christians sought to identify "*the* theology of the New Testament" behind all the writings, believing that scripture contained one divine revelation, which was inspired and therefore not contradictory. Modern scholarship reveals a quite different picture, recognizing a plurality of theologies within the New Testament. Consequently, less attention is placed on "spirituality," except as it is implicit in "theology," but it is now equally clear that we can no longer expect to find only one spirituality or *the* spirituality of the New Testament, and have every reason to detect many. In that respect, we can speak of a Markan spirituality, but also of a Matthean, Lukan, Johannine, and Pauline spirituality.

There are a number of ways people approach the New Testament. Most people do so for religious reasons, approaching it from the perspective of faithful believers. Many people revere the Bible as the Word of God and want to know what it can teach them about what to believe and how to live. However, there are other equally valid ways of approaching the New Testament. In addition to religious reasons, there are literary reasons. The New Testament contains great literary gems, such as Matthew's Sermon on the Mount (Matt 5–7), the gospel of John's portrayal of Jesus and his teachings, the apostle Paul's Hymn to Love (1 Cor 13), and the symbolic imagery of the book of Revelation.

Nevertheless, however we approach the New Testament, we must read and interpret it historically, that is, in its own historical context. The books of the New Testament emerged out of the life of the Christian community, particularly out of the hopes and fears of early Christians in a Greco-Roman world. To understand the New Testament, we must acknowledge and appreciate not only the context of individual passages, but the broader Greco-Roman context as well. Those who don't understand the New Testament in its historical context necessarily take it out of context, thereby changing its meaning. Furthermore, to understand the New Testament from a historical perspective also means readers must initially suspend their own belief or disbelief about its message and meaning, something nearly impossible to do, at least without guidance.

One important aspect of the context of the New Testament is the religious and political environment of the Greco-Roman world. When scholars used the term Greco-Roman, they are referring to the political, social, and cultural conditions prevalent in the Mediterranean world from roughly the time of Alexander the Great in the fourth century BCE to the time of the Roman emperor Constantine in the fourth century CE, that is, a period of some 650 years. Alexander (356–323 BCE) was the great military genius who conquered most of the Mediterranean and lands east, including Persia and India. As he conquered, he spread Greek religion and culture, so that by the time of the New Testament, most of the educated elite throughout the Mediterranean world spoke Greek, in addition to their native language. The Roman empire arose in the context of the Hellenistic world and took full advantage of its unity—promoting the use of Greek language, accepting aspects of Greek culture, and even taking over features of Greek religion—to the point that the Greek and Roman gods came to be thought of as the same, only with different names.

Romans eventually conquered most of the Hellenistic world, ruling Palestine, Syria, North Africa, Asia Minor, Greece, and much of Europe during the emergence of Christianity, and establishing the Pax Romana (the "Roman peace"), a period of peace and stability that lasted for about two hundred years. The Roman world enjoyed a common language, coinage, and legal system, and had a good road system and other benefits that helped the spread of Christianity.

To maintain peace, prosperity, and stability, Rome ruled with an iron fist. In addition, it required tribute from conquered peoples. Roman provinces were ruled by governors, chosen from the Roman aristocracy with two major responsibilities: to raise tax revenues and to keep the peace. To achieve these objectives, they were granted near absolute authority. It was assumed that the governor, on location, would know how best to handle any situation, using whatever means necessary to maintain public order and maximize revenue collection. Using any means necessary meant having the power of life and death. Christians were occasionally persecuted and prosecuted, not because their religion violated Roman law, but because they were perceived as public nuisances. Authorities took care of problems on an ad hoc basis. This is what we see in the crucifixion of Jesus. From a Roman administrative point of view, Pontius Pilate was completely justified in condemning Jesus to death, not only as a political threat, but mostly as a public nuisance who might stir up trouble and create riots.

Jesus as Apocalyptic Jew

To understand early Christian spirituality, we must situate it in its historical context. To do so, we begin with Jesus, who set the tone for Christian spirituality by establishing a pattern for his followers. To understand Jesus' life and teachings, biblical scholars distinguish between the "Jesus of history" and the "Christ of faith." While the New Testament writers had a great deal to say about the latter, what about the former? Who was Jesus of Nazareth? What was his self-understanding? How did he understand human history, and what role did he believe he was playing in it?

To understand Jesus we must situate him in his own historical context. Jesus was a first-century Palestinian Jew, and as such lived in a period of foreign subjugation by Rome. One consequence of foreign subjugation of Palestine included the formation of Jewish sects, which exercised some power and offered religious options for Jews living at the time. The Essenes lived at the margins of society, maintaining their own purity through separation from institutional Judaism. Through unique lifestyle and fervent study of scripture, they lived in anticipation of the imminent apocalypse in which God would judge the world, thereby ending Roman rule and purifying Judaism. The Zealots emphasized Jewish autonomy and their divinely appointed duty to reestablish Israel as a sovereign state, by force if necessary.

Despite the somewhat favored treatment of Jews by Rome, Roman rule was nonetheless felt by many Palestinian Jews as an unbearable burden. Jews responded to Roman rule in a variety of ways, from silent protest to armed rebellion. During the first century CE, various Jewish prophets arose to speak against Rome as God's enemies and were often killed as troublemakers. One form of resistance ideology, apocalypticism, became prominent in the period. This ideology claimed that the forces of evil that were currently in charge of this world and responsible for its suffering would be overthrown by God in a mighty act of judgment. This imminent event was thought to be the prelude to the appearance of God's kingdom in a utopian age on earth. John the Baptist was an apocalyptic prophet of this sort, and we have compelling reasons for thinking that Jesus held such apocalyptic views.

The only way to know what Jesus actually taught is through the sources that survive from antiquity, namely, the four gospels. However, these books must be examined critically. To reconstruct the historical Jesus, it is not enough simply to quote verses from the Bible; every verse of the gospels must be examined carefully, not just to see what it says and to determine what it means, but more importantly, to establish whether it actually goes back to Jesus.

The view that Jesus was an apocalypticist was first popularized by Albert Schweitzer in his 1906 classic text, *Quest of the Historical Jesus*. In this book Schweitzer showed how previous critical scholars had portrayed Jesus incorrectly, because they failed to recognize that he was an apocalypticist. When we examine our gospel sources critically, we find that Schweitzer was right. To understand Jesus correctly, it is important to follow a primary rule used by historians, namely, that we should prefer sources that are closest to the time of the events they narrate and that are not tendentious. In the case of Jesus, a clear perspective emerges when we examine the earliest sources at our disposal: Mark, Q (an early "sayings source" said to underlie Matthew and Luke), M (a source unique to Matthew), and L (a source unique to Luke) but not in later sources, such as John or the second century gospel of Thomas. Each of these early sources are independent of one another, and all portray Jesus apocalyptically. Interestingly, later sources, such as John and the gospel of Thomas, do not.

In the earliest accounts of Jesus' teachings we find numerous apocalyptic predictions: a kingdom of God will soon appear on earth, in which God will rule. The forces of evil will be overthrown, and only those who repent and follow Jesus' teachings will enter the kingdom. Judgment on all others will be brought by the Son of Man, a cosmic figure who may arrive from heaven at any moment. Jesus is said to have proclaimed this message in all of our earliest surviving sources.

This is clearly the case in Mark 1:15 and 13:14–27, the latter passage ending with Jesus' proclamation: "Truly I tell you, this generation will not pass away until all these things have taken place" (Mark 13:30). The same message is found in Luke 17:24, 26–27 and Matthew 24:27, 37–39 (this is Q material), Matthew 13:40–43 (M), and Luke 21:34–36 (L). Some of these apocalyptic traditions are toned down in later traditions. For instance, contrast Mark 9:1 with Luke 9:27 and then with Luke 17:21 (found only in Luke). In this later gospel, Jesus no longer says that his disciples will see the kingdom come in power, but only that the kingdom will arrive in the ministry of Jesus. In Luke 17:21, Luke has Jesus state that the kingdom is "in your midst." This clearly differs from Mark's earlier "coming with power."

The author of Luke's gospel does not seem to think that the coming of a real kingdom would occur in the lifetime of Jesus' companions. Evidently, because he was writing after they had died, and he knew that the end had not come, he deals with the "delay of the end" by making changes in Jesus' predictions. Later sources eliminate the apocalyptic material altogether. Thus, in the gospel of John, the kingdom is not described as imminent but as already present to those who believe in Jesus (3:3, 36). Here, in passages written near the end of the first century, the older apocalyptic idea that a day of judgment is coming and that the dead will be resurrected at the end of the historical age is replaced by a newer view, that in Jesus a person can already experience eternal life (11:23–26). This "de-apocalypticizing" of Jesus' message continues into the second century, as we see in the gospel of Thomas, which contains a clear attack on anyone who believes in a future kingdom on earth (sayings 3, 18, 118).

From this evidence a clear picture emerges. It appears that, when the expected end did not arrive, later Christians changed Jesus' message accordingly. However, when we examine the earliest sources, it is clear that Jesus was an apocalypticist. First-century Palestine had many apocalyptic

Jews, some of whom left writings (such as the Essenes, who wrote the Dead Sea Scrolls). Other apocalyptic Jews were activists, including John the Baptist and prophets such as Theudas (see Acts 5:36–37) and "the Egyptian," mentioned by Josephus.

In Mark 8:38, Jesus talks about a cosmic judge of the earth (the Son of Man), without any suggestion that the reference is himself, even though early Christians did make this association, equating Jesus with the coming heavenly judge. That, however, is not what Jesus taught. In some cases he clearly did speak about himself using the term "son of man" (that is, son of a human), as a reference to his humanity, but when speaking about the future coming of the heavenly Son of Man, Jesus does not appear to have been speaking about himself.

As noted above, the tradition about Jesus as an apocalypticist is confirmed in a study of early Christian sources such as Mark, Q, M, and L. In addition to this evidence, another argument seems convincing. Not only did Jesus begin his ministry apocalyptically, through association with the apocalyptic prophet John the Baptist, but his ministry concluded with apocalyptic Christian communities, such as those established by the apostle Paul, who believed he was living at the end of the age (see 1 Thess 4:13—5:10). If Jesus began his ministry as an apocalypticist, and if the first Christian communities were apocalyptic, then it seems most likely that the middle—Jesus' life and teaching—was also apocalyptic.

Jesus, as we have seen, proclaimed that God's kingdom was coming to earth imminently (Mark 1:15). These words in Mark, the first words Jesus is recorded to have said in that gospel, provide a summary of Jesus' teaching. This would be a real kingdom with real rulers, a kingdom that would welcome some people but exclude others. Before the kingdom arrived, a scene of judgment would take place, in which the Son of Man, a cosmic figure from heaven, would appear to destroy God's enemies. This coming judgment would involve a massive reversal of fortunes; those who had prospered in this world through siding with evil would be displaced, but those who had suffered would be exalted. The judgment would come not only to individuals, but also to institutions and governments. In particular, the Jewish temple in Jerusalem, the heart of all institutional Jewish worship, would be destroyed.

Throughout his authentic teachings, when Jesus refers to the coming kingdom, he seems to mean an actual earthly kingdom, with actual rulers. Consider Jesus' teachings found in Q, perhaps our earliest source: "Truly I tell you, at the renewal of all things, when the Son of Man is seated on the throne of his glory, you who have followed me will also sit on twelve thrones, judging the twelve tribes of Israel" (Matt 19:28; cf. Luke 22:30). While the arrival of the kingdom was "good news" for Jesus' followers, it was not good news for everyone. In a mighty act of judgment, evil rulers would be toppled and punished, and the oppressed would be raised up (Luke 13:23–29; cf. Matt 8:11–12). This coming judgment would involve a serious reversal of fortune, one that makes sense in an apocalyptic context (Mark 10:31; Luke 13:30).

Likewise, Jesus' ethical teachings make best sense in an apocalyptic context. These teachings, however, have come down to us today as perfect examples of how people ought to live normally. Nevertheless, it is important for us to understand that the meaning of Jesus' ethical teachings might have been quite different in their original context from their meaning in ours. In our context, Jesus' teachings assist us in knowing how to get along with one another, so that we can contribute to a healthier and more wholesome society, allowing us to experience peace and wellbeing for the long haul. However, for Jesus there was not going to be a long haul. The Son of Man would soon come in judgment, and people needed to prepare for entrance into his kingdom by showing that they sided with God rather than with the forces of evil that were opposed to him. Jesus' ethical teachings were ethics of the kingdom—they both reflected what life would be like in the kingdom and qualified one for entrance once it arrived.

In the kingdom, there would be no hatred; thus, people should love one another now. In the kingdom, there would be no oppression; thus, people should work for justice now. In the kingdom, there would be no war; thus, people should work for peace now. In the kingdom, there would be no sexism; thus, people should work for equality now. Only those who lived in ways that are appropriate to the kingdom would be allowed entrance when it arrived.

According to Jesus' teachings in the Sermon on the Mount, his followers should regard entrance into the kingdom as their most prized possession, and even be willing to give up all their possessions for the sake of the kingdom (Matt 6:25–33). Later on, Jesus indicates in his parable of the Pearl of Great Price that the kingdom is like a merchant in search of fine pearls who finds a perfect pearl and then goes out and sells all that he has to buy it. The pearl is the kingdom, and it demands our ultimate allegiance; that's how valuable it is. For Jesus, nothing made sense apart from the kingdom of God that was on the verge of breaking into history. If its coming found one unprepared, all would be lost.

If Jesus' ethical teachings make best sense in an apocalyptic context, we need to rethink their meaning for his followers. Jesus, it appears, did not deliver timeless truths to guide individuals in leading long and productive lives. His teachings were meant to show people how to live in order to enter the kingdom that would soon appear. When we examine teachings such as "love your neighbor as yourself," and "love your enemies and pray for those who persecute you," he was teaching ethics of the coming kingdom. How else can we understand Jesus' teaching to the young ruler, that he should give up everything—all possessions and everything that binds one to this world (Mark 10:17–31)—except in this context? This emphasis on giving up everything for the kingdom means that Jesus was not a major proponent of what we now call "family values" (see Luke 14:26; 12:51–53). As with other hard sayings of Jesus, these should not be explained away so that they no longer mean what they say. Instead, they should be placed in an apocalyptic context.

Understood apocalyptically, Jesus' command to love one's neighbor and God above all else points to the coming kingdom, when God will provide such things as food and clothing (Matt 6:25–33). To those who trust God, all things are possible, for that is how God will care for us in his kingdom that is soon to come. Jesus, then, did not see himself as inventing a new system of ethics, so much as explaining the law of Moses in view of his own apocalyptic context.

While later sources have Jesus proclaiming the kingdom as a present reality, this is not what Jesus actually taught. For him, the kingdom was imminent, but it had not yet arrived. Understanding Jesus' message of the coming judgment of the Son of Man, including the destruction of the temple in Jerusalem, helps explain Jesus' actions in the temple prior to his crucifixion. Viewed apocalyptically, they become a symbolic expression of his teaching, a prophetic gesture or enacted parable of the coming of God's imminent judgment on the earth, beginning with institutional Judaism. In cleansing the temple, Jesus was demonstrating on a small scale what would soon occur in a large way.

Jesus was betrayed by one of his own followers, Judas Iscariot. What is not clear, though, is what it was that Judas betrayed, or why he acted as he did. Some believe that he betrayed Jesus for financial gain; others argue that Judas grew disillusioned when he realized that Jesus had no intention of becoming a political Messiah; yet still others have reasoned that Judas wanted to force Jesus' hand, thinking that if Jesus were arrested, he would call out for support and start an uprising that would overthrow the Romans. While each of these explanations has merit, the clearest explanation is that Judas may have divulged insider information that the authorities could use to bring Jesus up on charges. Jesus, it appears, taught his disciples things in private that he did not state publicly.

We have several hints as to what Jesus taught about himself that Judas might have divulged to the authorities. Almost certainly, the charge leveled against Jesus by the Roman governor Pontius Pilate was that he considered himself to be the King of the Jews (Mark 15:2; John 19:33; 19:19). However, Jesus never called himself this in any of the gospels. Why would he be executed for a claim he never made? Jesus did teach that after the Son of Man executed judgment on the earth, the kingdom would arrive. Kingdoms, by their nature, have kings. Who would be the king? Ultimately, of course, it would be God. However, Jesus probably did not think that God would physically sit on the throne in Jerusalem. Who, then, would?

The earliest traditions indicate that Jesus thought he would be enthroned. For one thing, only those who accepted his message would be accepted into the kingdom. Jesus also told his disciples that they would be seated on twelve thrones to rule the twelve tribes of Israel. Who would be over them? It was Jesus who had called them to be the Twelve. Moreover, his disciples asked him for permission to sit at his right hand and his left in the coming kingdom (Mark 10:37). Of course, the current textual context, modified by later authors and redactors, changes the original meaning of Jesus' teaching. Rightly understood, his disciples would have viewed him as ruler in the kingdom, just as he was their "ruler" now.

Judas, then, betrayed this private teaching of Jesus to the Jewish authorities, and that explains why they could level the charges against Jesus that he called himself the Messiah, the King of the Jews. Of course, he meant it in the apocalyptic sense, but they meant it in a this-worldly sense. Once the local Jewish authorities learned this insider information, they had all the grounds they needed to make a quick arrest to get Jesus out of the public eye, and thus avoid any recriminations from their Roman overlords over disturbances caused by Jesus and his followers.

From Prophecy to Apocalyptic

To consider properly the eschatological element in the New Testament, we must turn to Israel's prophets, for eschatology was basic to their message. They consistently looked beyond the present, in which God's purpose seemed to be temporarily opposed by Israel's rebellion, to a time when God would triumph over the forces of evil. Prophetic predictions of the triumph of God's purpose were expressed in phrases like "the Day of the Lord," "the Age to Come," and "the kingdom of God." For Israel's prophets, the consummation of history was to be a time of reckoning, when all rebellious powers would be judged and destroyed. It was also to be the beginning of a new creation in which nature and human nature would be transformed. No longer would there be war, and even wild animals would be tame (Isa 65:17–25). The pictures of the messianic age remind us of the idyllic peace and harmony of the Garden of Eden prior to the expulsion. The prophets proclaimed that the Day was imminent, as the very next moment of history.

The prophetic message was further elaborated in a type of literature called "apocalyptic," which flourished in the postexilic period. The theme of apocalyptic, as in the case of prophecy, is the nearness of the time when God will assert sovereignty over history and nature. It is characteristic of apocalyptic, however, that specific historical events recede into the background, and the contest between God and rebellious forces assumes a cosmic scale. Apocalyptic writers were dualistic in their view of history. They perceived two dominions (kingdoms) struggling for dominance. The kingdom of God stands opposed to the well-organized kingdom of Evil that is under the leadership of Satan. They did not view this metaphysically, as a dualism rooted in ultimate reality or in the depths of divinity, for God's original creation was good. Rather, this was a postcreation dualism rooted in creaturely rebellion against God—rebellion that is evident not only in human sin but also in cosmic revolt by celestial beings. The conflict between the forces of God and the forces of evil was eventually expressed in terms of the myth of Satan, a heavenly being who revolted against God and set up a rival kingdom into which human beings are enticed. These two dominions may also be described as two "ages" or "worlds," that is, as periods of history. The present "age," in the apocalyptic view, is under the dominion of evil, and it will be succeeded by the "new age," when evil is overcome and all things are made new.

The End will be heralded by unusual "signs" and cataclysms in nature. On the Day of Judgment God (or God's messianic agent) will destroy all powers of evil and will create a new heaven and a new earth. As we see in the book of Daniel, the purpose of apocalyptic writers was to encourage the faithful to remain steadfast in a perilous hour when

Apocalyptic Spirituality

allegiance to God was temporarily eclipsed by foreign tyranny or the victory of evil. (In this light, see the account of Daniel's friends cast into the "fiery furnace" [Dan 3] or of Daniel cast into the "den of lions" [Dan 6], symbols of the Maccabean faithful under the forced Hellenization by the tyrant Antiochus Epiphanes around 165 BCE.) The use of fantastic imagery in books like Ezekiel and Daniel clearly indicates that the language was intended to be imaginative. The heart of the apocalyptic message was the certainty that God's purpose could not be frustrated—a certainty that found expression in the nearness of the End. This is the only way that a new age of peace and justice could come: God must destroy the whole evil system.

The movement from classical prophecy to apocalyptic can be traced within the book of Isaiah, from its inception in the message of the eighth-century prophet Isaiah of Jerusalem (chapters 1–39), to the message of the so-called Second Isaiah during the exile (chapters 40–55), to the message of the so-called Third Isaiah, dated to the postexilic period and found at the conclusion of the book (chapters 56–66). To appreciate the theological significance of this shift, we turn to the message of Second Isaiah, which represents the transition from prophecy (First Isaiah) to apocalyptic (Third Isaiah).

Like a pastoral theologian, Second Isaiah offers comfort to a dislocated, suffering people whose faith in God has been strained to the breaking point: "Comfort my people, says your God. Speak tenderly to Jerusalem, and cry to her that she has served her term, that her penalty is paid, that she has received from the Lord's hand double for all her sins" (Isa 40:1–2). The substance of the "good news" that is to be carried from heaven to earth is that the time of the coming of God's dominion is near. While Second Isaiah does not refer directly to the Mosaic covenant, the people are told that though they have suffered the penalty for their sins, and they are assured that God's covenant promises made of old are still valid: "the word of our God will stand forever" (Isa 40:8). Like the former exodus from Egyptian bondage, God is about to do a "new thing," which will be so wonderful that the former things pale in significance: "I am about to do a new thing, now it springs forth, do you not perceive it?" (Isa 43:16–19). The heart of Second Isaiah's message is the proclamation that the new creation is happening in the present as God conquers the chaos of the Babylonian exile and makes a path through the sea for his redeemed to pass over and return with singing to Jerusalem (Isa 51:10). The prophet has taken creation completely out of the realm of mythology.

For him creation is a historical event in the now. Here is a faith that turns not to the archaic past, longing for the good old days, "but stands on tiptoe, facing the new age that God is about to introduce."[1]

Second Isaiah turns to the Davidic covenant, announcing the rebuilding of the temple through the agency of a foreign ruler, Cyrus of Persia, here called God's anointed (Messiah) because he will accomplish God's purpose (Isa 44:28—45:7). The Davidic covenant is reaffirmed by shifting the promises of this "everlasting covenant" from the Davidic dynasty to the new community (Isa 55:3). The poet continues by stating that this community will be instrumental in including other nations in the saving purpose of God, as promised in the Abrahamic covenant (Isa 55:5; see Gen 12:3; 22:18).

The final section of the book of Isaiah, Third Isaiah (56–66), is sometimes designated proto-apocalyptic or the "dawn of apocalyptic," since it is not apocalyptic in the full-blown sense. In the final edition of the book of Isaiah, materials of more definite apocalyptic character were added, including "the little apocalypse" of Isaiah 24–27 and chapters 34 and 35. In these passages we notice a shift in emphasis from the history of the people Israel to the cosmic dimension, which includes heaven and earth and the whole course of human history from creation to consummation. Nations like Assyria and Babylon are no longer agents of God chastening the people Israel, but are symbols of sinister powers at work in history, threatening God's divine plan for Israel and the nations. God's victory over these forces of evil represents a new creation in which God vindicates Zion, the city of God, and ends the suffering of the poor and helpless of the earth (see Isa 65:17–19).

Whereas classic prophecy explained suffering as retribution for the people's failure or sin, apocalyptic writers found this explanation of evil to be inadequate. It was not enough to call for repentance or to blame the people for their irresponsibility. They perceived that Israel and all peoples were caught in the grip of monstrous forces that challenged the sovereignty of God. Evil, in their view, is located not in the human heart but in oppressive empires and other structures of power. Accordingly, apocalyptic writers revived the ancient myth of the battle of the Divine Warrior against the powers of chaos and the decisive victory that demonstrated God's power as King. This ancient myth influenced the pattern of the Song of the Sea (Exod 15:1–18), a poetic response to the exodus.

---

1. Anderson, *Contours of Old Testament Theology*, 294.

At one point Second Isaiah invoked the myth to portray Yahweh's power to create a people and give them a future. In this poetic view, the victory over the army of the Pharaoh is symbolized by the monster of chaos, Rahab (Isa 51:9–10), and the author addresses Yahweh to achieve a similar victory in the future.

In apocalyptic imagination, the Divine Warrior's victory is not restricted to Israel's history but belongs to a universal drama, in which the kingdom of God opposes the powers of evil that afflict people. These visionaries portrayed a New Jerusalem, a new age, indeed, a new creation. In this perspective, the coming of God's kingdom on earth would be the time of God's triumph—not only over human sin but also over all the powers of evil that have corrupted human history. In the Isaiah Apocalypse (Isa 24–27), the writer portrays the final triumph of the Divine Warrior over the monster of evil known as Tiamat in Babylonian tradition and as the sea serpent Leviathan (Rahab) in Canaanite mythology (Isa 27:1).

Thus, in apocalyptic literature, the whole historical drama, from creation to consummation, is viewed as a cosmic conflict between the divine and the demonic, creation and chaos, the kingdom of God and the kingdom of Satan. According to this view, the outcome of the conflict would be God's victorious annihilation of the powers that threaten creation, including death, which apocalyptic writers regarded as an enemy hostile to God. Seen in this perspective, the role of the Messiah would be not just to liberate humanity from the bondage of sin but to battle triumphantly against the powers of evil.

A line can easily be drawn from this apocalyptic message to the apocalyptic teaching of Jesus and Paul, and to the portrayal of the consummation found in the book of Revelation. In this Christian apocalypse, at the time of the final triumph of God, Isaianic optimism and symbolism are invoked yet again, as the powers of evil—symbolized by "the great dragon . . . that ancient serpent, who is called the Devil and Satan" (Rev 12:9)—will be overcome. Moreover, "the sea"—the locus of the powers of chaos—will be no more (Rev 21:1).

The Life, Death, and Resurrection of Christ as Eschatological Events

When we place the resurrection of Jesus into an apocalyptic context, it makes complete sense that it represents the new reality that is expected in the coming age. Jewish apocalypticists did not expect to be taken to heaven in the new age. Rather, that new age would be a golden age on earth. Associated with this expectation was the belief that when the time had been fulfilled for the current evil age, there would be a general resurrection of the dead (see Matt 27:51–53). Followers of Jesus who believed in the resurrection of Jesus would draw an obvious conclusion, namely, that the new age had already begun. In 1 Corinthians, Paul makes this connection, finding in the resurrection of Jesus clear proof of the anticipated general resurrection of the dead (1 Cor 15:12–24). In Paul's mind, Jesus was the "first fruits" of resurrection, that is, the beginning of God's final winnowing or harvesting process. This meant, for Paul and other early Christian apocalypticists, that God's end-time judging and rewarding was to occur shortly. Jesus had been exalted to heaven, but would soon return as the heavenly Son of Man to judge the earth.

During his lifetime, Jesus had spoken of the coming Son of Man as a divine emissary, not to be equated with himself. Now, however, his followers began thinking of him, not as a prophetic forerunner of the final apocalypse, but as the actual coming judge referred to in Daniel 7:13–14. Whereas Jesus had taught his disciples that he would have a place of prominence in the coming kingdom, after the Resurrection his followers assumed that the kingdom had already begun, and that Jesus was already its ruler. In fact, Jesus was now ruler of all things in heaven and earth. No longer merely King of the Jews, they now understood him to be Lord of all.

The New Testament is saturated with the belief that something new happened in the history of humanity, in and through the life and death of Jesus Christ, and above all through his resurrection from the dead. Like their Old Testament counterparts, the followers of Jesus were shaped by an event so profound that it continues to be celebrated as decisive for Christians around the world. The early Christians found in Easter a correlation with the exodus—a path from darkness to light, despair to hope, inability to possibility, bondage to freedom—and with the creation, for the resurrection of Jesus constituted a new beginning for humanity.

In order to make sense of the New Testament, we need to begin with Easter, for Easter is central to Christianity. Whatever occurred on that first Easter, it had incredible power. Before the Easter experience, Jesus' followers forsook him and fled. After the Easter experience, they were willing to die for their conviction that whatever their understanding of God, it had to include Jesus of Nazareth. This shift in God consciousness revolutionized the theology of Jesus' followers so dramatically that the world has never been the same. In addition, the Easter event led Jewish Christians to create Sunday, a new holy day, different from yet fulfilling the notion of the Jewish Sabbath.

While the line between the eschatology of Jesus and that of the church cannot be clearly drawn, it seems likely that Jesus thought in the framework of Jewish apocalyptic. However, this changed over time, and it led early Christians to view the appearance of Jesus as an eschatological event. It became their conviction that in Jesus the *eschaton* (the final and decisive event) had already entered history, giving assurance of the near approach of the Day of Judgment and "the time of universal restoration" (Acts 3:20–21). The cross, no longer viewed as a naked act of Roman cruelty, instead became God's sentence of judgment upon human sin and the powers of darkness, making possible through resurrection a "new creation" for those who are in Christ.

Christian Transformation of Apocalyptic

While early Christians shared basic convictions with Jewish apocalyptic, one finds not only similarities but also striking differences. For example, the New Testament transformed the Jewish apocalyptic perspective by announcing that God has done something totally and radically new through the life, death, and resurrection of Jesus Christ. A "new creation" has begun to appear (2 Cor 5:17).

The New Testament portrays Jesus not merely as an apocalyptic visionary who announces the mystery of God's kingdom to a select few; rather, he himself is the sign of God's kingdom in the present historical age. Jesus' crucifixion, crowned with resurrection, signifies that Jesus is the victor in the long struggle with evil. The New Testament announces that the period of waiting is over, for the king has come and the dominion of God has already been inaugurated. In other words, the Christian gospel has altered the time scheme of apocalyptic, with its sharp separation of "the present evil age" from "the age to come," so that the old must pass away before the new can come. In the New Testament, the two ages are like overlapping circles, for already God has introduced the new age through Jesus

Christ even while the old age persists. In the Christian reinterpretation of apocalyptic, the supreme sign of the new age is the resurrection of Christ from the dead. As Paul argues in 1 Corinthians 15, this end-time event has already occurred in the midst of the present age. So near and certain is God's triumph that Paul can go so far as to say that not everyone will die (1 Cor 15:51; likewise, Matthew's gospel refers to a strange apocalyptic event occurring at the moment when Jesus was crucified, when many who were dead are said to have come forth from their graves; 27:51–54).

To be sure, the Christian community lives in the tension of the "already" and the "not yet." Using the symbolic language of apocalyptic, the trumpet signaling God's final triumph has not yet sounded. There is still a period of waiting for the final consummation, the coming of God's kingdom fully on earth and the appearance of Jesus Christ in glory. But this waiting is not the expectation of counting the days or speculating on an apocalyptic timetable. For already God's triumph has been manifest in the resurrection of Christ.

Finally, "apocalyptic has given to the early Christian community a profound grasp of the meaning of God's triumph in Jesus Christ. God's victory is liberation from the power of sin through divine forgiveness, displayed in the vicarious and atoning death of Jesus. The apocalyptic perspective, however, pushes Christian interpreters to go beyond the prophetic message of sin and forgiveness and to proclaim God's triumph over all the powers of darkness, chaos, evil, and death."[2] Paul lists some of those powers in his great victory proclamation at the end of Romans 8, where he declares that through Christ we are "more than conquerors" (Rom 8:37).

The call to conquer is fundamental to the structure and theme of the book of Revelation, the apocalypse that brings the Christian canon to a close. Everything that is said in the seven messages to the churches has this aim, expressed in the promise to the conquerors that concludes each (Rev 2:7; 11, 17, 28; 3:5, 12, 21). Like Jesus, the real victors are the martyr-witnesses, those who are faithful to God even to the point of death. Conquering is not represented as something to which only some are called, but as the only way for Christians to reach their eschatological destiny. According to Revelation 21:7–8, there are only two options: to conquer and inherit the promises, or to suffer the second death in the lake of fire. John's message in Revelation is a call for resistance against evil, not, however, through violence but through kingdom living and witnessing.

---

2. Anderson, *Contours of Old Testament Theology*, 335.

Questions for Discussion and Reflection

1. Explain and assess the author's view that there is not one spirituality but rather many spiritualities in the New Testament.
2. In a sentence or two, define the word "apocalyptic." In your estimation, why have Christians been so attracted to this perspective?
3. Modern scholarship is divided regarding Jesus' self-understanding. Some scholars view Jesus to be an apocalyptic prophet, whereas others envision a non-apocalyptic Jesus. How do you view Jesus, apocalyptically or non-apocalyptically? Explain your answer.
4. In your estimation, how are the Christian doctrines of salvation and the afterlife associated with the apocalyptic perspective? In your estimation, what do Christians mean by the phrase "the kingdom of God"? How do popular notions of God's kingdom differ from what Jesus taught and believed about God's kingdom?
5. Which of Jesus' ethical teachings do you find most significant and transformative? Why?
6. In your estimation, did Jesus envision an imminent end to human history? If so, does this understanding of Jesus' motivation and perspective affect how you view and apply his ethical teaching?
7. If Jesus were to appear today, what would he want us to know about his nature and his mission?
8. Explain the origins of apocalyptic thinking in Judaism. In your estimation, what role did this perspective play in shaping the early Christian movement?
9. Without belief in Jesus' resurrection from the dead, it is safe to say that Christianity would have been just another failed messianic movement. What role did belief in the general resurrection of humanity from the dead play in apocalyptic theology?
10. While apocalyptic passages are scattered across the New Testament, the book of Revelation is its sole example of apocalyptic literature. What role has this book played throughout Christian history, and how has it contributed to Christian eschatology?

5

Mystic Spirituality
Early Medieval Christian Piety

While most Christians consider themselves disciples of Jesus and try to follow his teachings, a smaller number focus on practical acts of service or solidarity. While these can be done in tandem, some Christians feel compelled to pursue a third option, the difficult mystic path. Throughout Christian history, many mystics followed the monastic path, pursuing spiritual perfection through self-denial, ascetic practices, and extreme devotion.

Unfortunately, the mystical path is often described in vague terms, making it appear unappealing or perhaps inaccessible to most. However, if we define "mysticism" to mean "experiential knowledge of spiritual things," as opposed to head knowledge, book knowledge, church knowledge, or other forms of secondhand knowledge, it appears more compelling.

Much of organized religion, without meaning to, actually discourages us from taking the mystical path by telling us to trust outer authority exclusively—whether in the form of scripture, tradition, or reliance on specific religious experts—instead of encouraging and supporting the value of inner experience. This first-half-of-life approach—trusting the "containers" instead of the "contents"—blocks access to experiential second-half-of-life spirituality. Discouraging or denying people's actual experience of God can create passivity and lead to the conclusion that either there is no God to be experienced or that such experience is not possible. This approach can result in distrusting our soul, and hence the Holy Spirit within us.

Contrast this with Jesus' common advice, "Go in peace. Your faith has made you well" (see Mark 5:34; also Luke 17:19). He said this to people who made no dogmatic affirmations, did not think he was "God," did not pass any moral checklist, and rarely belonged to the "correct group." They were simply people who trustfully affirmed, with open hearts, the grace of their hungry experience, and that, in that moment, God cared about it.

Admittedly, personal experiences are easy to misinterpret, and we cannot assume that our experience is always from God. We must develop filters to clear away our own agenda and ego. We need a solid grounding in theology, psychology, and sociology, along with good and wise counsel. We cannot forget Paul's reminder, which is meant to keep us humble, "For we know only in part, and we prophesy only in part" (1 Cor 13:9).

The Augustinian Paradigm of Spirituality

In the history of Europe, the medieval period (the thousand-year period said to last from the fall of the Western Roman empire in 476 to the fall of Constantinople in 1453), altered the Western and Middle Eastern worlds profoundly. However, the start of the fourth century, beginning with the Edict of Milan in 313, changed the fortunes of Christianity forever. With the conversion of Constantine to Christianity in 312, state persecution of Christians ceased, and Christianity was on its way to becoming the official religion of the Roman empire (an event made official by Emperor Theodosius in 380).

This dramatic change of church-state relations, with Christianity no longer endangered but established, had a profound effect upon prayer and spirituality. On the one hand, it led to an impressive display of liturgical worship. Spacious churches were built and richly decorated, where the Eucharist could be celebrated in formal splendor. At this time there was also a rapid development of pilgrimages, the cult of the saints, and devotion to the Virgin Mary. On the other hand, ascetic piety, present in Christianity from the start, assumed a more articulate form with the emergence of monasticism as an organized movement, distinct from the life of the parish. Both the "way of affirmation" and the "way of negation" became sharply differentiated.

While there are many things in medieval spirituality that modern people find extreme or self-deprecating, medieval Catholic spirituality is not all excess and abuse. There is also a wonderful spiritual legacy here, from which we have much to learn.

Medieval spirituality is about a journey to God. Being with God is regarded as the destiny of believers, our heritage, our home. For this we are created, and here we belong. The journey, called by Augustinian scholar Phillip Cary "The Augustinian paradigm of spirituality," goes back to the church father Augustine (354–430), who lived during the church's conciliar age, near the end of the Roman empire. Augustine's thought established the fundamental theological categories for medieval thought, meaning that all medieval church theologians lived and thought in an Augustinian framework. Despite notable exceptions, for one thousand years, the Augustinian spirituality was nearly every Christian's paradigm.

For medieval Christians, the goal of the spiritual journey was finding happiness, often called "beatitude," "bliss," or simply "the blessed life." In this context, ultimate or eternal happiness meant finding God, or, as Augustine put it, "seeing" God. Of course, this did not happen with one's physical sight, but with what Augustine called inward or "intellectual" vision, seeing with one's mind and heart. Such vision is what we experience when we struggle to understand something before we finally "see" or "get" its meaning. That intuitive way of knowing, that recognition, is what Augustine meant by "seeing" or experiencing God, who, we might add, is not only final and absolute truth, but the Truth at the center of the universe from whom come all other truths. Imagine having this knowledge, this certainty, this relationship, at the center of your life. Imagine living within the context of the eternal "Aha! Now I get it!" That happiness, joy, and bliss, seeing God with your mind's eye, is what Augustine's spirituality had as its goal. This, for Augustine, is what it means "to see God eternally," and also what it means to speak of "heaven."

This, of course, is the end of the journey. During the journey, we might have glimpses of God, but there is yet no finality. The journey is long and arduous, and what we need for the journey are values, morality, and commitment. What we need for the journey is not vision—that comes at the end—but faith, hope, and love, moral characteristics of the soul that power the soul on its journey. The journey begins with faith, which means, essentially, believing what you are told. Then there is this long road to travel, a road we travel by love—of God and others. For Jesus and Paul, this is the summation of the religious law, which goes back to the Old Testament, and Augustine puts it at the heart of Christian ethics. Love is like gravity—a force of attraction—but it pulls us upward, not downward. Love for God attracts us to God, pulling us upward, like sparks from a fire, ultimately uniting us with God.

A central concern of medieval Christianity is knowing God, a form of knowing that often focused on the incomprehensibility of God, a mystery beyond understanding. While Augustine, like many Christians, conceived of God as incomprehensible, he interpreted the concept differently from most theologians. For Augustine, the human mind is like an eye, made to see the light of divine Truth. However, due to human sin, no one can see God naturally. As a result, our human soul—including our will, intellect, and understanding—is corrupted. However, if our mind's eye is healed by grace, and we are guided on our way to God by divine love, we will—by the nature of our intellect—be able to see God. That is what our intellect was made for—to see the truth. For Augustine, it is natural for humans to seek God. This is the path we humans have been on our whole lives—the path of love—and when we receive God's grace, we finally find the truth we have been searching for. This is the happiness we desire; it is joy in the truth, says Augustine. In this respect, when human beings receive God's grace, God is intelligible, and it becomes possible for humans to look directly at the "sun" and not be dazzled.

This notion is unique to Augustine. The rest of the Christian tradition, in both East and West, says it is not natural for humans to see God—like the natural eye is not made to look at the sun. However, at its best, this way of seeing is partial and transitory, Augustine admits, enabling only a glimpse of God. Just because the physical eye can see an object does not mean it can comprehend it. While the eye might see an object such as a cup, it can only see one side at a time. Thus, the eye can see a cup, yet not comprehend it. The same holds true for God. We may be able to see God by our intellect, but we cannot comprehend God.

Following Augustine, the West faced a problem that had to be solved. The Western tradition believed that human happiness depends on seeing God. Yet the West also inherited the view of Eastern theologians such as the apophatic theology of the pseudonymous sixth-century theologian called Denys or Pseudo-Dyonisius, whose work was translated into Latin and influenced nearly all major Western theologians. In his treatise on the *Divine Names*, Denys reminds us that all affirmations fall short of God, that no human concept can describe what is unknowable, and this leads to his apophatic spirituality, with its realization that "the most divine knowledge of God" is known through "unknowing." In Greek, "apophatic" means "negation" or "denial." The West picked up some of this apophatic way of thinking, speaking of the *via negativa*, saying what God is not, such as immutable (not changing), immortal (not mortal), and incomprehensible (above human understanding). In this respect, the fourteenth-century English work known as *The Cloud of Unknowing*, written in the apophatic tradition, is a masterpiece of negative mystical theology.

The resolution of the doctrine of the incomprehensibility of God came in the thirteenth century, in the theology of Thomas Aquinas, a brilliant thinker viewed by Roman Catholicism as the supreme medieval theologian. Aquinas agreed with Augustine that happiness consists in seeing God with the mind's eye, and that this is the ultimate goal of life. On the other hand, he agreed with Denys that no created being can see the divine essence. This raises the million-dollar question: "How can humans have happiness, if with their natural mind's eye they try to gaze on an incomprehensible God?" Eventually disagreeing with Augustine, Aquinas declared that it is not possible naturally for humans to have a "beatific vision" of God (a vision of God that makes a human being happy or blessed). Nevertheless, he argued, comprehending God (seeing God) is possible for a mind that is elevated by "supernatural grace."

In so arguing, Aquinas introduced a new concept of grace, one that elevates the mind above itself, so that it can see what no natural capacity is able to see. Grace, in this new sense, doesn't just come to our aid, doesn't just heal us so that our natural mind is strengthened to see God. Rather, supernatural grace actually enables humans to do what they cannot do by nature. This gift of grace, when given, is said to reside in one's soul, making it habitual—a habit of the soul—to see God. Aquinas, influenced by the Greek philosopher Aristotle, came to understand grace as a skill or habit that enables one's heart and soul to see what is beyond their inborn capacity to see and comprehend. Hence, it is possible to look directly at God and find in that brightness, not dazzlement or blindness, but rather happiness and beatitude. While the beatific vision—the ultimate goal of human life—cannot be achieved independently, such experience, such finding, requires faith, hope, and charity, supernatural gifts of divine grace. One, alone, however, is not sufficient. Knowing God requires all three gifts simultaneously.

Unlike Aquinas, in Augustine's attempt to know God and understand God's will, he began exclusively with faith. For Augustine, faith is not some nebulous cognitive act by which one hopes God exists, but an activity requiring the whole of one's being—heart, mind, soul, and strength. In his commentary on the gospel of John he writes, "Understanding is the reward of faith. Therefore, seek not to understand in order that you may believe, but believe in order that you might understand." Augustine shortened this to the motto: *credo ut intelligam*—"I believe in order that I might understand," taking this motto from Isaiah 7:9: "If you do not stand firm in faith, you shall not stand at all."[1] In other words, unless one begins by accepting certain truths, one will not understand later on. While modern versions of Isaiah 7:9 read somewhat differently, Augustine was working with Old Latin texts of the Old Testament, before Jerome (a contemporary of Augustine) produced the Vulgate, which became the standard Latin Bible in the medieval period and the basis of Catholic Bibles to this day.

Building on passages from the gospels of John and Matthew, Augustine notes that Jesus first invites followers into a relationship with himself and through him, with the Father (see John 17:3), and it is on the basis of this relationship of knowing and trusting God that he says to his disciples in Matthew 7:7, "Search (seek), and you will find." Thus, people are to believe first what they later come to understand. Augustine was not asking believers to scrap or compromise reason—he was not asking for "blind" faith—but simply subordinating reason to revelation. For Augustine, divine revelation, as given in Christ, is the precondition for all religious knowledge. Once believers begin with God, then they are to seek to understand all truth in light of God. In our journey toward God, the task of reason is to seek deeper understanding of what we already believe by faith.

Truth, for Augustine, requires God's illumination of the mind. In this respect, religious truth is real, objective, and unchanging. It is truth because it is illumined to our minds by God. While truth is rational (capable of rational explanation), it is not rationalistic (not dependent on abstract human reason, which is prone to usurp divine revelation in Christ; see John 1:9). For Augustine, both faith and reason are needed in the search for truth, not as cognitive processes, that is, as ways of requiring belief, but as affective processes involving our desires, our will, and our commitments. As Augustine made clear, knowledge is not simply a means of knowing for its own sake, as a purely rational endeavor. For Augustine, such knowledge is likely impossible.

Augustine believed that everyone's search for truth begins with the acceptance of authority, not merely in religion, but in all areas of human

---

1. In his reading from Isaiah, Augustine followed a different version than the one upon which modern translations are based.

life. Historical claims in particular must be accepted or rejected on the basis of authoritative testimony. Christianity involves such historical claims, and Augustine sought to show that it is reasonable to accept the testimony upon which Christianity rests. Thus, we have three distinctives in Augustine's search for truth: (1) that all knowledge involves our affective side, meaning that to know and relate to God, our heart must be right; (2) that the purpose for seeking truth is that it lead to knowledge and love of God; and (3) that knowledge involves acceptance of authority. For Augustine, faith is indispensable, but it is only the start of the journey to God. The journey requires grace, which increases our love and brings us closer to God. Relying on authority is not, however, a substitute for reason. Augustine viewed authority as no more than a short cut: authority discloses what reason later comprehends.

For Augustine, grace increases human merit or worth. In speaking of merit, Augustine utilized an argument central to Roman Catholicism, but not for Protestants, who, following Martin Luther, speak of faith alone, or grace alone. For Augustine, humans must cooperate with God, and when our wills cooperate with grace, the resulting works of love have merit. In this regard, Augustine distinguished between "operative grace"—the initial gift of grace that changes our hearts, turning our will toward God—and "cooperative grace," which works together with our good will to produce meritorious works of love. As the late medieval theologian Thomas Aquinas argued in the thirteenth century, following Augustine, "operative grace" is the divine help given to humans whereby "God is the sole mover," and "cooperative grace" is our response, whereby we become active participants in our salvation. While Protestants often think that Catholics emphasize "works" as essential to salvation, that is not altogether true, for Catholics are Augustinian, and as Augustine noted, salvation requires grace.[2]

Although Augustine considered grace and free will as compatible, the human propensity is to sin—that is, to love in the wrong order (loving self more than others, or things more than God), seeking happiness in lesser things, when only God can make us truly happy. Grace enters our will and strengthens it to love the right things. For Augustine, the will's

---

2. Of course, Roman Catholics do not believe they can "earn" salvation. For Catholics, sin continues throughout the believer's life, for which there is forgiveness. The important thing is to be on the journey, and on the right road. As Catholics believe, Christians don't get home to God until after death. However, life should be an ever-improving journey toward one's destination with God.

primary role is to love, and grace helps it to love the right things, in the right order. Operative grace is where God works in the human will apart from its cooperation. Operative grace is God's grace entering deep into one's heart, transferring it from selfishness (self-absorption) to selflessness (authentic, selfless love of God and others).

In the sixteenth century, Protestant Reformers such as Luther and Calvin denied Augustine's notion of cooperative grace, arguing that humans cannot merit God's grace or contribute in any way for their salvation. They understood salvation more as a guarantee of eternal life with God in the afterlife than as a journey that begins in the present and continues into eternity. They certainly valued Augustine's understanding of operative grace, which they called "grace alone." Such grace results in what later revivalist called "conversion," where the will is turned, not by coercion, but by sheer delight, as fulfillment of one's deepest longing and truest happiness.

When we are on the journey home toward God, our desire to love is strengthened by grace. Augustine called this strengthening grace, "assisting grace." He also spoke of "healing grace," since humans are wounded by things other than God, things they pursue such as money, alcoholic drink, sex, and power—any impulse that distracts them from love of God and neighbor. Augustine viewed these distractions as a disease, and just as people addicted to things seek them in excess, so the diseased heart seeks things that are not for its good. God's grace, both operative and cooperative in nature, is necessary in our journey toward greater love of God and others, stimulating, healing, and strengthening our will to love.

The goal of the journey, for Augustine, is to know or "see" for oneself. Nevertheless, as in the classroom, pupils begin with certain beliefs or principles, given to them by their parents or by other authority figures. However, the goal of all learning and knowing is intellectual knowledge, that is, understanding truth for oneself. Likewise, for Augustine, believers begin with what the Bible and the church teach, but that is only the beginning. Our deepest desire is to "see" God for ourselves. To reach that goal, we start by believing what we are told. What keeps us moving on our journey is not faith, however, but love, by which Augustine meant "desire for union." This is what all love requires, whether it be union with one's beloved, one's desire for food, or, less beneficially, one's compulsion for drugs, vice, or attachment to material possessions. The greatest of these desires, that which fulfills and transcends all others, is the desire for union with God. While love is the engine that drives us on this journey, the reward is not material or even spiritual blessing, but intimacy with God. Heaven, in this respect, is not a place of eternal bliss, or a reward in itself, but another way of speaking about this mystical union with God.

Medieval spirituality, then, is about cultivating this desire, this longing for God. There is no sense of finality on earth, however, no claim of having arrived at the goal. Believers are on the way, but they are not yet saved, Augustine would say, for they are saved in hope. This notion came to be central not only for medieval Catholicism, but for Catholicism to the present. Christians are saved in hope, but not yet in reality. Believers are on the way, but not yet home; dangers and pitfalls await.

What grace meant for Augustine is that one's love of God is a gift of God; as the scriptures make clear, we love God because God first loved us (see 1 John 4:7–12). The implication is that even our desire to fall in love with God comes from God; it is this desire for love, this delight in love, that pulls us upward and onward. This raises again the question of free will, for apart from free will, we cannot truly love. If God turns our will apart from our cooperation, does that violate free will? For Augustine, it does not. Even in those moments when grace holds the initiative, grace and free will are compatible. It is not a matter of free will responding to grace, but of grace turning our will. However, grace turns our will freely, through the action of inner delight, without violating our free will. The journey starts with grace, but we engage our will by praying for more grace, in order to love God with greater intensity and delight. During the medieval period, such ways of life would be worked out not only by priests, but most fully by monks and friars, who lived monastically.

Augustine made an important argument for the necessity of grace that became central to Luther and the Protestant Reformation. At one point in his reasoning on the necessity of grace, Augustine brought up an interesting psychological point. What happens, he says, when we read in the Bible that God's law is fulfilled when we love God with all our ability and others as ourselves? When we hear that command, do we obey? Augustine argued that we cannot, because as a result of Adam's sin, the human will is "unable not to sin" (*non posse non peccare*). According to Augustine, when we hear the law, we actually resent it. We would rather not have to keep it, and find that even if we wish to fulfill its demands, we are unable to do so. However, out of fear of punishment, we try to love God fully, and fail, because fear cannot be a motivation for love.

How, then, does love work? How is God's law fulfilled? Such fulfillment requires an inward change in our will, which only occurs through grace. When we pray for grace, God provides it, thereby transforming our heart. As a result, we find we want to love God. The grace we need, which God provides, yields not only compliance, but becomes an inner gift of delight (see Rom 5:5), increasing our longing for God and our love for others. If things are delightful, they are easy. Even hard work, if it is delightful, is easy (see Matt 11:30).

Augustine worked out the implications of grace in his treatise *On the Spirit and the Letter*, based on Paul's argument in 2 Cor 3:6, "the letter (the Jewish law and its commands) kills, but the spirit gives life." Building on Paul's contrast between the external and the internal, Augustine notes that the help we need is not additional outward legislation, but rather the inward grace of God's Spirit. The role of the religious law is not to drive us to guilt or terror but to the grace of God, and that gift of grace—acquired through prayer, worship, and a life based on faith—transforms us so that we end up loving God for others' sake and others for God's sake, and that becomes our salvation.

In speaking of free will, Augustine's spirituality recalls the issue of merit. For Augustine, one of the reasons why human beings have free will is because they must have merit. Augustine believes that humans merit reward or blame, since such language appears regularly in the Bible, to the effect that we are judged according to our works (see, for example, 1 Cor 3:12–15). Augustine does clarify that the earning of merit is entirely due to grace, since all our works are due to love, which is a gift of grace. There is therefore no merit apart from grace. This teaching became central to most medieval spirituality. During the Reformation, however, Luther would take this notion to its extreme, arguing that there is no merit whatsoever in human works.

In Augustine's view, the more believers progress along their spiritual journey, coming ever closer to God, the more we become like God. And the more Christlike we become, the more worthy we become, and this is where merit enters the picture. As our love for God grows, we become morally and ethically better people, and the closer to home we get, including our final arrival, somehow the more deserving we are of God. At some point, we are fit for home, worthy of our place close to God.

Merit, however, is not about "earning" or achieving salvific status. It can degenerate to that, but that is not how most medieval theologians understand merit. In the twelfth century, Anselm of Canterbury (1033–1109) aptly captured the best of Augustinian spirituality in a prayer he wrote in his *Proslogion*.

> What shall your servant do, most high Lord, what shall this exile do, so far away from you as he is? What shall your servant do, tormented by love of you, and yet cast off far from your face? He yearns to see you, and your countenance is too far from him. He desires to come to you, and your dwelling place is inaccessible; he longs to find you, and does not know where you are . . . Lord, you are my God and my Lord, and never have I seen you. You have created and recreated me, and you have given me all the good things I possess, and still I do not know you. I was made in order to see you, and yet I have not accomplished that for which I was created . . . O miserable condition of humanity, who have lost that for which we were made. We have lost the blessedness for which we are made, and found the misery for which we were not made. Humanity did once eat the bread of angels, yet now it is the bread of sorrow.

By so praying, Anselm recognizes Augustine's doctrine of original sin, the loss of being driven from Paradise, the loss of fellowship with God. As a result, he longs to return to God, to get back home, to recover what he has lost. "Look with grace upon us, O Lord," Anselm continues, "Take pity on us, for without you we can do nothing." At this point, Anselm acknowledges Augustine's doctrine of grace. "Let me find you by loving you, and let me love you when I find you."

Notice how this prayer works. Anselm is not afraid of hell. He is dealing with the misery of his condition—distance from God. How does he draw closer to God? That is his dilemma. He is in exile; how does he go home? His experience here is not fear, but longing, desire for God. What he fears is his current condition, his absence from God.

From Augustine's view of grace come several important implications, one of the most important being his view of evil. The presence of evil in the world perplexed Augustine before his conversion to Christianity—not only cosmic evil, but ethical evil, his double inability as a young adult, like Paul's in Romans 7:15–20, to enact the good he desired, or to prevent the evil thoughts or actions he opposed. Despite his pessimistic views, Augustine wrote in his *Confessions* that "whatever is, is good." In saying this, he was not ignoring evil, but affirming that everything created by God is good. All that exists is God's creation, and God only creates good things.

For Augustine, when evil appears, it takes the form of privation. Like darkness, evil is the absence of light. In speaking of darkness, of course, we are not referring to blackness, which is a real color, for darkness does not exist ontologically, but only as the absence of goodness. While, according to Augustine's definition, evil might appear unreal, as the absence of something, nevertheless it is real, as shadows and absences are real. The results of evil have effects on us, like stumbling in the dark. Despite having no substance or reality of its own, the presence of evil is like a vacuum, simultaneously real and unreal. The universe is good because God makes all things inherently good, including human nature. Even the devil—an agent of evil in traditional Christianity—is good by nature, though evil by free will. Likewise, sinners have a good nature, and though they might reject God, they cannot escape the notion that they are God's good creatures.

Thus, in a deep philosophical sense, Augustine is an optimist, though he does leave a legacy of deep and sometimes terrifying thoughts in his doctrine of grace. Yet through them all come wonderfully winsome concepts, such as his concept of inner delight in God, this love for God that grace instills in human beings. Augustine's legacy deeply influenced future Christian thinkers—not only in the medieval and Reformation periods, but modern theologians as well.

Monastic Spirituality

The rise of monasticism may well be one of the most beneficial institutional events in the history of Christianity. For over a millennium, in the period between the reign of Constantine and the Protestant Reformation, almost everything in the church that approached the highest, noblest, and truest ideals of the gospel was done either by those who chose the monastic way or by those who were inspired in their Christian life by monks. Protestantism, we might recall, began with the monastic experiences of Martin Luther. Luther and Calvin turned repeatedly to the work of Augustine, including his monastic order. In fact, Luther began his adult life as an Augustinian monk. Throughout the ages, monasticism provided an alternative lifestyle that enabled Christians to express discipleship in a more radical way. Monasteries became important centers for reform and in the early medieval period of the West, monks enhanced education, copying manuscripts and preserving for other Christians a great body of teaching about the discipline necessary to be an authentic Christian.

The breadth and depth of monastic influence in the church is comprehensive. If we read scripture in our native language, we benefit from a tradition inspired by the monk Jerome (342-420). If we sing hymns, we follow the pattern established by the monks Gregory (540-604) and Bernard of Clairvaux (1090-1153). If we pursue theology, we find ourselves indebted to the monks Augustine and Thomas Aquinas (1225-1274). If we focus on Christian missionaries, we think of efforts pioneered by the monks Patrick (387-461), Boniface (680-754), Cyril (826-869), and his brother Methodius (815-885). If we are interested in the early record of Christianity in English-speaking areas of the world, we cultivate a concern begun by a monk known as the Venerable Bede (673-735). If we relish in nature and its goodness, we follow the friar Francis of Assisi (1181-1226). Monasticism may not be a perfect answer to the question of how to live the Christian life, but its impact is sizeable.[3]

Throughout the Middle Ages, the monastic life provided one of the few venues where women were allowed to participate in the religious life. Early praise for virginity played a part, especially after the Virgin Mary became prominent in the church's liturgy and theology. Thus Hildegard of Bingen (1098-1179), an early example of female leadership in a monastic setting, became founder and first abbess of a Benedictine community on the Rhine River. A Renaissance woman, she was renowned not only for her mystical visions but also for a remarkable set of writings on scientific, theological, and musical subjects. In addition, she provided advice to kings, bishops, and leaders of other monastic institutions, as evidenced by a significant body of letters.

Because the monastic movement often challenged the church, it served as a source of renewal. Following a period of striking ecclesiastical degeneration in the ninth and tenth centuries, the founding of a monastery at Cluny in 910 ushered in administrative and spiritual reforms that were felt over the next century and a half, even to the highest reaches of the Vatican. Over time, however, wealth and power had a corrupting effect on the rigor of monastic life. The entry of the nobility into the monastery and their inevitable ascent to power led, in turn, to the election of abbots of Cluny as bishops, and even as popes. By the year 1100, more than one thousand Benedictine monasteries belonged to the Cluniac order.

The emergence of the Dominicans and the Franciscans in the thirteenth century sparked another cycle of renewal in the life, thought, and service of the church. These orders became known as mendicant (the term comes from the Latin word for "beggars"), and the term "friar"

---

3. Noll, *Turning Points*, 79.

distinguished them from monks because, unlike monks, they went forth to live and serve among the people. Just as monastic houses arose to minister in the countryside, so the mendicant friars focused on meeting the spiritual needs of townspeople.

The first approved mendicant order was founded by Francis of Assisi (1182–1226) in 1209. Abandoning his wealth and status to serve Christ in poverty, the charismatic Francis left home in ragged clothes, wandering the countryside with followers he called his "little brothers." Preaching the joys of poverty and paying attention to outcasts, they survived by depending on alms. A noblewoman named Clare, a friend of Francis from Assisi, established a corresponding order of women known as the Poor Clares. The early history of the Franciscans is complex, and over time it became difficult to maintain Francis's original, radical ideals. The order eventually committed to scholarship and gave rise to great theologians and mystical teachers such as Giovanni di Fidanza, better known as St. Bonaventure (1217–1274), and Duns Scotus (1265–1308).

The second order of mendicants, the Dominicans, was founded by the Spaniard Dominic de Guzmán (1170–1221). He studied arts and theology, and then sold his possessions during a famine to help the poor. He became enthralled with the ideal of preaching the gospel to pagans before founding an order of preachers, approved by Innocent III in 1216. The great learning and dedication of this order produced great theologians such as Thomas Aquinas and great mystics such as Meister Eckhart, John Tauler, and Henry Suso.

Because of their zeal to oppose heresy, both Dominicans and Franciscans were used by the papacy in the process of inquisition. Together, these mendicant orders not only served as instruments of papal policy, but they energized evangelization and the care of the poor. Their commitment to the intellectual life also made them leading movements in the development of medieval universities.

Mysticism, an expression of Christian faith, flourished during the fourteenth and fifteen centuries. Mysticism was particularly evident in England in the fourteenth century. Among the most powerful and remarkably beautiful of the mystical works of this period is *The Cloud of Unknowing*, an anonymous guide to the contemplative life written for monastic readers. The book recognizes that between humans and God there is an impenetrable cloud, so that the point is not knowing God but loving God. Of the writings of the mystics of the late Middle Ages, one still widely read is *The Imitation of Christ*. Attributed to the fifteenth-century Thomas à Kempis, the book may be based in part on earlier works. It begins: "He that followeth Me walketh not in darkness, saith the Lord . . . Let therefore our chief endeavor be to meditate upon the life of Jesus Christ." For the author, as for Christians in general, the life of Christ exceeds all others.

Among the anchorites (those who live as hermits within the context of the cathedrals) are two English figures, Richard Rolle (1300–1349), known for his beautiful poems on the passion of Christ, and Julian of Norwich (1342–1416), who uses female attributions to the divine in her series of visions she calls "Showings." Her *Revelations of Divine Love*, written around 1395 and widely acknowledged as one of the classics of the spiritual life, is the first book in the English language known to have been written by a woman.

During the Reformation of the sixteenth century, Protestant thinkers began questioning doctrines and practices established during the medieval period, including ecclesiastical hierarchicalism, the authority of the pope, the estrangement between laity and clergy, sacramentalism, monasticism, the veneration of relics and saints, the emphasis on good works as meritorious for salvation, and the sale of indulgences. In so doing, most Protestants were not rejecting church authority, but rather subordinating it to biblical constraints. While retaining the ancient creeds and the theological formulations of the great ecumenical councils of the fourth and fifth centuries, mainline Protestants rejected those doctrines, practices, and ceremonies for which no clear warrant existed in the Bible, or which seem to contradict its letter and intent.

It took the Church of Rome some time to respond fully to the Protestant challenge. At first the defiance was local and personal, but when Catholicism finally realized the seriousness of the revolt, it responded comprehensively. Some historians interpret the response as a counterattack against Protestantism, while others describe it as a genuine revival of Catholic piety. The truth is the movement is both a Counter-Reformation and a Catholic Reformation. The mystical experience was a large part of Catholicism's recovery. The sixteenth century produced a remarkable variety of Catholic saints, including the English humanist Thomas More, the missionary Francis of Sales, the Spanish mystics Teresa of Ávila and John of the Cross, perhaps the preeminent mystical authorities of Western Catholicism, and the most influential of all, the Spanish soldier Ignatius Loyola.

Questions for Discussion and Reflection

1. How would you describe "the Augustinian paradigm of spirituality"?
2. Explain and assess Augustine's emphasis on "seeing God eternally." In your estimation, is such perception possible today?
3. What did Augustine mean when he spoke of love as a force pulling us upward, not downward?
4. In your understanding of God, do you tend to side with the Western church's emphasis on the comprehensibility of God or with the Eastern church's emphasis on the incomprehensibility of God? Explain your answer.
5. Compare and contrast apophatic theology (with its emphasis on knowing and experiencing God by unknowing) and kataphatic theology (with its emphasis on knowing and experiencing God analogically and sacramentally).
6. In your estimation, why is the doctrine of salvation also called the doctrine of grace? In your understanding of grace, do you tend to side with Augustine, Aquinas, or the Reformers? Explain your answer.
7. If this world is created good by God, how do you explain the existence of evil?
8. Describe and assess the contributions of monasticism to the development of second-half-of-life spirituality.
9. The Christian mystical tradition produced numerous spiritual mentors. Is there one you find more attractive than others? If so, whom? Explain your answer.

6

Penitential Spirituality
Late Medieval and Renaissance Christian Piety

To UNDERSTAND LATE MEDIEVAL piety, we begin with the medieval distinction between clergy and laity, not the distinction between ministers and congregants, as Protestants tend to think of it, but of two distinct spiritual groups, one holding power, the other subject to that power.

In the medieval church, priests were ordained so that they might receive the power to say the Mass, by which bread and wine are transformed into the body and blood of Christ. This spiritual power is only available to clergy, according to Catholic teaching, and hence, a power unavailable to the laity. That power, spiritual in origin, extends to other realms in society, influencing politics and economics. The Mass had benefits, not only for congregants, but also for those deceased, for whom Mass could be given.[1]

Masses could be said for those in purgatory, the place where, according to Catholic teaching, souls might go if they were not yet ready for heaven and not destined for hell. Of such souls, further purification awaited, hence their purgation. Their suffering could be reduced significantly through interventions made on their behalf by family members and friends still alive. In addition, people could set up endowments or provide payment in their wills for Masses to be said on their behalf after death. Costs and payments for such Masses became a significant part of

---

1. In Catholic settings, this can happen today as well, but it does not carry the economic weight it did during medieval times.

the medieval economy, making one's future spiritual condition a commodity that could be purchased and sold.

In late medieval times, when someone entered a cathedral and proceeded down the main aisle, called the nave, heading toward the high altar at the front, he or she would pass numerous side altars. Frequently during the day, particularly at times devoid of public worship, one might see priests saying Mass at these side altars, often without parishioners in attendance. The reason for these Masses was that they had been paid for in advance. For example, in the church at Wittenberg, as late as 1519, two years after Martin Luther tacked his 95 Theses to the church door, some 9,000 masses were paid for in Wittenberg, which meant that on most days, dozens of Masses were said, many at altars in vacant side chapels.

The Mass was believed efficacious just by being performed. Most of the time, even when attendees were present, no one received the Eucharist, for this sacrament was only obligatory at Easter. For later Reformers, paying for spiritual services looked like magic, and Protestants worked hard to abolish such practices and the belief system upon which they were based.

In addition to the division between clergy and laity, another medieval distinction was between laity and monastics such as monks and friars. Called regular clergy because they lived under monastic rule, the latter included many who were not priests. Living under a rule (*regula*) set them apart from secular clergy such as parish priests, who lived in ordinary society with ordinary people. Regular priests lived apart, bound by special rules that included vows of poverty, obedience, and chastity. The implications of this way of life were many, as monks and friars were not allowed to own property or form families, and their ultimate allegiance was to their religious superior as opposed to a civil ruler.

Surprisingly, while individual monks and friars were committed to economic poverty, monasteries were not. As institutions, many medieval monasteries became wealthy and politically powerful. For example, when William the Conqueror took over England in 1066, the monasteries owned one-sixth of the landed wealth of England, giving them vast wealth and power. At the end of the Middle Ages, when King Henry VIII inaugurated the English Reformation, he dissolved the monasteries, gaining a large amount of wealth. In medieval times, then, monasteries came to acquire significant economic wealth and political influence.

During the medieval period, temporal and spiritual powers were intertwined, for clergy had political power, particularly bishops and popes, whose office included benefices, an ecclesiastical fief. In feudal times, kings granted fiefs to nobility in exchange for military service. A fief consisted of landed wealth, and it included serfs who were bound to the land. In return for this economic advantage, nobles owed their lord political allegiance. Likewise, bishops acquired fiefs, including peasants to work the land and reap its produce. In return, they owed such spiritual services to their political overlord as saying the Mass and overseeing the sacramental life of the community, which services contributed to the general law and order of the society and to the eternal salvation of its members.

As with political and spiritual powers, medieval society also intertwined economics and politics, meaning there was little if any secularization. Bishops were regularly involved in politics, and that meant that power then, as today, was double-edged, for those who hold power in one sphere inevitably come into conflict with those who hold power in other spheres, and winning is not guaranteed. To have power meant one had powerful enemies, and this created competition between bishops, lords, and other rulers.

One of the implications of holding a benefice was that the holder could not pass it on to an heir or a descendent. This meant that whenever a bishop died, his benefice became vacant, and this often led to power struggles between competing parties, secular and religious alike. The king sought people loyal to himself, but so did the pope. The king didn't want the beneficiary loyal to the pope, for this reduced his power and influence. While local rulers desired the wealth to stay locally, popes desired the wealth for themselves and their purposes. Another source of conflict during the Middle Ages was a practice called *annates*, whereby popes claimed the right to tax the first year's income from each benefice, often a hefty sum. The papacy was expensive, and popes came to rely on this income.

In addition to his spiritual authority, the pope was also a temporal ruler of significant stature. His benefice at the time consisted of most of central Italy. This territory served not only as a source of wealth, but it also involved military rule, for the pope was called to war frequently during this period. While modern times are marked by the idea of autonomous, sovereign states without religious affiliation, with the church functioning as a voluntary association apart from the rest of organized society, these ideas did not exist in the Middle Ages.

At that time, three competing views emerged regarding society and the church's role in the world: (a) the Constantinian (Justinian) view, whereby the church and state are united *under the state*, (b) the Augustinian view, which views state and church as *independent but cooperative*, neither supreme over the other, and (c) the medieval view, whereby church and state are united *under the church*.

Augustine's model of the "City of God" and the "City of Man" led to the doctrine of two authorities or swords by which God orders society. The spiritual sword of the church works to bring people under the rule of the City of God, while God uses the temporal sword of the state to restrain sin and keep order in society. The Augustinian model views church and state as separate institutions and yet as working together for the benefit of earthly order and welfare. This view led to the American view of society, with its separation of church and state.

The Justinian model regards the state as holding both swords but lending one to the church (this model is operative in the absence of a strong institutional church). According to this political theory, modeled in the Byzantine empire (but also traditionally in state churches in Europe and Latin America), God advises the emperor (ruler), whose reign thereby makes holy the empire (nation).

The medieval view, implemented in the absence of a strong central government, regards the church as holding both swords but loaning one to the state. During the tenth century, Europe experienced almost total collapse of civil order and culture. Everywhere church property either was devastated by invaders or fell into the hands of local nobility such as feudal barons in France and kings in Germany. Bishops and abbots thus became vassals, receiving fiefs for which they were obligated to provide feudal services. This loyalty to higher lords created unusual conflicts for bishops, who looked to the pope for support. However, in the tenth and early eleventh centuries, the pope was politically powerless. Without imperial protection, the papacy fell into decay.

By the eleventh century the church was in a better position to influence for the better the behavior of the feudal barons. In addition to attempting to add Christian virtues to the code of knightly conduct called chivalry, the church tried to impose limitations on feudal warfare. After the German king Otto the Great revived the Roman empire in the West in 962, some sense of unity was restored. With the renewal of the empire, however, came renewed rivalry between church and state.

During the eleventh century the controversy between church and state centered on the problem of lay investiture. Theoretically, bishops or abbots were subject to two investitures: church officials bestowing spiritual authority and a king or a noble bestowing feudal or civil authority. In reality, however, feudal lords and kings controlled both the appointment and the installation of clergy. This practice was most pronounced in Germany, where control of the church was the foundation of the king's power.

Before the church could challenge kings and emperors, however, it needed to set its own house in order. This began with a far-reaching revival within the Benedictine order of Cluny, founded in 910. The Cluniac program began as a movement for monastic reform, but in time it called for the enforcement of clerical celibacy and the abolition of simony (the purchase or sale of a church office). The ultimate goal of the Cluniac reformers was to free churches and monasteries from secular control and subject them solely to papal authority. The reform led to two significant changes: the freeing from lay control of hundreds of monastic houses, and the creation of the College of Cardinals, which henceforth elected the popes.

The person behind the reform of the papacy was Hildebrand, who in 1073 was elected Pope Gregory VII (1073–1085). Holding as his ideal the creation of a Christian commonwealth solely under papal control, in 1075 he formally prohibited lay investiture and threatened to excommunicate any laypersons who participated in its practice. This act virtually declared war against Europe's rulers, since most of them practiced lay investiture. The climax to the struggle occurred in Gregory's clash with the German king, who ruled as Emperor Henry IV (1056–1105).

In addition to forbidding lay investiture, Gregory decreed that priests must no longer be married, that emperors could not appoint popes, and that the pope, not the emperor, should appoint bishops. The German clergy rebelled at the decree against their marriage, and Emperor Henry responded by appointing a bishop in Milan. He announced that Gregory was no longer pope but a false monk. The pope excommunicated Henry and deposed him, freeing Henry's subjects from any duty to obey the emperor. Following a revolt among the German nobles, Henry appeared before Gregory at Canossa, a castle in the mountains of Italy. Dressed as a penitent, the emperor stood barefoot in the snow for three days, begging forgiveness. The pope relented and withdrew the decree. Eventually, however, Henry invaded Rome and forced Gregory to flee. A rival pope was elected to office, and Gregory died in exile. The conflict of church and state would continue.

During the late Middle Ages, when Europe longed for unity, the church attained a level of power and influence such as it has never known since. During the twelfth and thirteenth centuries, the papacy led an admirable attempt to constitute a perfect society on earth, achieving incomparable power and majesty. Germanic rulers continued to call themselves Roman emperors and continued to go to Rome for their coronations, but they were merely the sovereigns of a cluster of kingdoms and municipal republics that constituted the Germany of the late Middle Ages. The papacy, by contrast, built upon the reforms of Pope Gregory VII and emerged as the most powerful institution in Europe. The pope's government was truly monarchical and centralized. All bishops swore fealty to the pope, and no religious order could be founded without his authorization. The papal court in Rome heard appeals from all over Christendom, and in every country legates from Rome executed papal orders.

In the hands of a strong leader, the papacy could overshadow all secular monarchs. The pope's first weapon in controlling monarchs and peasants alike was the threat of excommunication. When implemented, excommunication threatened individuals with the loss of grace essential for salvation. While under excommunication, persons could not act as judge, juror, witness, or attorney. They could not be guardians, executors, or parties to contract. After death, they received no Christian burial. Without the sacrament, people were condemned to hell. The second weapon was the interdict, a curse aimed not at individuals but upon a nation. Its power included the suspension of all public worship, and even the withdrawal of the sacraments from the lands of disobedient rulers. Under interdict, nobody received the grace they needed to escape hell.

In one power struggle, Pope Innocent III (1198–1216) excommunicated King John of England (1199–1216). Of course, this was a battle King John lost, at least temporarily. As a result, all of England became the pope's official fief, required to pay a huge sum of money to the pope annually. The agreement, signed by King John, did give him some benefits. For example, in 1215 John had signed the Magna Carta, a charter granting concessions to local barons, a decree Pope Innocent promptly annulled. Acquiescing to the pope had its benefits, at least temporarily.

Trained in canon law (church administration), Innocent III held an exalted view of his office. "The successor of Peter," he announced, "is the Vicar of Christ. He has been established as a mediator between God and man, below God but beyond man; less than God but more than man; who shall judge all and be judged by no one." Innocent III successfully applied or threatened the interdict eighty-five times against uncooperative princes. Wielding these spiritual weapons, Innocent and his successors during the thirteenth century led Christianity to its peak of political and cultural influence.

The period between 1300 and 1500 marked a turning point in Western history. It witnessed what has been called "the decline of the Middle Ages" because the idea of Christendom came under attack. During this period we see not only the further decline of the empire, but the dramatic loss of papal prestige. The fourteenth century is perhaps too early to speak of nations in the modern sense of the term, but more and more, people were getting used to the idea that they were English or French whenever their allegiance came into question, and more importantly, they found it possible to think of their "state" functioning without direct papal guidance. Europe was slowly moving away from its feudal past, and land was becoming less important than cash. Earlier, in their need to finance costly military campaigns, secular rulers in England (Edward I) and in France (Philip the Fair) simultaneously hit upon a controversial solution: tax the clergy within their realms. The pope fought back; in 1296 Boniface VIII (1230–1303) issued a document threatening excommunication for any lay ruler who taxed the clergy. Edward and Philip, believing themselves above church law, responded by threatening to seize clerical properties, thereby depriving the papal treasury of a major source of revenue. In 1302 Boniface issued *Unam sanctum*, the most extreme assertion of papal power in church history. "It is altogether necessary," he declared, "for every human being to be subject to the Roman pontiff." Allegorizing the passage in Luke 22:35–38, he announced that in the church there are two swords, the spiritual and the temporal. Both are in the power of the church, the temporal authority subject to the spiritual.

Philip burned the papal decree and began immediate proceedings to have Boniface deposed, sending a lawyer armed with authority to bring the pope to France for trial before a special church council. Boniface, now eighty-six, was arrested and died within weeks, shamed and reviled. An unpopular pope, he was the target of widespread criticism. Shortly thereafter Dante, author of *The Divine Comedy* (written between 1308 and 1320), reserved a place in hell for Pope Boniface.

This episode came to symbolize the descent of papal power. When Boniface's successor in Rome died after a brief, ineffectual reign, Philip's daring coup bore fruit. In 1305 the College of Cardinals elected a Frenchman as Pope Clement V. Clement never set foot in Rome, preferring to stay close to home. Clement's election marked the start of a seventy-two-year period in church history called "the Babylonian captivity" of the papacy. Following Clement, six successive popes, all of French origin, chose to reside in the small town of Avignon rather than in Rome. One pope supported France in its war with England, and other nations chose sides and entered the fight.

By 1360 turmoil in Italy made it clear that the Avignon papacy could not continue indefinitely. In 1377 the aged Pope Gregory XI returned to Rome, to be succeeded a year later by Urban VI, an Italian. All the cardinals were present. The next months, following unpopular decisions by Urban, the cardinals suddenly declared that the people of Rome had forced the election of an apostate and declared the proceedings invalid. A month later, Urban responded by creating a new College of Cardinals, electing the French Clement VIII in his place. Clement moved to Avignon, and now there were two popes, one in Avignon and one in Rome, marking a chapter in papal history called the Great Schism. Various nations and groups supported one or the other, and the popes became involved in armed conflict with each other. In an effort to stop the scandal, an attempt was made to depose both and set a new one on the throne in Rome. The result was that for a few years there were three popes.

Finally, in 1414, the Holy Roman Emperor Sigismund assembled at the German city of Constance the most impressive church gathering of this era. For the first time voting took place on a purely national basis, each nation receiving one vote. The structure of the Council of Constance was highly significant, indicating that the church was accepting a new alignment of power. In 1417 the Council of Florence persuaded one incumbent pope to step aside and deposed the others, effectively ending the schism.

The conciliar movement aimed at limiting the power of the papacy. Constance decreed that general councils were superior to popes and that councils should meet regularly. Political corruption and immorality in the Vatican continued, however, reaching unbelievable depths under Rodrigo Borgia, who ruled as Alexander VI (1492–1503). The challenge of the Protestant Reformation was at hand.

The Renaissance Papacy

The thirteenth and fourteenth centuries witnessed the flowering of the period known as the Renaissance, the rebirth of classical ideals, with some of the greatest minds of all times. The Renaissance reached its peak in the fifteenth and sixteenth century. It produced some of the finest works of art, architecture, and engineering the world has ever known. No other period of Western civilization can boast of producing so much genius.

About 1450, Johannes Gutenberg invented the printing press, and this helped produce a cultural revolution. Now the works of scholars could be disseminated and ancient manuscripts copied and preserved relatively free from error. The Latin Vulgate had been the only scripture most had known, but the new interest in ancient manuscripts focused attention on the study of the Bible in its original languages of Greek and Hebrew. By 1380, John Wycliffe led a team of scholars at Oxford in the translation of the Bible into English, inspiring Martin Luther (1483–1546) in Germany and William Tyndale (1494–1536) in England, and it was only a matter of time before laypeople would begin reading the scriptures in their vernacular language.

In the late fifteenth and sixteenth century, the papacy changed dramatically under the Italian Renaissance popes, who disregarded pronouncements of church councils and assumed powers for themselves. They acquired tremendous wealth, took on expensive building projects, and fought wars. One pope, Julius II (1503–1513), after whom the Sistine Chapel was named, became involved in a conspiracy to murder the Medicis of Florence. He succeeded in assassinating one family member, but another, named Lorenzo the Magnificent, survived. Lorenzo's son, Leo X (1513–1521), was pope when Luther attempted to reform the church.

Italian family politics played a huge role in the late medieval and early Reformation periods, money and power given by popes to nephews and illegitimate sons like Cesare Borgia, the son of Pope Alexander VI (1492–1503), whose struggle to establish his own principality in central Italy was a major inspiration for Machiavelli's classic book, *The Prince*. The Renaissance papacy was awash in money, buying and selling religious offices in Rome while profiting from benefices. In addition, a great deal of money was flowing into Rome from other territories, much of it from Germany. Such abuses led to the movement that arose in Germany known as the Reformation.

The Role of the Conscience in Late Medieval Spirituality

In late medieval spirituality, the Augustinian metaphor of the journey was abandoned, replaced by the concept of judgment. There was little possibility of merit now, for no one stood before God's throne of justice confident or worthy. While Augustine had believed in the judgment of God, it was not central to his spiritual sensibility as it would be for Luther, Calvin, and the Reformers. What happened between Augustine, Anselm, and the Reformers was the development of something called the "late medieval conscience," a mindset concerned with the judgment of God. The causes of this development were varied, including the outbreak of pandemics and, in the East, a surge of Muslim invasions that culminated in 1453 with the fall of Constantinople to the Turks. After eleven centuries, the Eastern Byzantine empire ended, and Eastern Christianity became a minority in a society run by Muslims.

The fourteenth century experienced the Great Plague, or the Black Death, which began in 1331 and extended to 1351. It decimated Europe as it did the rest of the inhabited world. The plague was preceded by the great famine of 1315 to 1317, caused by centuries of moderate climate followed by what climatologists term "the little ice age." Between 1310 and 1330 there were severe winters and cold summers. Beginning in 1315, this climatic shift brought decreased crops and a famine that spread across Europe, leading to the death of some 10 percent of the population of Northern Europe. The starvation caused extreme social crime, including widespread theft and murder. A mere nine years later, the plague hit. The bubonic plague, spread by fleas carried by rats, killed half the population of China before spreading to the Middle East and Europe, were it yielded similar results.

During this period the papacy was also caught up in the dynastic struggles of the Holy Roman emperors as well as other kingdoms. From 1337 to 1453, England and France fought the "Hundred Years War," partly as an expression of nationalism and partly as a distorted version of holy war.

To understand the late medieval mindset, we need to understand the meaning of the word "conscience." Originally, the Latin word *conscientia* referred to someone who shared a secret with another, meaning literally "someone who knows with you." The word *scientia*, which we translate as "science," originally meant "knowledge." If someone knew you had broken a law, for example, that person could be a witness against you in a trial. Thus, one's "conscience" eventually came to mean "one's witness inside you," which, in religious terms, can bear witness against you at the judgment throne of God. In this regard, conscience is awareness of your standing before God. For some medieval Christians, this notion led to a sense of guilt, but for those of greater religious sensitivity, it led to terror.

Religiously speaking, what led to emphasis on an accusing conscience was the development of the sacrament of penance, which required that believers attend private confession. At these sessions, pious Christians were expected to probe their conscience to see if there was any hidden sin within, anything in their heart and memory that might be offensive to God. Of course, if you had a vivid or guilty imagination, you might find all kinds of sins that might bring you condemnation by a perfect, all-seeing and all-knowing God.

Medieval piety, thus, was driven by a condemning sense of inwardness, fueled not only by acts of commission, but also by acts of omission. Sin included not only external deeds, but also inner feelings of bitterness, resentment, envy, and jealousy. In their investigation, confessors were guided by manuals filled with penetrating questions to ask penitents, designed to probe their innermost fears. Such questions went like this, "Are your prayers, alms, and religious activities done to impress others? Are your good works intended to atone for your sins, or solely to please God? Have you loved friends and relatives more than God? Have you had doubts about scripture, the sacraments, or the judgment of God in the afterlife? Have you accused God in your mind for anything bad that has happened to you? Have you skipped Mass without a good excuse? Have you insulted or disobeyed the clergy? Have you failed to offer prayers or endow Masses for those who have died?"

These manuals contained a long list of questions, each associated with breaking one or more of the Ten Commandments. Such interrogation invariably drove devout or well-meaning Christians to fear and self-doubt, for each of these sins could potentially send you to hell, or certainly to purgatory. Penitents felt they had to root such sins from their hearts, else they might die in a state of mortal sin rather than in a state of grace, meaning there was no hope for their salvation.

This form of piety led many penitents to extremes of despair, even to visions of demons, such as Margery Kempe described in her autobiography, speaking of how, after having brought a secret sin to her confessor, he berated her, terrifying her into moments of insanity. Finally, she had a vision of Jesus, who brought her great comfort, calling her "daughter" and telling her that her new confessor pleased him very much because he assured her that Jesus loved her and accepted her as she was, rather than as her previous confessor had done, increasing her sense of guilt and self-loathing. Such new and freeing emphasis on "gospel" rather than on "law" would be the good news proclaimed by the Reformers.

Unlike the Augustinian or mystical forms of spirituality, based on grace and love, late medieval spirituality emphasized "the art of dying well." However, in helping people focus on their moment of death, this piety utilized art forms that focused on satanic assault, often in the form of demonic temptation and accusation, designed to drive believers to despair. To accentuate the agony, religious artists created woodcuts, paintings, and tapestries filled with horrors, often brought to one's deathbed.

Thankfully, such piety, manipulated by extremists, is now viewed as perverse and unhealthy, more "the art of dying poorly" rather than "the art of dying well." A far better approach is trusting God, a form of "good news" designed to uphold believers through the trial of death, when the conscience is most susceptible to guilt, doubt, and despair.

In medieval spirituality, nothing was feared more than sudden death, when one might die with mortal or unconfessed sin. Under such conditions, the church provided the sacrament of "last rites," today known as the "anointing of the sick," though even this remedy came to be associated more with religious duty, law, and a vengeful God than with the loving God of the gospel. Imagine the damage done to family members of one who died without receiving final absolution by the church. What hope is there for those who die with unconfessed sin? This was the situation Martin Luther faced, and his answer would significantly advance Christian spirituality.

Questions for Discussion and Reflection

1. Explain the medieval distinction between clergy and laity. How is this distinction dualistic, and can it be viewed nondualistically? Explain your answer.
2. Explain and assess the role of penance in Christianity. Compare and contrast its role in Catholicism and Protestantism.

3. Compare and contrast the three medieval views regarding the church's role in society. How is the Augustinian view modeled in American society?

4. Explain and assess the medieval practice of lay investiture and the church's response to such practice.

5. Assess the medieval church practice of excommunication and the interdict. In your estimation, should church institutions or representatives hold absolute power on earth? Explain your answer.

6. When the institutional church becomes corrupt, as during the Renaissance papacy, is it appropriate and necessary for clergy and laity to rise in opposition to such abuse? Explain your answer.

7. Explain and assess the mindset known as "the late medieval conscience." Where do you draw the line between the church as "hospital" and the church as "cult"?

7

Faith Spirituality
Reformation Piety

THE SPIRIT OF REFORM erupted with surprising intensity in the sixteenth century, giving birth to Protestantism and challenging papal leadership of Western Christendom. According to church sociologist Ernst Troelsch, Protestantism is a variation of Catholicism, asking four traditional Catholic questions and arriving at different answers. The four questions that Protestantism answered in a new way are: (1) How is a person saved? (2) Where does religious authority lie? (3) What is the church? and (4) What is the essence of Christian living? During the sixteenth century, Protestant Reformers agreed on the essentials, but fresh answers emerged in Martin Luther's conflict with Rome.

To the question, "How is a person saved?" Luther replied, "not by works but by faith alone." To the question, "Where does religious authority lie?" he answered, "not in the institutional Catholic Church but in the Word of God found in the Bible." To the question, "What is the church?" he responded, "the whole community of Christian believers, since all are priests before God." And to the question, "What is the essence of Christian living?" he replied, "serving God in any useful calling, whether ordained or lay." To this day, any classical description of Protestantism must echo those responses.[1]

Martin Luther (1843-1546) is familiar as the founding figure of Protestantism. The sixteenth century featured a huge upheaval in

---

1. Shelley, *Church History*, 257.

Western civilization, politically, economically, and socially. Because of the Reformation, the Western world was changed forever. However, while these forces influenced the development and course of the Reformation, spiritual and moral issues were primary. Above all else, the Reformers sought to correct the doctrine and life of the church. Their movement represented "a revolt of conscience."

Luther's contributions to religion and society were often deeply controversial, stirring people and nations even to violence and warfare. His own methodology, however, was nonviolent, and his movement was disseminated, not by the sword, but by the power of his preaching and his writings, his ideas spreading like wildfire across northern Europe, thanks to the newly invented printing press. Consequently, Catholics and Protestants fractured the church irreparably, initially into four major denominations—Lutheran, Anabaptist, Reformed, and Anglican—and eventually into hundreds of religious sects and subsects. Bloody struggles between Catholics and Protestants followed, and Europe was ravaged by war before it became obvious that Western Christendom was permanently divided.

Thankfully, ecumenically minded Protestants and Catholics are now talking with one another differently, emphasizing the unity of the church and how they represent different members of one body rather than different bodies, building on the famous Pauline analogy in 1 Corinthians 12:12–26. For example, some Catholics today look at Luther and find in his teaching something their own church is missing. Conversely, some Protestants regret the excesses of the Reformation and the eventual loss of church unity. On a larger scale, such regret also takes us back to the schism of 1054, which occasioned the break between Eastern and Western Christianity.

Young Luther's Spirituality

As we noticed in medieval spirituality, there was a strong emphasis on death and dying as preliminaries to divine judgment. Believers feared dying suddenly, in part because one might not die in a state of grace, and, hence, be subject to eternal damnation. This is why people at this time feared thunderstorms, for it was like the feeling we might have if someone held a gun to our head; within a second or two, we might be dead. People living during the Middle Ages were superstitious. Having little knowledge of science, they imagined lightening as divine thunderbolts hurled by God. In a split second, one might face the judgment of God and be unprepared.

This is what happened to young Luther, who, at an early age, was caught in a thunderstorm. To please his father, he had recently enrolled in law school. In 1505, on his way to school, he found himself in a thunderstorm, the "gun" pointed at his head. Struck by a bolt of lightning, he panicked, fearing the worst. The son of a miner, he prayed to the patroness of miners, "St. Anne, save me, and I'll become a monk." He kept his vow and two weeks later entered an Augustinian monastery. Martin's father had wanted his son to become a lawyer, and now young Luther found himself disobeying his father's will, joining a monastery willfully, thereby opposing his father's will. Struggling with his conscience, he found the wrath of God too great. Obsessed with his own sin, he tried austere acts of penance such as prolonged fasting, sleeping outdoors in freezing weather, and self-flagellation. The purity of God, however, proved to be too great, and no amount of penance soothed his spirit.

The troubled monk was assigned to the chair of biblical studies at the recently established Wittenberg University, where he found a different view of God. He wished, above all, to live in a state of grace, and he knew that to live in this state meant to love God. In 1515, while pondering Paul's epistle to the Romans, Luther came upon the statement that "the just shall live by his faith" (1:17). Here was the key to his dilemma. The answer lay in Christ's identity with sinful humanity. Luther understood clearly now the gospel message: salvation is only by faith in Christ. As a gift of God's grace, it cannot be earned, but merely affirmed by an act of faith. Luther had come by his famous doctrine of justification by faith alone. He saw how sharply it clashed with the Roman Church's doctrine of justification by faith and good works. The implications of Luther's discovery were enormous. If salvation comes through faith in Christ alone, the intercession of priests, masses, and prayers to the saints was unnecessary. The mediation of the institutional church, through hierarchical, sacramental, and monastic means, was superfluous.

As his 1516 lecture notes on the epistle of Romans reveal, his search for a deeper understanding of love led him to the writings of the twelfth-century mystic, Bernard of Clairvaux. In his writings, Bernard revealed a progressive spirituality of love, moving from (1) loving self for self's sake, an initial state of selfishness, to (2) loving God for self's sake, a deeper but still immature state in which one relates to God by wanting something from God, to (3) loving God for God's sake, a mature relational state of love, to (4) loving self for God's sake, an advanced state of grace, whereby the believer loves God by loving what God has made, understanding oneself as an instrument of God's love.

In his early professional life, Luther struggled to make his love increasingly less self-willed, or, as he put it, less "curved in on itself." At this time, be thought of impure motives as evil. He was still tormented by sin, for he had not yet been freed from the late medieval mindset to discover what he later called "the gospel." His understanding of salvation came close to what we might call "self hatred," for it was only in despising himself that he could hope to be acceptable to God.

Young Luther was not yet in a good place, for his spirituality was all law and no grace. What grace he sought, he sought only in law. It is as if good works come before grace, something alien to Augustinian spirituality but which Luther found in late medieval spirituality, a form of spirituality still alive in traditional Christianity. "Do the best that you can," it taught, "and learn to love God by sheer will, after which you can hope for God's grace." That approach, Luther discovered, does not work. Love works by delight, he learned, and not by demand or by sheer force of will. Good deeds can be done that way, but that is not how spirituality works. Spirituality *starts* with grace, lives by grace, and reaches its goal by grace. In a manner of speaking, God does it all. Like a great tide, love lifts all lives. Living by the confessional and by penance only confirmed the premise that we are sinners, unacceptable to God. Such an approach did not lead to joy, peace, and the other benefits of love, but only to begging and sighing, always seeking and never finding acceptance, grace, or righteousness.

At this point, Luther believed that God was more concerned with judging and condemning than with loving and forgiving. This form of spirituality, masochistic in nature, never focuses on what is good and right, but emphasizes what is sinful and wrong. According to this theology, God is Judge and Accuser, not Friend or Lover. The bottom line of young Luther's spirituality was this: To love God is to hate oneself. His confessor at the time, a priest named Staupitz, had to bring Luther to his senses by telling him, "Martin, you say that God is angry with you, but it is you who are angry with God."

Such an approach never works, for as Jesus regularly declared, we are not made to hate ourselves, but to love ourselves, and to love God and others with appropriate self-love. As we learn from the biblical and Augustinian paradigms, we must want good things, not bad things, for ourselves and for others. What we want and truly need is a loving God; nothing else will do. Martin Luther had yet to discover the transformative element in spirituality. He was seeking condemnation, but what he needed was acceptance.

In 1510, young Luther had visited Rome, then under Pope Julius II, known as Julius the Terrible. Luther was an unknown priest at the time, and he found Rome to be worldly, cynical, and even atheistic. Italian priests were more secular that religious, more opportunistic than believing. Their word for a "faithful" Christian was a "fool." Luther was shocked by their behavior, for these priests kept the "red light district" going; many had mistresses, prostitutes, or both, bearing numerous illegitimate children. In this environment, Luther was attempting a religious pilgrimage, seeking God's grace for deceased relatives in purgatory. For his deceased grandfather, he climbed the sacred steps on his knees. These were the steps supposedly of the Jerusalem house of Pilate, where Jesus had been on trial, moved to Rome. According to church tradition, if penitents climbed these steps one at a time, pausing at each step to recite the Lord's Prayer, when they reached the top, the departed soul was released from purgatory.

Much of the wealth of Renaissance popes came from pilgrims or parishioners from other European nations. Their spirituality was based on the late medieval piety of fear and anxiety about divine punishment in the afterlife, a condition exacerbated by the clergy. Average parishioners had little peace in this life, for death came suddenly, and if you died with unconfessed venial sin, you was destined for punishment. However, if you died with unconfessed mortal sin, your soul would go straight to hell with no chance of escape. Of course, if you died and went to purgatory, your punishment could be reduced, but this required financial and penitential acts by concerned relatives or friends.

Of course, such activity proved lucrative for the church. To supplement this income, the church devised a practice known as indulgences, whereby devout believers could pay money in exchange for a written guarantee that the souls of their loved ones would be released from purgatory or their punishment in the afterlife lessened or reduced. An entire economy was built on religious anxiety and superstition, much of it manufactured by greedy and cynical clergy in search of financial gain.

Luther, like other Reformers, had no desire to start a new religion, denomination, or sect, but rather to reform the church of its excess. He had no idea where his spiritual discovery was leading, but he knew it was important. It took flagrant abuse of church finances through the sale of indulgences to propel him into confrontation with papal authority. Luther's displeasure increased noticeably during 1517, when the Dominican John Tetzel traveled throughout Germany on behalf of a papal fundraising campaign to complete the construction of St. Peter's basilica in Rome. In exchange for a contribution, Tetzel boasted, he would provide donors with an indulgence that would free souls from purgatory. "As soon as the coin in the coffer rings," went his jingle, "the soul from purgatory upward springs."

The Reformation is said to have begun on October 31, 1517, when, protesting the sale of indulgences, Luther nailed his 95 Theses to the bulletin board on the door of the Castle Church at Wittenberg. While these theses did not present his theology, they proposed theological debate. Copies of Luther's theses were published and republished all over Europe, sparking a theological revolution. Luther came to regard the printing press as one of the great gifts of God.

In this context, Luther's gospel hit like a bombshell. Sincere parishioners in Germany became unhappy with this state of affairs, and they erupted in protest, with Luther at the center of the revolt. In the midst of this debate about the afterlife, Luther announced that believers could have certainty of God's grace. The guarantee, he declared, is in scripture. Instead of paying money or performing deeds of penitence, wondering whether they made any difference, one could go to scripture and simply trust in God's promise of love and forgiveness.

Luther's stress on the gospel not only gave believers peace of mind, it also had enormous economic and political consequences. It meant parishioners were no longer dependent upon clergy and the sacraments for divine grace. Through prayer, believers had direct access to God. No longer were penance, indulgences, or payments to the papacy needed. The gospel was free, for payment had been made on our behalf by Christ. That is what Jesus meant when he told his followers, "This is my body, given for you."

In part, the situation at the start of the Reformation could be characterized as a disagreement between German and Italian Catholics. Germans, essentially pious folk, were anxious about the afterlife, and they were paying dearly for promises they could not trust. Meanwhile, their money was being used by cynical priests to fund wars, extravagant buildings, and artistic projects in Rome. Pious Germans, with Luther as their spokesperson, were fed up. They discovered they didn't need all their religious baggage. All they needed was Jesus Christ and the gospel. Once they heard that, tremors resulted, and the earthquake came to be called the Reformation.

Within a short time, German Dominicans denounced Luther to Rome as preaching "dangerous doctrines." The Vatican issued a series of counter-theses, arguing that anyone who criticized the sale of indulgences was guilty of heresy. Luther decided to put his case before the German people. Utilizing the printing press, his reply came through a vast literary production. In one year alone (1520) he published five major works, relying on biblical arguments for support. His *Treatise on Good Works* demonstrated how faith in Christ was the only good work that God expected from repentant sinners. In *The Papacy of Rome* he attacked the pope directly, calling him Antichrist because he kept people from understanding and heeding the message of the gospel. His *Address to the Christian Nobility of the German Nation* called on the princes of northern Europe to throw off the tyranny—economic and political as well as spiritual—that bound them to Rome. His *Babylonian Captivity of the Church* examined the sevenfold system of sacraments, claiming to find only baptism and the Lord's Supper (and perhaps confession) as authorized by Christ in the New Testament. In contrast to the sharp polemics of these works, Luther published *Freedom of a Christian*, a conciliatory effort explaining how saving grace results in doing good works.

Among the ideas in these writings, three gained emphasis: (1) the supremacy of scripture as the only source and rule for Christian faith and practice (*sola scriptura*), (2) justification by grace received by faith alone (*sola gratia/sola fide*), and (3) the priesthood of believers (all church members are called to be "priests" to one another, the keys of the kingdom having been granted to the entire faith community and not only to the clergy [cf. Matt 18:18]). Known as the "three principles of Protestantism," these ideals countered essential aspects of medieval Catholicism: (1) "scripture alone" opposed Roman emphasis on the twofold authority of scripture and tradition, which made the decrees of popes and councils the only legitimate interpreters of the Bible; (2) "grace alone" opposed the Roman theory that faith and good works cooperated as sources of justification; (3) "the priesthood of believers" opposed the theory of the church as a vast hierarchy, which made ordained priests the necessary mediators between God and humanity.

In June 1520, Pope Leo X issued a decree condemning Luther and giving him sixty days to turn from his heretical course. Luther received his copy in October. At the end of his sixty-day period of grace, he led a throng of students outside Wittenberg and burned copies of medieval church documents, adding for good measure a copy of the decree condemning him. That was his answer. In 1521, the pope declared him a heretic, making complete his excommunication. The problem now fell into the hands of Charles V, a young man of twenty-one who, in addition to serving as king of Spain, had recently been elected Holy Roman Emperor. He summoned Luther to the imperial Diet (assembly) meeting at the German city of Worms to recant. Before the assembly Luther again insisted that only biblical authority would sway him: "I will not recant, for to go against conscience is neither honest nor safe. Here I stand, I cannot do otherwise." With these words, Protestantism was born. Protestants would obey the Bible before all other authorities. Europe—and the church—would never be the same.

Charles V gave Luther twenty-one days before the sentence fell. It never came. Luther was saved from arrest and death by the prince of Saxony, Duke Frederick the Wise, whose domains included Wittenberg. The duke gave Luther sanctuary at Wartburg Castle, where he remained for nearly a year, disguised as a minor nobleman. During this time, he translated the New Testament into German, an important step toward reshaping public and private worship in Germany.[2] Meanwhile the revolt against Rome spread and new reformers appeared on the scene. Princes, dukes, and electors defied the condemnation of Luther by giving support to the new movement. In 1522 Luther returned to Wittenberg to put into effect the spiritual reform that became the model for much of Germany. He called for the abolition of the office of bishop, arguing that the churches needed pastors, not dignitaries. Advocating for the abandonment of celibacy for monks and nuns, in 1525 Luther married Katherine von Bora, herself a former nun.

Luther's Understanding of Gospel

The central concept of Luther's theology and thought, which became the core teaching of Protestantism, is the phrase "justification by faith," a concept perhaps best captured by Luther's use of the phrase "the gospel." When asked what he meant by "the gospel," Luther often replied by citing the Apostles Creed, something all mainstream Christians of his day

---

2. In 1534 Luther completed his translation of the entire Bible, on which he worked with the help of colleagues for over a decade.

confessed and that most Christians affirm to this day, be they Orthodox, Catholic, or Protestant. In other words, Luther did not think that the gospel he proclaimed should be unique to him and his followers, but believed it underlay all Christian thought and belief. Luther disclaimed the terms Lutheran or Lutheranism, asking that his followers call themselves Christians. As Luther emphasized, the gospel he preached was not the gospel of Luther, but rather the gospel of Christ.

When Luther spoke of "the gospel," he had in mind not one or more of the four gospels in the New Testament. For Luther, there was only one gospel, only one story of Jesus Christ, but there are many ways of telling the story. The notion of the gospel as genre, as always in narrative form, was significant for Luther. However, the gospel story contains doctrines, that is, teachings about Christ, his life, death, and resurrection. We have, then, "the gospel," but we also have teachings about the gospel, and this is where Luther became controversial. The controversial aspect in Luther's teaching was that believers are justified (that is, are "made righteous" before God) by faith alone, apart from works of the law (that is, apart from requirements or laws found in the scriptures). This meant that a person's relationship with God is set right simply by believing the gospel, this story about Jesus. Apart from believing the gospel story to be true, there is nothing devout believers need to do for their salvation. Simply believing the gospel transforms believers into children of God. This happens by faith alone, by which Luther means grace alone, for even faith is God's gracious gift to us. The implication is simple: God does it all. We accept what God does, and that acceptance changes us.

To understand Luther's point, however, we must add an additional concept, namely the notion of promise. A good way to understand this concept is to think of a wedding ceremony. A person can put a ring in the hand of his beloved, but unless that gift is followed by a promise, the ring remains a token. It is the promise of love, of commitment and loyalty, that gives the ring its significance. Thus, a promise is more than words; a promise gives what it promises, but only if one is willing to receive it. The ring can be rejected, but if it is accepted, this means that the promise is believed. That, for Luther, is the meaning of faith. Faith is not about what we do, but about what God does.

To underscore his point, Luther gave the example of the Last Supper, where Jesus told his disciples, "This is my body, given for you." In this act, Jesus gave his followers, not just something to eat, and not simply his body, but himself. That, then, is the significance of the Eucharist;

Jesus gives himself in the sacrament. The same is true of a wedding vow. In exchanging rings, promises are given, but underlying the vow is the promise of the giving of self by each individual—without reservation—to the other. The willingness to receive this promise requires faith, by which Luther meant, not mere belief, but rather trust. As Luther would say, "Believe it, and you have it."

The point, for Luther, is that God keeps his promise. The gospel contains power, and that is how it saves. Its power comes from God's promise, for God is always faithful, always trustworthy. This is what Paul means in his writing by "the righteousness of God," and how it is that faith imparts God's righteousness to believers (see Rom 1:17; Gal 3:11; Phil 3:9; Heb 10:36, 38).

Thus far, we have established two points about Luther's view of the gospel, and they go together. The gospel is a story with a promise. To these points we add a third, that the gospel is a story with a promise "for us." To believe the gospel is not to believe something objective or theoretical. Rather, to believe the gospel is to personalize it: the gospel is "for me." Accepting the gospel is like accepting a ring, which includes the promise. In the gospel, God is saying, "I give myself to you. I belong to you, and you belong to me." Ultimately, however, the gospel is a story about Jesus. This means it is a story about Jesus, not a story about us.

When we examine the story as it appears in the Apostles Creed, we realize the gospel is about Jesus. He is the subject, but we are the beneficiaries. Luther's point in reciting the creed is that when the believer does so, it is done with the understanding that Christ lived for me, died for me, and was raised for me. The believer is the object, not the subject. Jesus is the doer in the story, and we are the recipients. The believer is not the one acting or doing. The story is about Jesus and his work. For Luther, believers are justified by faith, not by works, that is, not by acts they perform or by doctrines they accept rightly or correctly. Ultimately, the gospel draws attention away from us as well as away from our beliefs. Luther would say, "Don't look at what is in your heart; don't even look at your faith. Look at Christ; he is the actor; he did everything necessary for salvation, and he did it for you." That, for Luther, is the meaning of the gospel.

Given this emphasis on the gospel, two concerns arise that must be dispelled. The first is the apparent egocentricity of the stress on the believer as beneficiary. Why this emphasis on me? The answer is, the emphasis is on God, not me. If God promises us a gift, what right do we have to reject it? By deemphasizing the gift, we are actually emphasizing *our* autonomy, *our* ability to determine our fate, *our* obstinacy in rejecting the gift. If we are being addressed by God, we ought to listen and believe God's promise, that is, trust in God's gracious love and acceptance.

An opposite concern—one we hear increasingly in today's pluralistic environment—is that of course God loves humanity. After all, God does not discriminate or have favorites. Aren't we all beloved of God? If God's nature is love, God wouldn't possibly wish to hurt or punish anyone, would he? At this point, Luther calls attention to the law, with its emphasis on sin and judgment. Building on Augustine, Luther stresses that humans are sinners who deserve nothing but condemnation and rejection. Apart from God's promise of mercy in Christ, humans can expect nothing but judgment.

This view of God's wrath is foreign to many of us today, so to understand it, we need some imagination. Luther lived in a world where everyone feared hell, and thus he spent a great deal of time speaking of hell, but it was not demons or hellfire or even details of punishment that concerned him. Rather, his fear was of God, and of the potential loss of relationship with God that defines human origin, meaning, and destiny. Just as the gospel is about God giving himself to us, so also hell, or what Luther calls "the law," is about God rejecting us, accusing us, and withholding himself from us.

In Luther's understanding, there are two ways God relates to us, (1) through gospel, in which God gives himself to us, and (2) through law, which condemns us not only for what we do, but also for what we do not do. Concerning our relationship with God, we have two options, to focus on God's law, whereby God condemns us, or to focus on the promise and comfort of the gospel, whereby God accepts us as we are.

For Luther, our fear should not be of hellfire or torture, for foremost in his mind is the fear, not of punishment, but of loss of relationship, of disappointing God to the point of being disowned or rejected by God. Such loss of relationship with one's Creator, with one's eternal Father, is, for Luther, unimaginable terror. However, accepting God's unconditional love and forgiveness, despite our unworthiness, is far better, equally incalculable and unimaginable. That is the consolation of the gospel. For Luther, simply believing the gospel—faith alone—changes the individual and, indirectly, society.

Luther's Understanding of Law

By 1520, when Luther wrote *Freedom of a Christian*, also called "A Treatise on Christian Liberty," he had worked out the distinction between law and gospel, that is, the distinction between human effort and human faith. The phrase "justification by faith" appeared early in Luther's writings, but it appeared initially in the context of law, namely, in reference to the justice of God. In this setting, law has an accusatory function that cannot save.

Luther discovered two functions of the law, the first its civil or political use, where it has a restraining function, threatening evildoers with punishment. While this use of the law does not make people internally righteous, it does help in ordering society. The law's second function, its spiritual and central purpose, is what Luther calls its evangelical use. This is a striking concept, for it means the "gospel use" of the law. In this sense, the law serves as a preparation for the gospel. This is the internal use of the law, its religious use, in that it humbles us, bringing our ego or sinful self under control. For Luther, the religious law "kills us" (it crucifies the old self, to use Pauline language; see Rom 6:6) in order to make us fully alive. The law, then, does not stand on its own, but it points to some kinder and more hopeful truth, namely, the gospel.

Thus, what for early Luther had been the basis of all theology, namely, accusation and humiliation, become in the mature Luther preparation for the gospel. As we saw earlier, the gospel is both genre and promise, a story about what God does in Christ, whereas the law is about what we do. On its own, the law is useless, because it focuses on us and our religious duty; its use is not in what it says about us, but in how it points to Christ and the gospel. In the spiritual life, then, telling people what to do is essentially useless, for in putting the cart before the horse, it assumes that sinners are able to please and obey God, something that, for Luther, they cannot do.

While Luther spoke of two uses of the law, later followers envisioned a threefold function of the law as:

- *spiegel* (mirror): as a summons to repentance, God's law provides moral guidance;
- *oregal* (curb or bridle): as a means of restraint, God's law provides civil guidance;
- *regal* (rule): as a means of instruction, God's law provides practical guidance.

The third use of the law, related in scripture to Paul's thoughts on the guidance of the church, may sometimes be expressed by means of the term "law," but when Paul speaks of the "law of the Spirit" (Rom 8:2) or the "law of Christ" (Gal 6:2), he is referring to the "law of love," the law which Christ exemplified and which he laid down when he said that the whole law and prophets depend on the twin commandments of love to God and love to one's neighbor (Matt 22:40). This use of the law is echoed by Paul when he says that the whole law is summed up in a single commandment: "You shall love your neighbor as yourself" (Gal 5:14) or that "Love does no wrong to a neighbor; therefore, love is the fulfilling of the law" (Rom 13:10).

Ultimately, however, Luther's distinction between law and gospel is singular and obvious; gospel is what Christ does, and law is what we do. So, if some religious authority declares, "This is what you must do to be saved," that is law and not gospel, and hence, part of the problem rather than the solution. Even faith is not something we "do," but rather about what Christ does. The gospel is not advice about how to live or how to be a better Christian, for that is law. The gospel is about what God does, and that makes all the difference, for it changes us from the inside out, which is the good news of the gospel.

What changes human being is not doing but hearing, an internal and spiritual form of hearing that Christians attribute to the inner working of the Holy Spirit, an agent of spirituality emphasized by Luther and key Reformers such as Zwingli, Calvin, and distinctively by Anabaptist Reformers. While hearing God's Spirit is essential to the gospel, so also is hearing God's Word (scripture). This is something all Reformers emphasize, for, as Luther declares, the gospel functions not just as authority for believers; the gospel is power. The Bible is God's Word, and God's Word as gospel is efficacious, accomplishing what it promises. The gospel is not, for Luther, theory or doctrine. If it were, it would be law, something Christians have to believe, something they have to do or apply to their lives. For Luther, it is not human effort, beliefs, or deeds that make us come alive spiritually. Rather, it is the gospel that revives, that gives life.

In *Freedom of a Christian*, Martin Luther compared the gospel story to a king who gives his son in marriage to a prostitute, where believers (the prostitute) become the bride of the king's son. The marriage changes the prostitute. She now dresses regally and acquires all the wealth of the king's son, which, according to the parable, she is to distribute to all in the kingdom.

There are good deeds in the gospel, Luther notes, but they come as the result of a change in the prostitute's status, and never as the cause of that status. At the wedding, the prostitute hears the promised vow (the gospel): "You are my beloved, and I am yours" (see Song 2:16; 6:3), and she realizes she is no longer a prostitute. She is now a princess, the beloved, joint heir with the prince. She is not just married to the king's son (Christ), but everything that belongs to the son is hers (righteousness, holiness, blessedness). Over time, the bride learns that being married to the king's son is better than having the son's belongings. Love and intimacy with the son supersedes any benefit she accrues, be it joy, peace, even salvation. What this means for believers is that we love God for love's sake alone, not for any benefit or reward that love might bring.

The first side of the story, what Luther calls the "blessed exchange," indicates that all that is Christ's is ours. The second half of the story, however, is equally true: all that is ours becomes his; our sin, suffering, even death, all is placed on the cross. Thus, the king's son takes upon himself all the bride's debts, wounds, anguish, and loss. The cross, for Luther, is the place of exchange. Ultimately, of course, it is God who takes our sins and dies on the cross, for what affects the son affects the father. Likewise, Christ's victory over sin is also God's victory. It is divine love that pays the price, and the result is forgiveness and newness of life for the prostitute, temporally and eternally. One result of the good news of the gospel is comfort: it cheers and consoles us, and like good therapy, we feel better—about ourselves and others.

For Luther, the consequences of this exchange carry with them the notion that the gospel is good news for sinners, for the king's son loves a prostitute. This is where the concept of law enters into the story, for as the law makes clear, the bride is a sinner. Thus, it is when the prostitute asks, "How can the king's son love a sinner like me?" that she is ready for the gospel message, "It is you, the sinner, whom I love" (see Rom 5:8).

When Luther speaks of sin, it is never ultimately about condemnation, but about redemption. As Luther understands, every human being is an unworthy sinner. Whereas the law prepares us for the gospel, telling us "You are a prostitute pretending to be a princess," the gospel is transformative, for it accomplishes what it promises. The law's role, for Luther, is not to instruct believers on how to be better Christians. Its sole role is to drive us to the gospel. The gospel, on the other hand, is not about adding laws and duties to our lives. Its role is to free us from the law, with all its baggage.

Nevertheless, when Luther speaks of believers, he notes that they remain sinners and saints simultaneously, for even after the prostitute becomes the princess, she still struggles with the "old self" (note the contrast between "flesh" and "Spirit" in Romans 7 and 8). In fact, she is a princess, but there is still unbelief and unrighteousness within, making her prostitute and princess at the same time. If we look at ourselves only, we see a wounded past; however, if we look at ourselves in Christ, we see God's beloved bride. Ultimately, then, we are defined, not by who we think we are, but by who God says we are, perfected and holy.

Despite his indebtedness to Augustine, Luther's conception of spirituality differed significantly from his mentor. Whereas for Augustine, the Christian life is like a journey toward God, in which one progresses toward a goal, for Luther, the Christian life is a gift already given. Hence, believers have already reached the goal. Whereas for Augustine, believers are motivated by longing and desire, for Luther, they are motivated by gratitude, for the Christian life is a gift one accepts by faith. Whereas for Augustine, the goal is "seeing," that is, contemplating God, for Luther, the goal is "belief," that is, trusting the promise of a trustworthy God. That is how we know God, by trusting what God says and does. Underlying Lutheran spirituality is what the apostle Paul called the "righteousness or faithfulness of God." What this meant for Luther is that God is trustworthy. God does not lie, but always keeps his promises.

Faith alone, trusting solely in God, is the central step in the Christian life, not believing certain things about God or living a certain way. These things come later, but they are not primary. Faith is inward, works are outward. Faith changes us inwardly, and good works flow from that center naturally, toward our neighbor. Good works do not contribute to faith, but they flow from faith. Good works are not requisite for salvation, but they exhibit faith's saving power.

As Luther strikingly puts it, once believers have saving faith, they become Christs to others. They live, think, and act as Christ does, for God's love flows to them and through them to others. God does not need our good works, but our neighbor does. That, for Luther, is the freedom of the Christian, freedom from servitude to the egocentric self, yet free for love.

Questions for Discussion and Reflection

1. In your estimation, how did the Protestant Reformation influence and change the development of Christianity as a religion and as a way of life?

2. In your estimation, how did the Protestant Reformation change Western society?

3. Explain and assess Luther's change of mind regarding the role of law and grace.

4. Do you tend to regard God more as Judge and Accuser or as Friend or Lover? Explain your answer.

5. Assess the significance of the Lutheran principle of salvation by faith alone for the development of Christian spirituality.

6. Explain and assess Luther's understanding of "the gospel." What did Luther mean when he spoke of gospel as genre?

7. Explain how Luther connected gospel with promise, and how this affects our understanding of "the righteousness of God."

8. Explain what Luther meant by "the evangelical use" of the law.

9. Explain and assess Luther's understanding of "merit" or "good deeds" in the gospel.

10. Compare and contrast Luther and Augustine's conceptions of spirituality.

8

Pietist Spirituality
Romantic Piety

DESIGNED TO REFORM THE church, the Reformation gave birth to Protestantism, challenging papal leadership of Western Christendom. While the Protestant Reformation fragmented Christendom, the idea of Christendom in the form of state churches survived the Reformation practically unscathed.

One Protestant principle that greatly affected the relationship between church and society is the Lutheran principle of the priesthood of all believers. The church, Martin Luther taught, does not need a priestly class to mediate between believers and God. Rather, each believer has immediate access to God through Christ. By virtue of one's faith in Christ, each believer stands before God as priest, needing no clergy or human institution as mediator.

While Luther in Germany and John Calvin in Switzerland were the leading Protestant Reformers during the sixteenth century, they were not viewed as infallible, and some of their followers began modifying their views. One group, later called Anabaptists or Radical Reformers, disagreed with the notion of a reformed Christendom altogether. Led by the Swiss Reformer Ulrich Zwingli (1484–1531), they disagreed with Luther, who allowed in worship and in practice whatever the Bible did not prohibit. Zwingli established the principle that whatever the Bible does not commend should be discarded. For this reason, the Reformation in Zurich stripped away traditional symbols of the Roman Church such as candles, statues, music, and pictures. Later, in England, people called this behavior Puritanism.

In 1527, an early conference of Anabaptists took place at Schleitheim, marking the first synod of the Protestant Reformation. The group adopted the Schleitheim Confession, a shared set of belief and values based on the following principles:

- *Discipleship.* To be a Christian one must have a relationship with Jesus Christ. Such faith transcends doctrines and leads to a transformed style of life. For the Anabaptists, discipleship refuses participation in worldly power, including bearing arms, holding political office, and taking oaths. In the sixteenth century, such abandonment of citizenship constituted treason.
- *Love.* The principle of love, logically developed from discipleship, requires pacifism. Anabaptists are not to go to war, defend themselves against attacks, or participate in any coercion by the state.
- *Congregationalism.* Decision-making rests with the entire membership, not with bishops, priests, or other church officials. In Anabaptist assemblies, all members are baptized as adults, upon profession of faith in Christ. In deciding matters of doctrine, the authority of scripture is primary, its interpretation given by the consensus of local members. In matters of church discipline, the believers also act corporately.
- *Separation of church and state.* The church, according to the Anabaptists, is distinct from society, even if society claims to be Christian. Christ's true followers are a pilgrim people, perpetual aliens in a sinful world.

Many of these beliefs are now accepted by other Christians. The distant relatives of the Anabaptists today include Quakers, Baptists, and, to some extent, Congregationalists. The first Anabaptists, wishing to restore apostolic Christianity, desired radical social change. Their goal was to restore apostolic Christianity. Unlike Lutherans, who followed the notion of the "territorial church," considering the population of a given territory members of their church, Anabaptists followed the notion of the "gathered church," where individuals have the freedom to join the congregation of their choice. Such freedom begins with conversion, and for Anabaptists, it is this experience of spiritual regeneration that makes one fit for baptism. The true church, the radicals insisted, is always a community of saints, dedicated disciples in a wicked world. Like the missionary monks of the Middle Ages, Anabaptists wished to shape society by their example of radical discipleship.

In England, a religious group emerged that, while not technically Anabaptist, followed the Schleitheim principles. Known as the Baptists, they arose as Puritan Separatists. As Separatists, the Baptists were considered illegal, since they rejected the concept of a state or national church, which in England meant the Church of England. While Baptists agreed on biblical authority, they upheld the right of private interpretation, unmediated by hierarchical tradition. Baptists became leaders in the fight for religious liberty for all, both in England and in America. Their dissent, and the price they payed for nonconformity, paved the way for disestablishment and the religious liberty citizens prize in the United States. Baptist individualism was reinforced in America by national commitment to democracy, and by a congregational approach to worship. By opposing state churches and insisting on religious liberty for all, Baptists were ideally suited for American denominationalism.

The seemingly endless debate on dogma, and the intolerance of nonconformist Christians that arose in England and on the European continent in the sixteenth and seventeenth centuries, led many Christians to seek refuge in inner piety. One such figure was George Fox (1624–1691), born of humble origin in a small English village. At the age of nineteen, disgusted by the licentiousness around him, he began a life of wandering, seeking divine illumination. His study of the Christian scriptures and his attendance of varied religious meetings led to the conviction that all religious sects were in error, and that public worship ws an abomination.

Church buildings, clergy, hymns, sermons, sacraments, creeds, liturgies—all seemed to him hindrances to life in the Spirit. Against all of these, Fox placed the "inner light," a pathway common to all human beings, no matter their race, faith, or creed. True Christianity is not a matter of conforming to a set of doctrines or performing rituals led by a professional priest. Rather true believers are illumined by an inner light.

Like Baptists, the Religious Society of Friends, as the followers of Fox called themselves, were inspired by the notion of radical immediacy, taking that notion much farther than the Baptists. Immediacy is a modern notion, which arises when one disagrees or finds irrelevant national churches, established churches, and governments that enforce religion through persecution. Citizens of modern nations find the notion of forced worship repugnant, not only for being undemocratic but because it actually suppresses religion.

According to the Quakers, there is only one requirement in religion, namely, one's relation with God. The central Quaker conviction, articulated by Fox and other early Quaker leaders, is that the same Holy Spirit that inspired the Bible also speaks today within the human heart. For that reason, Quaker meetings have no liturgy or clergy but only members of the congregation speaking as they are moved by the Spirit. When they speak, their words have the same authority as scripture. Quakers believe that the inner light of divine revelation is available to all, for every human has the Holy Spirit.

In America, the most famous Quaker was William Penn, after whom the state of Pennsylvania is named. In 1681 Penn received a charter to found a colony in North America in which there would be complete religious freedom. Under Penn, the first governor of the colony, relations with the Indians were excellent, and for a long time his dream of a peaceful settlement was a reality. In the seventeenth century, if you were Roman Catholic in the American colonies, the only place you could celebrate the Mass freely in the British world was in Pennsylvania, because as a Quaker colony, it advocated freedom of worship for all. In England it was not until the "Glorious Revolution" that accompanied the accession of William and Mary that full religious tolerance for Quakers and all other dissenting groups was made into law

Early Continental Pietism

Modernity arose, in part, from the Protestant Reformation, which dissolved the unity of medieval Catholicism and resulted in competing churches or denominations. This movement fostered secularism, especially as national churches became less acceptable. As sectarian groups developed, they ran into opposition from the national church in their region, often suffering persecution as a result. In turn, groups like the Baptists and Quakers became critical of the established churches, and for good reason, since the ruling churches often used the existing governments to suppress their rivals. So modernity tended to push against national or established churches, against conformity with authorities external to the individual, favoring secularized government, one with decreasing responsibility for the religious welfare of its people.

As Western society and politics became more secularized and fragmented, modernity provided an environment more suitable to low rather than high churches, favoring theologies of the Spirit and experience over theologies of word and sacrament. High churches were more hierarchical and institutionalized, affirming distinctions between laity and clergy, while enforcing doctrinal orthodoxy. Low churches, like Baptists and Quakers, moved in the opposite direction, toward anticlericalism, though there was always the temptation toward holiness, purity, and withdrawal from social influences. In many ways, these groups represented the future of modernity, arguing for a form of individualism known as immediacy, a phenomenon called "inner light" by Quakers and "soul competency" by Baptists, thereby opposing institutional mediation between the individual soul and God.

Most Protestants were not that radical, but as modernity unfolded, they, too, tended to oppose institutional mediation. Thus, modernity favored a turn toward experience, toward the inner self, a view that says, "I can find God on my own, with little or no help from clergy or the church." This turn away from sacraments toward the Holy Spirit characterizes many Protestants, certainly those opting for the "gathered church" and away from highly ritualistic forms of worship.

In the seventeenth century, this mindset was particularly prevalent in the Puritan movement in England, and then among German pietists in the eighteenth century. At some point early in their development, Puritans encountered an issue that became all-consuming, namely, the question of how knowledge of salvation is possible, and in particular, how one can have assurance of salvation. This issue of skepticism concerning knowledge is a characteristically modern concern, both in philosophy and in theology. And the turn to experience is a typically modern way to answer that question, assuming that inner certainty is the solution.

Among early Lutherans and Calvinists, faith was regarded as a form of certainty, because it is based on the Bible, believed to be God's Word and therefore absolutely true. At a certain point, pietists placed an additional requirement on individual faith, namely, having the assurance that one's faith is adequate for salvation. Only those with true saving faith were said to be saved, and not those with merely acquired or intellectual faith. At this point, assurance of salvation came to be based not solely on scripture, but rather on the inner evidence of grace in the heart, manifest through personal salvation. Of course, such evidence is fragile, susceptible to uncertainty and doubt.

In the seventeenth century, these concerns were taken to Germany, where they were adapted to the Lutheran tradition and become known as pietism. The beginning of German pietism is customarily traced to a German Lutheran pastor named Jacob Philip Spener (1685–1705), who in 1675 wrote *Pia Desideria* (Pious Desires) because he was concerned about the lack of piety (sincere faith and practice) in his congregation and among his colleagues. He desired to promote personal piety, and he did so by gathering people together in small groups for the study of scripture—like small-group Bible studies today. Those small groups were meant to intensify Christian life. Spener's efforts are said to be based on a devotional book, *True Christianity*, written in 1606 by the German Lutheran pastor Johann Arndt.

The background to the problem of insincere worship and behavior by the majority of Lutheran clergy and laity in seventeenth-century Germany was a phenomenon called "Protestant Scholasticism," whereby Lutherans of that period turned faith into a mental exercise. This form of theology, modeled after medieval scholasticism, led to formality in worship and turned faith into a matter of outward conformity, something pietists rejected. One of Spener's key complaints was that Lutheran ministers were mostly careerists, trained in German universities to become successful rhetoricians, proving the superiority of Lutheran doctrine to Catholic, Anabaptist, or other forms of Christian belief. To accomplish this, university-educated pastors were trained in Latin disputations, learning to argue the merits and logic of certain beliefs and practices. Pastors then translated these disputations into German, using such proofs for Christian doctrine as the basis for their sermons. Imagine going to church and listening to sermons that consist exclusively of intellectual argumentation. As a result, spirituality suffered, and worship turned into an extension of the classroom. Many pastors became careerists, lacking in pastoral care and in ability to help with the faith-formation of their parishioners.

The head-heart split seems to be a good way of describing what was taking place, an emphasis on head knowledge rather than on religion of the heart. By "heart" I do not mean simply the emotions, but rather the original Hebrew emphasis on unity of emotion, perception, and thought. As the eighteenth century progressed, however, those who emphasized head knowledge viewed heartfelt piety narrowly and pejoratively, whereas those who emphasized heart knowledge viewed theology as purely intellectual and irrelevant to the Christian life.

That split became most evident in the work of the Protestant theologian August Hermann Francke (1663–1727), an early eighteenth century Lutheran pastor and a protégé of Spener. Francke was one of those Lutheran ministers in training who enrolled in a German university with the intention of training for a good career. At this point, theology was still the "queen of the sciences," still the reigning academic discipline. That changed shortly, as modern science entered the curriculum. As a careerist, his head filled with knowledge, Francke found that theology hardly affected his spirituality. For a while, he questioned whether he was a Christian. He lacked the "true Christianity" Arndt had spoken of decades earlier, and feared he might be an atheist. This was perhaps the first time in Christian history when that worry arose. Luther's struggle with God concerned whether God was merciful, but Francke's struggle was new, the struggle over whether God exists. This phenomenon grew virally in the eighteenth century, especially when Christianity was evaluated solely through the lens of reason, where it was found unconvincing.

Francke narrated his own conversion experience as follows: "One day I fell on my knees. When I did so, I did not believe there was a God, but when I stood up, I believed it to the point of giving up my blood, without fear or doubt. Reason stood away: victory was torn from its hands." Reason, here, is the enemy of faith, for reason can only produce arguments in the head, not true piety in the heart. To grow spiritually—to live authentically—one needs to put reason aside, so that one can fall to one's knees and experience the Holy Spirit, who makes one a new person. Unlike Luther, who found regeneration in baptism, Franke found regeneration in a conversion experience, where one is fully committed—body, heart, and soul—rather than through a sacrament like baptism, where infants remains passive and uninvolved. For pietists, one knows one is Christian through experience, by turning inward, into one's heart.

Pietism made an enormous contribution to Christianity. It shifted emphasis from theological controversy to the care of souls. It made preaching and pastoral visitation central to Protestant ministry. It enriched Christian music and underscored the importance of the laity for a vital church. Perhaps its greatest legacy, however, was its emphasis on small groups and the devotional reading of the Bible. Supporting all these emphases was regeneration, the pietist's dominant theme, by which they meant not doctrinal renewal but experiential renewal. The intensely personal way that pietists described regeneration often turned Christianity into a drama of the human soul, the scene of a desperate struggle between good and evil. In this sense, pietism was the foundation of all modern revivals.

Despite its private and sectarian nature, pietism shaped Western religious thought, initially through Kant, and later through Friedrich Schleiermacher. Kant's pietistic upbringing had an enduring religious impact on his life. Both members were devout members of a pietist church. Of his mother, Kant would say: "my mother was a sweet-tempered, affectionate, pious and upright woman and a tender mother, who led her children to the fear of God by pious teaching and virtuous example. She often took me outside of the city, directed my attention to the works of God, expressed herself with a pious rapture over His omnipotence, wisdom, and goodness, and impressed on my heart a deep reverence for the Creator of all things."

Pietism, as Kant describes it, was a religious movement that opposed the theoretical, philosophical, scholastic pursuit of Christianity, emphasizing (a) a renewed study of the Bible, (b) cultivation of devotional life, and (c) the practical side of Christian life equally important with doctrine. While at home, Kant encountered pietism at its best, but subsequent experience with the daily regimen of required Bible study and prayer in a Lutheran pietist boarding school had such a negative influence on him that in his adult life he virtually denied any value in prayer and worship. At school, students were expected to exhibit deep religious feelings, which fostered insincerity; the strengths of pietism led to its weakness, individualistic moralism and hypocrisy. The eight years he spent at this school were painful for Kant, an experience he later described as "youthful slavery." Nevertheless, he continued to see the good in pietism, which was a tribute to his family life. Later, in refuting the three traditional proofs for the existence of God—ontological, cosmological, and teleological—he showed deep respect for the latter, based on the perception of harmony and order in the universe, arguing that despite its deficiencies, this argument should be held in esteem, in part because it is the oldest, the clearest, and the best suited to ordinary human reason.

Friedrich Schleiermacher's Romantic Spirituality

In the nineteenth century, a theologically sophisticated movement arose that provided a plausible picture of Jesus, while maintaining a non-dogmatic faith. It was based neither on reason nor the authority of the church but rather on experience. The name for that movement, especially as it flourished in Germany, is Romantic Theology, initially a movement within Protestantism, though in the twentieth century it also influenced Catholicism.

The demise of rationalism in the second half of the eighteenth century led to dramatic changes in sensibility. Instead of viewing reality as rational and ordered, people turned to mystery, imagination, and feeling as the basis of truth. The new sense of the human self that captured the imagination of influential Europeans often goes under the name "Romanticism." This romantic worldview was initiated by the German secular philosophies of Johann Wolfgang von Goethe (1749-1832), Friedrich von Schiller (1759-1805), and Gotthold Ephraim Lessing (1729-1781). Rebelling against the rationalist thought of the Enlightenment, these authors emphasized emotion. Their view became integrated into all aspects of European society and culture. Their sense of human transcendence flourished in such English Romantic poets as Wordsworth, Coleridge, Shelley, and Byron. It inspired Goethe, drove the musical compositions of Beethoven, Mendelssohn, and Wagner, and undergirded the spectacular rise of the novel as the dominant form of European literature.

Like rationalism, Romanticism is a form of humanism, for it elevates the human being to a position of prominence in knowing and valuing. Unlike Enlightenment thought, however, which emphasized reason as the means of knowing, the Romantics stressed spontaneity, creativity, imagination, and intuition, attempting to reclaim the deeper dimensions of life. Whereas Enlightenment intellectuals viewed nature as orderly and mechanical, functioning independently of humans and solely according to natural laws, Romantics looked to nature with eyes full of wonder, pointing anew to the mystery of life. They valued relationships with others and with nature, seeing individuals as part of an organic whole.

Perhaps the best spokesperson for a Romantic view of Christianity is the German theologian Friedrich Schleiermacher (1768-1834). Called "the father of modern theology," he not only summarized the theological insights of progressive Protestantism for his time but he set the course for subsequent Christian thought. He attempted to rehabilitate religion among intellectuals, insisting that the great debates over proofs of God and the abstract doctrinal descriptions of faith were, at best, a secondary expression of religion. The theological task, he argued, cannot be separated from the great movements and concerns in society. He believed that theology no longer had the luxury of being isolationist. From now on, theology had to come to grips with society, culture, and technology, and with the growing authority of science. In particular, theology had to embrace the scientific method, with its stress on experience, observation, and experimentation.

In 1799, ordained as a pastor and serving a church in Berlin, Schleiermacher fell in with a group of Romantic thinkers, for whom feeling, rather than reason or even morality, was central. Schleiermacher agreed that feeling is at the heart of true piety, yet he also wished to retain much of his Christian conviction. Throughout his life, therefore, he sought to harmonize Romanticism and theism. At one point, his Romantic friends asked him to clarify his thought, and he did so in his *Speeches on Religion to Its Cultured Despisers*, his first influential work and the first great document of Romantic theology. There he pled with his friends not to discard religion, but to realize that the rationalism they disdained distorts religion by subordinating it to reason and conscience.

The title alone tells us a great deal about Romantic theology. First, it addresses the cultural elite, to whom Schleiermacher says, in effect, "We Christians can show you how what you desire as the cultural elite is best represented in Christianity. The feeling that you Romantics cultivate, the awareness of unity and continuity with the universe, the awareness that the self exists not for its own sake but rather as part of the whole— as representative of the Infinite in your lives—is actually at the heart of Christian spirituality." This perspective—that religion is not primarily about dogma, ritual, or morality, but rather about intuition and mystery, about the innate sense of the Infinite behind the finite—lies at the center of Schleiermacher's argument. For Schleiermacher, the human sense of feeling, of dependence upon something ultimate and Infinite, is preconceptual and religious in nature. Christian spirituality is this experience of the Infinite in all things. To seek and find this eternal factor in our lives, and to experience it directly, in the present—something all humans sense by nature—that feeling, says Schleiermacher, is what we mean by religion.

In arguing against the opponents of religion, Schleiermacher viewed religion as basic to human existence. Contrary to the rationalists, who view reason (the mind) as the source of certainty, religion is not about knowledge or knowing. Contrary to the Kantians, who view conscience (the human will) as the seat of religion, religion is not about morals or doing. Going beyond the dialectic of knowing and doing, Schleiermacher carved out for religion a third dimension of human consciousness, prior, independent, and more essential than knowing and doing. In addition to knowing and acting, humans also feel. According to Schleiermacher, the essence and source of religion lies in the realm of feeling—the aesthetic realm.

For Schleiermacher, the deepest feeling of one's heart aims at the Infinite, by which he meant what we call "God," even if he didn't always make this clear. In his *Speeches*, Schleiermacher avoided using the term "God," preferring instead terms such as "the Universe," "The One and Whole," or the "World Spirit." Not surprisingly, his theological language led to charges of pantheism. His language, however, was typically romantic usage. Schleiermacher was uncomfortable with personalistic descriptions of God, not wishing to confuse God with ideas about God. At the same time, he recognized the inadequacy of impersonal or non-personal descriptions of God. They, too, remain ideas, abstract and religiously empty. Schleiermacher's point, however, is that without religion as a vital and living awareness, neither personal or impersonal descriptions of God have value. Ultimately, experience is necessary.

Schleiermacher's hesitancy with "God language" is best understood by looking at the predominant Kantian philosophical background of the era. German philosophy at that time was in the shadow of Immanuel Kant, who argued for a turn to philosophical experience, and for whom the structure of human consciousness was the structure of human knowledge, which in turn is the structure of the world. In other words, if one wants to know the structure of the universe, one has to examine human consciousness and experience, because that is what structures our world.[1] For Kant, knowledge is based on experience.

The Romantics took Kant one step further: the root of all experience is not reason, which our mind constructs, nor is it moral or ethical action, which theological liberals find compelling, but rather it is feeling. What feeling provides is immediate, unmediated contact with the Infinite in the finite. Thus, when a Romantic poet looks at a waterfall or writes a sonnet, its beauty opens up the very essence of the universe, which

---

1. As students of modern philosophy know, Kant performed a task similar in scope to that of Plato. However, whereas Plato provided a synthesis in cosmology (combining the rationalism of Parmenides with the empiricism of Heraclitus), Kant provided a synthesis in epistemology, showing how knowledge takes place. Kant viewed the mind as a pseudocreater rather than a knower. Kant's fundamental premise was that although all knowledge begins with sense experience, not all knowledge arises from experience. The mind receives simple sensations from the world, but then it imposes organization and structure upon those impressions to create knowledge. The world, as it exists apart from our experience of it, is unknowable. For Kant, humans cannot know the essence of an object in itself (*ding an sich*).

religion calls "God." That sense of immediacy and awe, Schleiermacher argued, is the source of religion, of which the rituals, dogmas, and morality of Christianity are external expressions. While some might argue that belief gives expression to experience, Schleiermacher and the Romantic tradition argued the reverse view, that it is experience that gives form to outward expression. For this reason, Romantic theology is revisionist, making doctrine conform to experience.

At this point, some background on Schleiermacher is helpful. He was raised in an extremely religious atmosphere. Like Kant, Schleiermacher's parents sent him to a Moravian boarding school, where he had a conversion experience and cultivated a heartfelt, Christ-centered piety. However, despite their efforts, the Moravians failed to protect him from modern ideas. Schleiermacher and his friends started a philosophy club and read prohibited books by Goethe and Rousseau. At age twenty-one, Schleiermacher wrote to his father saying he no longer believed in the incarnation (the deity of Jesus) and vicarious atonement (the substitutionary death of Jesus on the cross). This resulted in a loss of faith in orthodoxy, but not in spirituality. In his schooling he awakened, he wrote later, to "the consciousness of the relation of man to a higher world. Here it was that that mystical awareness developed that has been so important to me, and has supported and carried me through all the storms of skepticism. Then it was questioning, now it has attained its full development, and I may say, that after all I have passed through, I have become a Herrnhuter (a Moravian in piety) again, only of a higher order." In this way, Schleiermacher did not actually claim to be a Moravian, but he was doing his theology in order to provide the intellectual scaffolding for the spirituality he learned among the Moravians.[2] What was valid about his experience among the Moravians was not their doctrines or their Lutheran theology in general, but rather their sense of piety. Schleiermacher's aim as a theologian was to give outward doctrinal expression to that inward experience of piety, an approach he called "a science of theology."

Interestingly, Schleiermacher became one of the founders of the University of Berlin, where he served as professor of theology. There, he became one of the most famous and influential professors in Germany. In German higher education, one's discipline is a science, and Schleiermacher was committed to making theology a science. Beginning with

---

2. Those familiar with my writings might recognize here an example of what I call "postcritical understanding" or "secondary naiveté"; see Vande Kappelle, *Adventures in Spirituality*, 33, and *Beyond Belief*, xxii–xxiv.

Romanticism, it was this science that articulates the meaning of Christian feeling of piety. His approach became "systematic theology," a perspective he laid out in *The Christian Faith* (1821), his *magnum opus*. As the first great systematic theologian of Romantic theology, Schleiermacher rethought Christian epistemology, soteriology (sin and salvation), and Christology (the person and work of Jesus Christ). If in his *Speeches* he answered the question, What is religion?, in *The Christian Faith* he answered the question, What is Christianity? (that is, what is theology?). Religion, he argued in his *Speeches*, "is nowhere so fully idealized as in Christianity."

Central to Schleiermacher's epistemology was his understanding of scripture. Rooted in his definition of religion was the view that true Christianity is not a set of dogmas but an inner individual experience. Building on this notion, Schleiermacher understood the Bible as simply the textbook of Christian dogma and doctrine. The scriptures, being only a reflection of the original Christian feeling, are thereby subordinate in authority to human feelings or intuitions about God, religion, and truth. On this account, Schleiermacher denied that the Bible provides truth revealed by God. The only absolute truth in Christianity comes from inner experience; objective theological knowledge does not exist.

Because of the centrality of Jesus Christ to his theology, Schleiermacher's approach is called "Christocentric Liberalism." Jesus was central to Schleiermacher because Jesus had perfect "God-consciousness," that is, the awareness of absolute dependence upon God, viewed by Romantic theologians as the ground of all human existence and being.

Unlike Jesus, other humans have a problem with "sin-consciousness," because our consciousness is attracted to finite things and to passions such as greed, power, and lust, to anything but God. Our sin-consciousness is our over-attachment to finite things. Unlike Christ, whose piety and spirituality were always directed to God, we live autonomously, falling prey to temptation and moral weakness.

Though he was a theological liberal, Schleiermacher had a strong doctrine of sin. For him, there is a tension in every human being between what the apostle Paul called spirit (God-consciousness) and flesh (sensual self-consciousness). Sin, for Schleiermacher, is "forgetting God," that is, giving in to autonomy and selfishness; because sin is related to human finitude, it affects all persons. In arguing that sin is a matter of the will, Schleiermacher sided with Augustine and the Reformers. Unlike rationalists, Kantians, and humanists in general, humans are unable to save themselves. Furthermore, reason cannot alter our will, but can only serve it. Schleiermacher understood this serious and deep understanding of sin as something that makes Christianity unique among world religions. Schleiermacher agreed with Christianity that even the best human piety—the best first-half-of-life spirituality, we might say—is inadequate and in need of reconciliation.

However, there is in Schleiermacher a twist to the traditional Christian doctrine of sin, for in his estimation, sin (moral evil) need not be viewed negatively. The Fall of Man (called "original sin" by Augustine and his followers) is not a step downward, but actually a step upward. While sin in itself is not praiseworthy, awareness of sin and admission of guilt actually lead to grace. In this sense and only in this sense, sin becomes the precondition to reconciliation with God, nature, and others, a *felix culpa* ("blessed fault").

Can anything overcome humanity's sin-consciousness? Schleiermacher's answer, again, sounds traditional: redemption in Christ. But how does redemption work? Humans need to have contact with Christ's perfect God-consciousness, something that can occur through preaching.[3] What clergy should convey in worship is an impression of Christ's perfect God-consciousness; this should be the focus of every sermon. Redemption, for Schleiermacher, does not consist in dogmas such as vicarious atonement or in events such as the incarnation or resurrection, but rather in Christ's perfect God-consciousness, something modeled for believers in scripture and through preaching. According to Schleiermacher, what is crucial about Jesus is not his deity but rather the central idea he taught and lived, "that all finitude requires higher mediation in order to gain union with the deity." For Schleiermacher, humans cannot save themselves. They need help (mediation), and the mediator (Christ) must not himself require mediation. In this way, subtly and gradually, Schleiermacher introduced what has been called his "reverse Christology," moving from Christ's office of mediation to his divinity. However, lest we place Schleiermacher firmly in the orthodox wing of Christianity, several additional twists appear in his theology. For example, if we ask, "Is Christ the only mediator?," Schleiermacher would answer that for Christians he is, but not necessarily in an absolute sense for all humans.

---

3. We need to keep in mind that Schleiermacher, in his position as university professor of theology, was primarily teaching seminarians; clergy are undoubtedly his target audience in *The Christian Faith*.

Because he argued that Jesus never claimed to be the sole mediator of God, Schleiermacher is accused of seeing Jesus as only one of "many Christs." Traditional Christians might question that assertion, arguing that in passages such as John 14:6, Jesus stated that his ministry was uniquely mediatorial. The authenticity of that passage, however, is disputed by many biblical scholars, who see it as an interpolation (an addition) by the author of the Fourth Gospel, denying its authenticity by arguing that this claim is unlike anything found in the synoptic gospels.[4] For those who maintain the saying's authenticity, one interpretation is that Jesus might here be speaking as a representative of regenerate humanity, that is, as one of those who have relinquished their false self (their first-half-of-life egocentricity) and replaced it with their True Self (their second-half-of-life spirituality).

Schleiermacher's greatest contribution was his attempt to move Christianity into the realm of the heart. To be human, he argued, is to be religious, for at the heart of human experience lies the awareness of humanity's absolute dependence upon God. After Schleiermacher, it became commonplace to view religions as differing expressions of a common inner religious experience shared by all people. The uniqueness of Christ, Schleiermacher argued, is not some doctrine about Jesus or in his miraculous nature. The real miracle is Jesus himself. In him we find a person who demonstrates the sense of God-consciousness to a supreme degree. The church is the living witness to the fact that down through the centuries individuals have come to a vital God consciousness through their contact with the life of Jesus. Religious practice, focused on God-awareness, can lead to the true reunion of humanity. Schleiermacher is the "father of modern theology" primarily because he shifted the basis of the Christian faith from the Bible to "religious experience."

Schleiermacher seems to have taught that Christianity was only temporary, and that it could one day be transcended by a more adequate faith. Part of the glory of Christianity, he believed, is its humble recognition of its own relativity. As he wrote in *The Christian Faith*, "It is possible to hope . . . that some day, the human race, if only in its noblest and best, will pass beyond Christ and leave him behind." This hope, however, contributes to Schleiermacher's dilemma: "But this [hope] clearly marks the end of Christian faith, which on the contrary, knows no other way to the pure conception of the ideal than an ever-deepening understanding

---

4. While each gospel contains editorial bias, most biblical scholars view the synoptics as reflecting a more primitive and hence more accurate view of Jesus.

of Christ." Will all humans ultimately experience salvation (perfect God-consciousness)? Yes, this is Schleiermacher's hope, the hope of universal salvation. However, for that to happen, each person must gradually relinquish sin-consciousness, which requires divine mediation.

Questions for Discussion and Reflection

1. Assess the significance of the Protestant principle of the priesthood of all believers for the development of pietist spirituality.
2. Explain and assess the significance of the beliefs and values adopted by the Schleitheim Confession for the development of Protestant spirituality. Rank them in their importance for American Christian spirituality.
3. After reading this chapter, what did you learn about Baptist spirituality?
4. After reading this chapter, what did you learn about Quaker spirituality?
5. Explain the origin and influence of German Lutheran pietism.
6. Why is Friedrich Schleiermacher called "the father of modern theology"? Explain your answer.
7. Assess the merits of Schleiermacher's idea that "sin-consciousness" or "original sin" is not a step downward but a step upward.
8. Assess the merits of Schleiermacher's definition of piety (spirituality) as one's experience of the Infinite in all things.
9. Do you agree with Schleiermacher that the essence and source of religion lies in the realm of "feeling"? Explain your answer.
10. Why is Schleiermacher's approach to Christian theology called "Christocentric Liberalism"? Assess his idea of "many Christs."

9

Existentialist and Neo-Orthodox Spirituality

Nineteenth- and Twentieth-Century Piety

DISPUTE OVER EPISTEMOLOGICAL ISSUES lies at the heart of modernity. In earlier periods of history, most members of Western societies agreed on a specific core of convictions. Those beliefs rested upon a widely accepted outlook. However, in the modern period, no such central core of beliefs unifies people because they now disagree about basic epistemological presuppositions. In reaction to Immanuel Kant, epistemology moved in a variety of different directions. In particular, his emphasis on the inner, subjective workings of the human mind stimulated the development of modern existentialism.

In modern times, existentialism achieved worldwide popularity in such diverse cultural fields as literature, drama, poetry, art, and theology. Its main themes were developed by Søren Kierkegaard in the mid-nineteenth century. Variations of existentialist themes also appeared in the works of Karl Marx, Friedrich Nietzsche, and in the twentieth century in the works of Karl Jaspers, Martin Heidegger, Gabriel Marcel, Jean-Paul Sartre, and Albert Camus. Spreading from the left bank of Paris to Greenwich Village in New York City, existentialism was popularized by such diverse sources as neo-orthodox theology, beatniks, hippies, the Theater of the Absurd, the films of Ingmar Bergman, and Zen Buddhism.

With its emphasis on individual existence, existentialism is in part a reaction against the dehumanizing tendencies of mass society. While existentialism may be characterized as a philosophy, it is more an attitude or a way of life that grows out of human anguish rather than out of theoretical contemplation in a scholar's ivory tower. Concerned more with what persons do than with what they think, existentialism is deeply subjective. It concentrates on human moods such as fear and dread, anxiety and guilt. These moods, for existentialists, reflect reality and reveal the nature of existence.

Common to all existential thinking is the concept that "existence precedes essence." This comes to mean that awareness of one's existence precedes personal identity or essence. Only by committing one's life to something can a person discover this essence.

Theologically speaking, existentialism has been divided into two camps, theistic and atheistic. Presupposing that there is no God, atheistic existentialism declares individuals "free" to make of themselves precisely what they choose. People act in "bad faith" whenever they allow the wishes of society, religion, or politics to interfere with what they want to be. For Sartre and Camus, there is no given human nature because there is no God to conceive it. Human beings merely exist and only later become their essential self. Humans, thus, become what they make of themselves. Theistic existentialists such as Kierkegaard, Nikolai Berdyaev, and Fyodor Dostoyevsky disagree. Believing God to be the ultimate source of reality, they argue that individuals discover their essence through commitment to God.

Existentialists, whether atheists or theists, make the existing individual their starting point or basic presupposition, rather than God. The existing individual is foremost to their method. For that reason, existentialism has been called humanism or philosophic anthropology.

Søren Kierkegaard's Theistic Existentialism

Søren Kierkegaard (1813–1855), a nineteenth-century Danish Christian philosopher and Lutheran theologian, is often seen as the founder of existentialism, not because he used the term, but because of his focus on the concept of existence, by which he meant *human* existence. Kierkegaard was interested in how human existence differs from the existence of non-human things such as trees, rocks, or chairs. For the latter, existence is not a task, nor do such objects think about death or worry about existence.

For humans, existence is a task, one that produces anxiety, even guilt and despair. Kierkegaard explored all those aspects of existence because for him, the task of human existence is ultimately the task of being a Christian. What it means to be a Christian became the key to his thought. Hence, he is called, not simply an existentialist, but a Christian existentialist. He is not, like Sartre and Camus, an atheistic existentialist who presupposes and acts as if there is no God, but a theistic existentialist, who, like Dostoyevsky and Berdyaev, believes God to be the ultimate source of reality in the universe, arguing that humans discover their essence through commitment to God.

Kierkegaard's nineteenth-century setting helps us understand his task. In that century, Christianity fared better than in the previous century. In the nineteenth century, Western civilization was spreading throughout the world, and it was Western Christian civilization that was spreading. Many Christian theologians were heartened by Christian spread and success, viewing these as proofs that Christianity was the true religion, the most advanced and progressive form of religion because it replaced older, more superstitious religions. In that century, Christianity was seen to be on the side of progress, enlightenment, and civilization, as opposed to paganism, animism, and the outmoded religions it replaced. Of course, this mindset was chauvinistic and Eurocentric, and Kierkegaard didn't accept it.

He saw institutional Christianity spreading, and he realized that head knowledge of Christianity does not make one a Christian. Indeed, at one point he uttered his famous dictum, "It is impossible to be a Christian in Christendom." Not only can institutional or corporate Christianity not make one a Christian, such Christianity can actually become an impediment to the existing individual, for, according to Kierkegaard, one can only become Christian through individual action, that is, by the passionate inward decision of faith. This means one does not become Christian by proving its truth or superiority, for such rationality actually replaces faith. When professors deliver lectures or scholars write books that simplifies truth or make it understandable, the result is not faith. Faith, for Kierkegaard, is a passionate inward subjectivity, not objective proof. Faith is what gives authenticity to human existence. Faith doesn't simply eliminate anxiety or produce steady inward peace, but rather faith is what helps us deal authentically with uncertainty and despair.

This focus on the negative in existentialism, on anxiety, guilt, and despair, is Lutheran in origin, and like Luther, Kierkegaard believed that terror, guilt, and despair can drive us to the gospel. The negative aspect of existentialism is not an accident. Viewed as a component of all individual human existence, anxiety can help us deal authentically with human existence and can lead to a faith that honestly confronts the problems of human existence.

Examining how Kierkegaard arrived at his perspective is important, for it reveals the strong correlation between his life and his writings. Known as "The melancholy Dane," Kierkegaard was no ivory-towered speculative thinker, for his thought was shaped by his life. His major works include *Fear and Trembling*, *The Concept of Dread*, and *The Sickness Unto Death*. These titles remind us of the macabre in Edgar Allan Poe's short stories, indicating Kierkegaard's preoccupation with the negative and the subjective dimensions of life.

Born in Copenhagen in a time of great social change, Kierkegaard preserved his interpretation of his life in a work published posthumously under the title, *The Point of View for My Work as an Author*. In that work, Kierkegaard called attention to three key events that shaped his thought: (1) the influence of his father on his early life; (2) his relationship with Regina Olsen; and (3) his relationship with institutional Christianity. All three relationships were turbulent.

Introduced into Lutheran doctrine by an intensely intellectual yet guilt-ridden father, Kierkegaard had been slightly deformed by an early accident, which led to unconventional behavior in his youth and a profound sense of social isolation. This seclusion was undoubtedly enhanced by the fact that only he and his older brother survived childhood, unlike his other five siblings, all of whom died in their youth.

In 1830 he enrolled in the University of Copenhagen, where he studied theology and the philosophy of G. W. F. Hegel (1770–1831). Hegel's influential philosophy attempted to explain rationally all of reality, but it seemingly ignored the actual existence of the individual. Kierkegaard reacted strongly against the abstractness of Hegel's system, which taught individuals to *think* rather than to *be*. Kierkegaard distinguished between the uninvolved spectator in the audience and the involved actor on the stage, arguing that only the actor is authentically involved in existence.

Kierkegaard's university experiences began a stormy period in his life. He almost discarded Christianity, and he became estranged from his father. His wit and taste for food and drink formed his reputation. His favorite places to visit were the café and theater, and he later referred to this period as the aesthetic stage of life. Eventually he re-established his relationship with his father, and in 1836 he experienced a kind of moral conversion, followed two years later by a conversion to Christianity.

At one point he began courting Regina Olsen, winning her from another suitor. However, after their engagement, he reneged, feeling it could not lead to marriage. While longing for a home and family, he eventually broke his engagement, which he attributed to incompatibility, his own melancholy, and eventually, to a special call from God to forego his security and happiness, a sacrifice he compared to Abraham's call by God to sacrifice his son, Isaac.

Kierkegaard became a polemical author, writing *Either/Or* in 1843, a code message to Regina, in part to break her from merely romantic and finite attachment to himself, but also opening a way for mature ethical choice. His writing career led to an attack on Christendom, criticizing church officials for not presenting New Testament Christianity in its full vigor. According to Kierkegaard, the central fact of the nineteenth century was that civilization that had been Christian was no longer so. He found the church of his day so thoroughly institutionalized and self-serving that it had become complacent and convenient rather than demanding total commitment to God.

Kierkegaard's one passion became Christianity, not philosophical or theological Christianity, but personal Christianity. His main purpose was to demonstrate through his life and writing what it means to be Christian. This, for Kierkegaard, and not the other questions that pastors and theologians discuss and philosophers debate, is the great fork in the road for the whole of humanity. Most of the other questions and concerns are frivolous, mere pastries rather than the main course. On October 2, 1855, only forty-two years of age, Søren was stricken with paralysis of the lower limbs, and he died soon thereafter.

Kierkegaard made an important contribution to the religious journey in his formulation of three levels or realms of existence, three progressive stages of life through which humans go in their ascent toward God. On the first level, which he labelled the aesthetic stage, individuals are ruled by their senses. Such persons live solely for the present, and particularly for self-gratification. The second level, the ethical stage, requires that one abandon attitudes of selfishness and embrace universal standards, making commitments to others. Here moral standards and obligations are adopted. The third and final stage, which Kierkegaard called the religious stage, entails a life of faith.

He further distinguished between Religiousness A and Religiousness B, associating Religiousness A—a natural form of religious life we call first-half-of-life spirituality—with the ethical sphere or stage, and Religiousness B—an ethical life lived in relation to God—with the religious sphere or stage.

In each stage, Kierkegaard selected a figure from literature or history as an example. For the model of the religious stage of life, the highest level through which humans go in their ascent toward God, he selected Abraham, whose trust of God and unwavering obedience led him to choose to sacrifice his only son Isaac, even in the face of absurdity, for to question God is to place reason over faith. In selecting this example, Kierkegaard was not denying the validity of ethics. He states that the individual who is called to break with the ethical must first be ethical, that is, must first subordinate to universal morality. The break, when one is called to make it, is made in "fear and trembling" and not arrogantly or proudly. In this final stage, the ethical is not abolished but dethroned by a higher purpose or end, a phenomenon he describes as the "teleological suspension of the ethical." The key to this final stage is not the commendable humanistic goal of universal duty to others, but the unqualified giving of oneself to God. For Kierkegaard, if one doesn't go beyond the ethical realm, beyond moral obligation, one cannot properly say one is related to God or obedient to God. Ethical duty, he believed, must ultimately lead to God, but since it usually leads to humanity (i.e. to humanism), then this stage must be transcended. An absolute relationship to an absolute (God) requires a relative relationship to relative ends. And for Kierkegaard, everything other than God is relative.

Feeling life to be fragile and frequently despairing of his purpose in it, Kierkegaard believed himself unable to take the acceptable path of a prosperous career. Rejecting both the established Lutheranism of his day and the dominant Hegelian philosophy of the intellectual world, he turned his attention to the ambiguities and uncertainties of his own life as an "existing individual," and this becomes the central feature of his thought. If Hegel was correct in his diagnosis of the nineteenth-century malaise as "spiritless," then the correct prescription for that way of life is not a passive immersion of the self into the Hegelian Absolute Spirit or World Soul, but rather the active, continuous vocation to a spiritual journey of the self before the personal God, life's essential being.

The essential longing of the soul to escape from the social swamp was for Kierkegaard "the umbilical cord of the higher life." And the biblical precursors of that path of salvation are lonesome knights of faith such as the beleaguered Abraham and the suffering Job. Since Kierkegaard was not ordained by any denomination and had serious doubts as to whether institutional Christianity represented the original gospel of Jesus Christ, he did not believe that his words held any intrinsic authority. Hence the modesty of some of his titles—"Philosophical Fragments," "Concluding Unscientific Postscript," and of his homilies, written largely on the occasion of festivals in the church's liturgical year—intended not as sermons to be preached but as "edifying discourses" to be read individually. He did not expect the success of his words to be dependent on persuasive eloquence but rather on the free response of the believer who learns to make the proverb personal, "Drink water . . . from your own well" (Prov 5:15).

One of Kierkegaard's familiar homilies, "Purity of Heart is to Will One Thing," an extended meditation on Luke 10:42 and James 4:8, was written for the Feast of Confession. Characteristic of Kierkegaard's spiritual writing is the opening prayer: "Father in heaven! What is a man without Thee? What is all that he knows, vast accumulation though it be, but a chipped fragment if he does not know Thee! What is all his striving, could it even encompass a world, but a half-finished work if he does not know Thee: Thee the One, who art one thing and who art all! So may Thou give to the intellect, wisdom to comprehend that one thing; to the heart, sincerity to receive this understanding; to the will, purity that wills only one thing."

While Kierkegaard's piety is simple, as opposed to his philosophy, often complex and convoluted, yet there is a high degree of intensity in his prayers, and the central paradox of creature in communion with Creator remains. The possibility of such communion, though implanted by the Creator, requires the free initiative of the individual, who must come to see, often by bitter experience, that his or her life is inadequate without the spiritual element. As Kierkegaard prays in his homily, "Whenever a man may be in the world, whichever road he travels, when he wills one thing, he is on the road that leads to Thee." This does not mean, however, that the wrong thing can be the object of one's desire or devotion. As he writes, "The person who wills one thing that is not the Good [that is not God], he does not truly will one thing. It is a delusion, an illusion, a deception, a self-deception that he wills only one thing. For in his inmost being he is bound to be double-minded." To will one thing, namely, God alone, is the heart's purity.

If the will to do one thing is the true Christian's spiritual goal, then the corresponding temptation is "double-mindedness"—a wavering of the will between the good and the evil, or between two goods, which makes for a divided self. For it is indecision that is at the root of the despair Kierkegaard faced before his decisive turn to Christian faith, and it is ever the fatal accomplice to disbelief.

Kierkegaard disagreed with most of his contemporaries in disputing that ultimate truth—what we might call religious truth—is something humans can access through reason or experience. For most of Kierkegaard's contemporaries, religious truth was a human endeavor, something humans basically contain in themselves or can somehow realize by themselves. Kierkegaard explored a different approach—that ultimate truth is a gift and that it comes to us from a transcendent source. Even the capacity for receiving truth and for recognizing it in the first place is a gift. For Kierkegaard, humans are created for communion with the truth—with God—but humans lose this gift through sin. Salvation—the ability to recognize and overcome sin—is only available to human beings through Jesus. Even the ability to recognize sin and to accept God's gracious forgiveness are divine gifts.

As Kierkegaard sees it, human reason takes "offense" at what he calls the "paradox" of faith. Faith, for Kierkegaard, is a kind of falling in love with Jesus Christ. It is not controlled by reason or will, but is like a gift one receives. Encounter with God through transformative love makes it possible for us to take a "leap of faith," and thus to "encounter" Jesus and receive the paradox not as something rational, but rather simply as paradox. For Kierkegaard, truth is not something cold and objective, a system of ideas to be grasped intellectually, but rather is personal and emotional. Truth is whatever an individual believes intensely. Such truth is active, not passive, and is paradoxical, for it is characterized by objective uncertainty. Active truth entails a leap of faith, for it requires trust and commitment before it can be known. To be valid, religious truth must penetrate one's personal existence, for if it does not become one's own, it is meaningless. Truth must be lived, passionately.

For Kierkegaard, Jesus is the divine teacher who enables us to grasp God's gift. Kierkegaard made it clear that Jesus was no ordinary teacher, but the only mediator of divine truth. It is an encounter with this teacher and not any other teacher or teaching that grants us awareness of sin and creates receptivity of transformative salvation. In this way, Kierkegaard rejected the significance of the historical study of Jesus and the gospels.

Kierkegaard wrote to free people from illusion, and the worst illusion, he felt, is the view that truth is objective, such that it can be compressed into a creed, doctrine, or dogma. Unlike mathematical truth, which is impersonal, religious truth must penetrate our own personal existence, becoming our own. For Kierkegaard, the task of philosophy is to convert people to the subjective. Objective truth make us observers, subjective truth makes us participants. Hence, for Kierkegaard, faith and truth cannot be universal, one size fitting all, as for Schleiermacher. Religious truth must be personal and individual, not driven by conformity. Such truth cannot be inherited or passed on. In that regard, faith is always characterized by objective uncertainty. For Kierkegaard, objectivity is a myth, and as he states in his *Concluding Unscientific Postscript*, "an objective acceptance of Christianity is paganism or thoughtlessness" (note how modern, even postmodern, this sounds).

Kierkegaard's lasting contribution to spiritual thought lies in his exploration of the relationship between each individual and the realm of the Eternal. This necessary relation is established in the area of "inwardness" where individual humans fully discover the one true source of their being and true goodness. For Kierkegaard, the means to nurture this inward life is prayer (contemplative devotion in general), which he describes as a person's "greatest earthly happiness."

Through the experience of his short life, Kierkegard forged the foundations of an existential theology in which the struggle and crises of the self become the focus of the search for God. Although his ideas may seem dire or desperate to outsiders, Kierkegaard had no doubt that he "lived with God as one lives with a father." That strong spiritual conviction of intimacy with God is the anchor of his existentialist thought.

Karl Barth's Neo-Orthodox Spirituality

At the start of the twentieth century, an influential movement emerged in Protestant Christianity known as neo-orthodoxy. The key figure in this movement was the Swiss theologian Karl Barth (1886–1968), considered the greatest Christian theologian of the twentieth century. In time, Barth became known for the manner in which he applied the theological concerns of Reformed Protestantism to the prevailing liberal theology. Barth gave his ideas systematic exposition in his *Church Dogmatics* (1930–1969), one of the most significant theological achievements of the twentieth century.

Neo-orthodoxy, sometimes called Religious Existentialism, has its roots in the existentialist thought of Kierkegaard, which initially profoundly influenced Barth. In the late 1920s, Barth began writing his *Dogmatics* and completed one large volume. When critics pointed out that it was dependent upon existentialist philosophy, Barth began over again. This became a decisive turning point in his theological development. Henceforth he determined to build his theology upon orthodox Christian thought, taking the incarnation of Christ as his starting point. Neo-orthodoxy is usually dated to 1919, with the publication of *Römerbrief*, Barth's commentary on the New Testament letter of Paul to the Romans. Seen as a synthesis of Christian orthodoxy and Protestant liberalism, Barth's theology later became a repudiation of many tenets of theological liberalism.

Barth started his career as a liberal theologian, hoping that modern values and human progress could revolutionize society, building the long-awaited kingdom of God on earth. In 1911, he began a ten-year pastorate in a small town in Switzerland. Trained by liberal theologians, for a time he repudiated theism. As a young pastor, he quickly realized that his training in theology had not prepared him adequately for his primary task as pastor. Preaching twice each Sunday, he questioned the role of preaching. He faced what Kierkegaard must have faced in Denmark, a Christianity that accommodated with secularism. As pastor, Barth faced classism among his parishioners, that is, tension between factory owners, managers, and common laborers. Barth experienced deep disappointment in August of 1914 when German intellectuals, including most of the theology teachers he confidently respected, signed a published statement endorsing the military and war policy of Kaiser Wilhelm II. Feeling betrayed, he sensed he could no longer adhere to their ethical and dogmatic formulations, including their exposition of the Bible or presentation of history. Like Kierkegaard, he wondered whether there was any future for nineteenth-century theology.

Finding no help in theology, Barth turned to the Bible, where he found a "strange new world" that was more alive than the latest philosophy. He did not intend to become a theologian, hoping only to offer a biblical correction to the theology of others. However, after his commentary appeared, he was catapulted to the center of theological discussion.

The First World War came as a shock to Barth's optimism, causing him to question the human capacity for goodness. As he watched the civilized nations plunge into an orgy of destruction, Barth felt the human situation was too desperate to be solved merely by changing political and economic structures. In 1921 he became a professor in Sweden, and in 1929 he relocated to Germany, where he taught at Bonn. He watched the rise of Hitler with concern and became one of the founders of the Confessional Church in Germany, which resisted attempts to unite Christianity with Nazism. He helped to draft the famous 1934 Barmen Declaration, which repudiated Hitler's totalitarian dictatorship, declaring that the church's allegiance is to God alone. In 1935, refusing to take a loyalty oath to Nazism, he fled from Germany, accepting a professorship at the Swiss university in Basle, from which he retired in 1962.

Initially, Barth called his approach "dialectical theology," referring to the give and take in an argument or conversation, especially in God's "No" and "Yes," because Barth was interested in the way in which God communicates with humans, first the negative and then the positive side of revelation. When Barth's biblical commentary appeared, it hit the public like a bombshell. Interestingly, Barth used the image of a bombshell regularly. Speaking of revelation as an "event" caused by God, Barth viewed God's communication with humanity the explosion. The crater left behind by the explosion of God's revelation is religion—the institutionalized Christian church, religious consciousness (so central to Schleiermacher's theological approach), and all other human religiosity. Revelation, for Barth, is an event through which God says both No and Yes to humanity, shaping the dialectic in Barth's theology.

Building his theological perspective, like Augustine, on the principle of "faith seeking understanding," Barth noted in his commentary on Romans that faith, which he defined as "knowledge of God," is an "impossible possibility." Knowledge of God is impossible for humans because human faith cannot reach God, but such knowledge becomes possible because God is able to reach humanity. Theology (faith), for Barth, is one-way communication, from God outward, and authentic faith must see things from God's point of view rather than from human perspective. This approach led to Barth's rejection of liberal values and perspectives such as the emphasis on human experience. For Barth, the event of revelation shattered human efforts and perspectives, and what it left behind (including human consciousness and awareness) is but the crater. Eventually, Barth's perspective resonated with a diverse group of thinkers, all of whom gathered around his understanding of revelation as "existential event."

Neo-orthodoxy parted ways with theological liberalism on many fronts, but especially on the issue of revelation. In the biblical tradition,

God's self-revelation to humanity takes two forms—general revelation, available to all people, and special revelation, given to humans in unique historical events such as the incarnation and resurrection. Besides Christ, the living Word of God, God's self-revelation occurs through scripture, which interprets and clarifies revelatory events in history, giving them meaning.

As its name implies, general revelation is available to all humans regardless of time, place, culture, or other historical factors. General revelation is non-verbal. It is God's self-disclosure in nature, the human mind (or conscience), and through the events of history. The purpose of general revelation is clear: all humans live in nature (viewed as God's created order) and in history, and through such experience humans can know God and gain insight into the qualities that give meaning and purpose to life. According to the Bible, if humans were not sinful, general revelation would be sufficient for them to know God accurately and relate to God authentically. However, as Paul indicates in Romans 1, sinfulness leads humans to "suppress the truth," distorting the truth about God's sovereignty, providence, and standards, resulting not only in ignorance but also in idolatry and autonomy.

Protestant liberals, it seems, focus on general revelation almost exclusively. Stressing God's immanence rather that God's transcendence, they limit revelation to what comes through nature, history, and the human mind, as well as to what is ideally exemplified in Jesus, who, though the exemplar of God's character, will, and nature, is merely mortal. Neo-orthodox thinkers such as Barth stressed God's transcendence, focusing on special revelation, though some argued that a fragment of general revelation remains available.

In claiming that the Bible is God's Word, orthodox Christians affirm that God inspires the authors of the Bible in such a way that what they write is what God intends for humans to know about salvation and spirituality in general. Most neo-orthodox theologians, however, distinguish between verbal revelation (that God speaks to humans by means of propositions or statements) and revelation through encounter (through existential, spiritual encounter that cannot be fully or even accurately conveyed in words), arguing that religious truth is neither objective nor subjective but something that occurs through encounter. Dialectic theology maintains that God does not reveal information or doctrine but rather reveals Godself, thereby overcoming the subject-object dilemma. God's revelation is not objective, that is, not an idea or object of thought, but rather self-revelation, as a person encounters another, establishing relationship with the other.

This view maintains that divine inspiration applies only to the *activity* of receiving revelation from God, and not to the *content* of the words themselves. Hence, believers should not directly equate God's Word and the Bible. According to Barth, the Bible is fallible—it contains errors, historical and scientific inaccuracies, and theological contradictions. However, despite its fallibility, the Bible *can become* the Word of God, but only in those parts and at those times when God chooses to reveal Godself. Consequently, the Word of God is not something humans can possess, not something that resides permanently in the Bible, for the Word of God resides only with God.

While the Bible can become a means of revelation, for Barth, revelation occurs only in Jesus Christ, and scripture is a witness, attesting to this revelation. However, although Christ is the primary form of revelation, there are actually three forms of the Word of God, (1) the written Word—scripture, (2) the preached Word—including proclamation and the sacraments, and (3) the revealed Word—Christ. Thus, scripture, preaching, and the sacraments may become the Word of God, but they only acquire this function as they reveal Christ. The first two forms—indirect witnesses—are primarily pointers to revelation.

In classic Christin formulation, the Trinity consists of three persons—Father, Son, and Holy Spirit. To understand God, Augustine, the great orthodox Trinitarian theologian, used the analogy of love: the Father is the Lover, who loves the world through the Son; the Son is the Beloved of the Father; and the Spirit is the bond of Love that binds all three. In Augustine's Trinity, knowledge of God is inseparable from love of God.

To understand God, Barth used the analogy of revelation: the Father is the Revealed, the Son the Revealer, and the Spirit the Interpreter of God's self-revelation. Unlike Aquinas, whose theological starting point for understanding God was rational proofs for the existence of God, Barth began his theology with the assumption of God's revelation; for Barth, God is a self-revealing God. The emphasis is on concrete relationship: God reveals Godself in relationship. However, what is significant about God's revelation is that it is never direct but always indirect. Like the proponents of apophatic theology, for whom God is Subject and never Object, God's revelation is always one of concealment. Barth's primary illustration for this is taken from Exodus 33, Moses's confrontation with God. "Face-to-face" encounter with God, the desire of every

Jew, was also Moses's desire, but even Moses did not see God's face; God remained incognito. However, for Barth, scripture is the message of the "passing before" of God; even the events of Christ represent God's secondary objectivity—a veil or sign of God's work. Whether it be "the crib of Bethlehem" or "the cross at Golgotha," revelation remains indirect, for that is how God intends it. Nevertheless, for that very reason, revelation is "real," for divine revelation requires faith. As Barth notes, "faith either lives in this sphere, or it is not faith at all," a view reminiscent of Paul's famous declaration, "now we see in a mirror, dimly, but then we will see face to face" (1 Cor 13:12).

Barth broke with other dialectical theologians by rejecting any foundation for theology that arises from theories of human nature or existence rather than exclusively from the revelation of God in Christ. For Barth, Christian theology is not fundamentally about experience, human consciousness, or human existence, but rather exclusively about God. Hence, whatever theology has to say about human experience, it must primarily be from God and about God. If humans wish to look within, they must begin with a divine vantage point. Looking within comes second. What comes first is looking at Jesus Christ, for he is the crucial event of revelation.

For Barth, nothing human or natural is capable of knowing God or even of adequately receiving divine revelation. Such reception requires not mere restoration of an organ or capacity, but rather complete re-creation, as in being reborn or resurrected from the dead. This is what the event of revelation is for Barth. Jesus' word is God's word; it gives people ears to hear, because it replaces death with life. There is no point of contact, no seeing or hearing, in a dead person, but God's Word can raise the dead. That, for Barth, is what happens whenever someone comes to faith. The foundation of theology is also the foundation of faith, namely, what God has done in Jesus Christ: "I was blind, but now I see" (John 9:25); "I was dead, but now I live" (see Rom 6:11; 8:10; Eph 2:5; Col 2:13).

Such points of emphasis led to what has been called Barth's Christocentrism, meaning that Christ is the only place where humans can experience God's grace. Human beings don't want to admit they are helpless, believing there is still goodness and righteousness within, or that they are unable to find God or grace on their own, but for Barth, there is nothing humans can do to gain salvation, that is, to come into a right relationship with God.

Unlike Schleiermacher, whose Christocentrism is about Christ's consciousness, Barth's Christocentrism begins with the Father. For Barth, God's revelation is the act of the triune God. In thinking about the universe and God's purpose in history, Barth begins with God's essence as Revealer. When God reveals, the revelation is of the Father, but the means is through Christ, and the content of that revelation in human beings is the Holy Spirit. While it is the Father who is revealed, that revelation remains hidden, because humans cannot see the Father; only the Son can. The Holy Spirit is the effective power that brings that revelation into our lives and changes us. So God—Father, Son, and Holy Spirit—is the structure of revelation.

Because God is by nature One who cannot be unveiled to humans, God does what humans cannot do. God the Father reveals Godself in the Son, in the form of what God is not (in the form of a human being), and the Holy Spirit takes this outward form and brings it into our lives by grace. There is a self-knowledge of God in the Trinity, we might say, where the Father is known in the Son. That, for Barth, is God's primary revelation; then the Son presents God to humans, which, for Barth, is God's secondary revelation.

The difference between the primary objectivity (the inner Trinitarian revelation, which is essential to the Being of God) and the secondary knowledge or objectivity of God (which God does not need to make known), is marked by the doctrine of election. For Barth, the person and work of Christ are one and cannot be separated. Christ is the sole mediator (reconciler) between God and humanity because he is fully God and fully human (see 1 Tim 2:5). Hence, for Barth, it is the incarnation that is the truly crucial aspect in reconciliation, not the biblical emphasis on the cross. In Jesus, God is both electing Creator and elected creature—both the giver and receiver of grace. In essence, Jesus is the elected man. As the elected man, Christ's atoning work—the salvation he accomplishes—is not partial or limited but rather universal in intent. It is for all humans. To understand Barth's doctrine of salvation, we must understand his doctrine of election.

To begin with, Jesus is the elected human. As the representative of every human being, he is the only condemned or rejected human. If the positive side of election is blessing (salvation), the negative side is reprobation (judgment). As we noted earlier when speaking of dialectical theology, in revelation God always speaks "No" as well as "Yes," but only one is ultimate. Behind God's No is always God's Yes. If God's No to human sin is penultimate, God's Yes to humans is always ultimate.

The doctrine of election, as formulated initially by Augustine and later by Calvin, involves predestination and atonement. Are some people chosen by God for salvation and others for damnation, as Calvin taught? For Barth, there are no frontiers to cross from rejection to election. There is only non-recognition and recognition of election. In his view, God is free to be gracious to every human. There is nothing in God's grace, or even in God's justice, that keeps God from electing every human being.

Neo-orthodoxy has been criticized on a number of fronts, particularly for its emphasis upon the otherness of God, which leads to God being viewed as distant and potentially irrelevant. Some find Barth's approach fideistic;[1] others fault him for dismissing other religions as distortions or perversions of God's truth, or for his unorthodox perspectives on predestination and the atonement. However, his doctrine of election may be his most controversial concept.

Building on the contributions of Augustine and Calvin, Barth used a unique Christological approach to arrive at a startling conclusion. For Barth, predestination refers not to the election of select humans for preferential treatment but rather to God's election of Jesus Christ to serve as mediator between humanity and deity. Barth's starting point is with God's free and sovereign decision to enter into fellowship with all humanity. Because Christ is elected to redeem humanity, it is he who is rejected, not humanity. The cross, representing God's judgment upon sin, is God's "No" to humanity. However, this "No" does not result in the exclusion and rejection of humanity, for God's "No" to sin is borne by Christ, who died for all. In Christ, then, we find God's judgment *and* God's redemption, God's "No" to sin and God's "Yes" to grace. Because Christ is the sole elected individual, his mediatorial role leads to God's final word to humanity, which remains "Yes." Barth's doctrine of predestination, pointing to universal restoration and the salvation of all humanity, eliminates condemnation of humanity. The only one who is predestined to condemnation is Jesus Christ, who from all eternity wills to represent humanity.

Barth, in effect, took Calvin's doctrine of election and says, "Why not suppose that this is about Christ? What happens if this doctrine is fundamentally about God's choice to reveal Godself to humanity in Jesus?" Barth pursued this idea through his *Dogmatics*, which comprise

---

1. Fideism, or "blind faith," is a belief system that so emphasizes faith as to drive an irreparable wedge between faith and reason.

thousands of pages and fourteen volumes, placing election at the heart of his argument. Election, for Barth, is always good news, because in Christ, God chooses to be *for* humanity. Election always serves blessing rather than condemnation. We saw this in chapter 2 in the election of Israel, whose election as the chosen people was intended for the blessing of all nations. Likewise, Abraham's call is not for his own sake, but for the blessing of all nations (see Gen 12:3; 26:4; Ps 72:17).

The biblical doctrine of election is not that some are chosen *instead of* others, but that some are chosen *for the sake of* others. Like Abraham and Israel, God chose Jesus to bless (save) others. In this respect, Barth was not an advocate of limited atonement, espoused by the Arminian opponents of Calvinism. In electing Jesus, God declared good news for the human race. In electing one human, God is electing all humanity. In some sense, all humanity is saved in Christ. In Christ, one sees deeply into God's character and eternal purpose: God chose, at the beginning of time, to be for humanity, not as our antagonist, but as our Savior. This is the Good News of the gospel, and it is the best of all possible news for a struggling, confused, and suffering humanity.

Barth's perspective, though hopeful, has been rejected by many evangelical and fundamentalist Christians, who consider that his methodology and conclusions compromise the traditional Christian doctrines of human nature, sin, and grace. While accused of universalism (that all humans will be saved by God's grace), Barth rejected the title, though he left the possibility open, arguing that while everyone might be saved in theory, this does not mean salvation is automatic. It still requires the response of faith. Nevertheless, while encounter is necessary, such intimacy is totally in the hands of God, else it would be based on human effort and not exclusively upon grace. In this respect, Barth is wholly Augustinian.

This conclusion leaves us with more questions than answers, but one thing becomes clear. For Barth, there is no private, no exclusive Christianity. As a result, no person is more beloved or special than any other. Is Barth's theology an alternative orthodoxy, a new orthodoxy, or simply neo-orthodoxy? The answer, like Barth's dialectical theology, is Yes and No. In the final analysis, Barth's theology demonstrates the resilience of Christian spirituality.

Questions for Discussion and Reflection

1. Describe how Kierkegaard's spirituality is existentialist.
2. What, for Kierkegaard, does it mean for someone to be Christian?
3. Explain the merits of Kierkegaard's three stages or realms of existence. Explain his distinction between Religiousness A and Religiousness B.
4. Explain what Kierkegaard meant when he described progression from the ethical to the religious stage as the "teleological suspension of the ethical."
5. Explain Kierkegaard's distinction between "double-mindedness" and "willing one thing."
6. Explain Kierkegaard's notion of the "paradox" of faith, and what he meant that truth requires a "leap of faith." Is this concept relevant to your faith? Why or why not?
7. Explain Barth's experience with liberal theology. Like Barth, has the theology of your upbringing or training let you down or left you wanting more? Explain your answer.
8. Explain and assess Barth's "dialectical theology."
9. Compare and contrast liberal and neo-orthodox views of general and special revelation.
10. Explain and assess Barth's understanding of "the Word of God."
11. Explain and assess Barth's view of the doctrine of election.

10

Ethical Spirituality
Enlightenment, Liberal, and Late Neo-Orthodox Piety

IN OUR DISCUSSION OF spirituality, we come finally to the topic of ethics. To explore ethical spirituality, we need to backtrack historically, going to the start of the Enlightenment period and even earlier, to early and medieval Christianity. However, before doing so, we start with theology, and with questions that connect spirituality with morality.

What is it human beings do when they profess belief in God? When they pray? When they join with others in rituals of worship? Based on their beliefs, how should Christians live? By what values should they be guided? Western philosophers and religious thinkers have asked these questions for centuries. However, in the seventeenth century, with the advent of modernity, the nature of these inquiries changed.

When we use the term "modernity," we are speaking of a historical period characterized by advances in science, philosophy, and politics. Modernity also marked a new attitude toward the world and humanity's place in it, where intellectual and cultural authority was no longer located in past traditions or in divine revelation but in the exercise of reason, and where humanity's sense of indebtedness to the past was replaced by confidence in its ability to shape the world for future generations.

In the modern context, Western intellectuals began to ask new questions about God, faith, religion, and morality. How do we know that God exists? Can reason defend any of the assertions about God and the world claimed by religious traditions? Is religion a force for good in human life, or is it something that belongs to a past age, a symptom of the infancy of humanity? Prior to the modern period, few serious thinkers questioned the existence of God or the importance of religion for human life. For medieval thinkers, the truth had been revealed, and the task of philosophy and religion was to understand this truth. Western medieval thinkers were engaged in the project of "theology" as "faith seeking understanding." However, once the Protestant Reformation of the sixteenth century divided Western Christianity, and with the successes of scientific inquiry into the workings of nature, such thinkers as René Descartes (1596–1650) sought to ground knowledge in "natural reason." Increasingly, they came to believe that they could identify a universal human rationality that worked independently of faith. With this development, modern philosophy separated itself from theology and gave birth to new ways of thinking about religion and new ways of living. Even though many philosophers continued to defend religion as "reasonable," others criticized it as irrational and harmful and developed methods for explaining religion as a psychological or social, rather than a divine, phenomenon. Atheism became a real possibility and criticism of religion became an intellectual responsibility.

With the birth of modern science in the seventeenth century, as human knowledge and technological accomplishment led to improvements in the human condition, the realm of faith gradually succumbed to the realm of reason. During the eighteen and nineteenth centuries, a growing minority of scholars and thinkers came to denounce religion, viewing it as irrational, illusory, and even as dangerous. While some philosophers continued to argue for the value and necessity of religion, others just as carefully argued against it, predicting its decline and eventual demise.

Modernity—a creation of the West, essentially over the past four hundred years—is a cultural mindset that increasingly persuaded leading scholars to turn from the authority of past tradition to the authority of reason, rejecting all authorities external to the individual thinker. We see this most clearly in the period we call the Enlightenment, a period in European history from roughly the late seventeenth century to the end of the eighteenth century. The modern ethos can be summarized in the injunction of the philosopher Immanuel Kant: "dare to know." In other words, don't take things by faith, from religious authority, but ask questions, become educated, and above all, use reason. Whereas traditional authorities looked to the past for guidance and truth, modern thinkers looked to the future, thereby remaining open to the realization of their full potential. For them, modernity meant progress.

In the past, thinkers used the term "modern," not to describe that which was simply current or up to date, but rather a cultural era. As way of thinking, modernity embraced a plethora of cultural, intellectual, political, scientific, and technological changes that radically transformed Western civilization. In the wake of this new and revolutionary mindset, people began to think of themselves as standing at the beginning of a new era of history. They saw themselves breaking with the past and forging a new vision of what it means to be human. However, as with any new era of major social and cultural change, this vision occurred in the context of debate.

Which aspects of the past remain important? What does the future hold? What does it mean to be human, or in this case, to be modern? At the center of these debates was the question of religion. Is religion a part of the past to be rejected, or can one be modern and religious simultaneously? While asking such questions, we need to be aware that not only were decisions about religion central to the debates of the eighteenth and nineteenth centuries, but that the very concept of religion itself, as we use it today, was a product of this debate. That is to say, "religion" as an idea emerged as people struggled with the question of what it means to be modern.

The Path toward Human Autonomy

Christianity has pervasively shaped Western culture through its ethical teaching. From the fourth to the twentieth centuries, morality in the West was tied to Judeo-Christian ethics. Since Christianity's inception, biblical principles have directed both the private and public lives of many Christians, and political, economic, and social institutions developed on the basis of biblical morality.

Building on theological, anthropological, epistemological, and cosmological presuppositions, Christianity provided a consistently theistic basis for ethics. By presupposing that God exists and that the cosmos has purpose, Christians argued that specific ethical behavior was not only possible but also necessary. If a sovereign, personal God created a morally significant universe, then human beings are obligated to discern the moral character of their existence.

During the Enlightenment, scientists, philosophers, and others began a piecemeal attack on Christianity's presuppositions, affecting beliefs about God, the church, salvation, and sin, among others. This resulted in questioning traditional Christian ethical values and practices. Earlier, however, gradual shifts in epistemology had begun influencing ethics, primarily during the medieval scholastic era. In his view of reality, Thomas Aquinas distinguished between two metaphysical realms—nature and grace. What was at stake was the relationship between philosophy and theology, better known as natural theology and revealed theology, the first representing the realm of nature and the latter the realm of grace.

In this regard, "nature" referred to that part of creation that was ordered by natural law, namely, the physical, natural world order, including human life and its institutions. "Grace" referred to transcendent, metaphysical reality, ruled by God's supernatural law. Whereas earlier, Augustine had argued that due to original sin, humans were unable to know or choose the good and therefore were completely dependent upon God's grace in matters of truth and salvation, Aquinas disagreed. Distinguishing between "natural" and "supernatural" virtues, Aquinas believed that humans could attain goodness through natural virtues such as prudence, justice, temperance, and courage. While Aquinas did not deny original sin, he believed that its effect upon the human race was not as radical as Augustine had taught. Though Adam's corrupted nature is transmitted to his descendants, humanity's rational powers are not impaired.

For Aquinas, reason and revelation were not contradictory. To attain truth, humans must begin with knowledge and reason—that is, with scientific and philosophical truths—and add to them the teachings of faith, that is, the truths of revealed theology. Thus, humans are redeemed through a twofold process, primarily through church sacraments but also through meritorious works (that is, through personal piety and spirituality). Following Augustine, Aquinas distinguished between two forms of grace, the first cooperative (whereby humans work with God), and the second operative (given by God through the church). However, whereas for Augustine, human beings are ultimately dependent upon God's grace for salvation and truth, for Aquinas, humans are motivated by both grace and works.

In the sixteenth century, Reformers such as Martin Luther and John Calvin denied such distinctions, repudiating any suggestion that people could merit God's grace. Modernist thinkers would challenge the distinction between operative and cooperative grace, disputing the claims of both reformation and medieval theologians by arguing in favor of natural theology. They maintained that human beings could live morally, discover truth, and find meaning in life through natural and scientific reason alone, apart from divine assistance. Building upon the distinction between natural and supernatural realms, modern philosophers, no longer committed to Christian beliefs, gravitated toward human autonomy, focusing on nontheistic naturalistic ethics.

Modern science arose in the sixteenth and seventeenth centuries, filling humans with optimistic visions of an age of peace and harmony. The pioneers of modern science created new ways to think about the universe. Nicolaus Copernicus (1473–1543) insisted that the sun, not the earth, is the center of our universe. Johannes Kepler (1571–1630) concluded that the sun emits a magnetic force that moves the planets in their courses. Galileo Galilei (1564–1642) made a telescope to observe the moons of Jupiter, adding further support to the Copernican theory of the universe. Isaac Newton (1642–1727), the most illustrious scientist of the Enlightenment, united all the laws of motion in his monumental work, *Mathematical Principles of Natural Philosophy* (1687). The universe, he argued, is one great machine operating according to unalterable laws, harmonized in a master principle of the universe, the law of gravitation.

Though a devout Christian, Newton's concept challenged the medieval notion of unseen spirits—angels and demons. His theory considered such beliefs superstitious, replacing them with a universe operated by physical laws, explained by mathematics. The sudden access to the mysteries of the universe seemed to magnify the role of human reason while minimizing the role of divine revelation. If the universe is a smooth-running machine with all its parts coordinated by one grand design, this freed humans to find meaning and happiness on their own.

This, then, is the fundamental idea of the Enlightenment, that humans are able to find truth by using the scientific method—an experimental approach that combines reason with the senses—rather than rely upon ancient values and beliefs, rooted in superstition and ignorance. The theological implications of such humanistic optimism are significant. In this environment, God seemed less necessary to sustain the world. In the new model, the sun displaced the earth as the center. Some believed that humanity was displaced as the crowning apex of creation in the center of God's world. Others felt that God was displaced as well.

Modern philosophers were primarily concerned with epistemology, that is, with the concept of knowledge, not simply with factual knowledge (what can be known), but with the process of knowing (how one acquires certainty). Until the 1600s, philosophy was concerned primarily with the nature of God and with existence itself. However, that concern changed dramatically in the seventeenth century. During modernity, philosophers and intellectuals in general became obsessed with epistemology.

At this time, the concern of philosophers was directed toward finding a new source of certainty. Protestant and Renaissance rejection of church authority, humanistic optimism in society, and the birth of modern science, all shook the foundations of medieval faith. Consequently, seventeenth-century epistemologies explored two basic alternatives: rationalism (that certainty arises primarily from human reason), and empiricism (that certainty arises principally from human sense perception).

The figure who perhaps best exemplifies modern rationalism is René Descartes. Descartes, above all, sought to know what is certain. He lived in a rapidly changing world in which long-held foundational principles were being challenged, including religious and scientific teachings. Skepticism flourished. Descartes, however, was not a skeptic. He was a devout Catholic who contended that human beings are capable of attaining certainty in knowledge, but that before people can obtain certainty, they must first become aware of how dubious or uncertain most of their accepted beliefs are. Descartes began his *Meditations on First Philosophy* with what he called "methodical doubt," and on the basis of this methodology he concluded that there is only one thing that he could not somehow doubt, and that was his thinking self. This discovery of an innate idea, clear and distinct to reason, he summarized with the Latin phrase, "*Cogito ergo sum*," which means "I think, therefore, I exist."

The important result of Descartes's approach is that knowledge in every case begins with knowledge of one's existence. Self becomes the starting point for knowledge, not God, and its justification is reason. Thus, human autonomy replaces divine sovereignty as the foundation of modern thought.

Thomas Hobbes (1588–1679), another great thinker of the seventeenth century, made significant contributions to the fields of political theory and philosophy. His father, a cruel and ignorant man who served as vicar of a British parish, abandoned his son after engaging in a fistfight with one of his parishioners at the church door. Fortunately, an uncle took care of Thomas, sending him to Oxford University.

Hobbes became a follower of British scientist and philosopher Francis Bacon (1561–1626). Hobbes was particularly influenced by Bacon's emphasis on the superiority of the physical sciences over any speculative inquiry of the supernatural. Like many seventeenth-century skeptics, Hobbes was not a thoroughgoing or consistent naturalist, since he believed in a supernatural being. His God, however, was not the Christian God of the Bible, whom we worship or with whom we can establish personal relationship, but rather was the God underlying nature, "the first of all causes." In Hobbes's view, God is totally transcendent and apart from nature, not having intervened in the world since its creation. This theological perspective became known as deism.

Deist Spirituality

Deism became the primary religious belief of intellectuals during the Enlightenment. After Hobbes and Descartes, as confidence in reason soared, many intellectuals begin dismissing appeals to scripture as superstitious nonsense. A group of French thinkers and writers known as the *philosophes* brought the Enlightenment to its climax. These were not philosophers in the academic sense but rather men of letters, observers of society who analyzed its evils and advocated reform. They aimed to spread knowledge and emancipate the human spirit. These were not atheists, as we might call them today, for most believed in a supreme being but denied that he interferes in the affairs of the world. They were deists, believers in the watchmaker God: God created the world as a watchmaker makes a watch, and then wound it and let it run. Since God is a perfect watchmaker, there is no need to interfere with the watch. Hence, deists rejected miracles and special revelations or anything that suggested God's interference in the world.

The most influential propagandist for deism was Voltaire (1694–1778), who personified the skepticism of the French Enlightenment. He achieved his greatest fame as a relentless critic of the established churches, Protestant and Catholic alike, sickened by the intolerance and petty squabbles that seemed to characterize organized religion. Voltaire, Jean-Jacques Rousseau (1712–1778), Denis Diderot (1713–1784), and other brilliant thinkers, championed tolerance, denounced superstition, and expounded the merits of deism. They held Jesus in high regard, urging contemporary Christians to emulate the morality of the ancient master and to discard the theological trappings.

While metaphysical and ethical questions formulated during the Christian centuries continued to preoccupy European intellectuals, the great philosophical influences of the nineteenth century—such as Immanuel Kant (1724–1804) and Georg Friedrich Hegel (1770–1831) in Germany and John Stuart Mill (1806–1873) in Britain—labored to replace traditional dependence upon revelation and religious tradition with what they believed were more secure foundations of the good, the true, and the beautiful. Kant's argument in his 1793 work *Religion within the Limits of Reason Alone* became an intellectual charter for many great minds of the nineteenth century. "True religion," he argued, "is to consist not in the knowing or considering of what God does or has done for our salvation but in what we must do to become worthy of it."

Enlightenment thinkers used the distinction between natural and revealed religion to understand the diversity of religions, especially Christianity. "Revealed religion" meant any religion based on a purported revelation from God, such as Judaism based on the Torah and the Talmud, Christianity on the Bible, and Islam on the Qur'an. "Natural religion" meant religious beliefs that were based on reason, which Enlightenment thinkers considered universal and common to all humanity. Later thinkers questioned naturalist premises as well, but during the eighteenth century, intellectuals favored natural religion.

The reasons are clear. They were looking back to the seventeenth century, a century filled with religious wars in Europe. These were sufficient to convince intellectuals that religious zeal was fanatical and dangerous. Many intellectuals concluded that being religious was a bad thing, State churches, whether Catholic or Protestant, viewed as oppressive, authoritarian, and dogmatic, were falling out of favor. The very words "dogma" or "dogmatic" became negative concepts, associated with repression and narrow-mindedness. The conflicting diversity of denominations within Christianity, from Catholic to Anglican to free churches, made revealed religions questionable and unappealing, by contrast with the rising modern sciences, which actually improved people's lives and made significant progress possible. Theology, by comparison, looked increasingly less reliable and helpful.

Modern physics, based on Newtonian science, began presenting nature as a closed system, functioning solely on predictable and knowable natural laws while leaving decreasing room for divine intervention, that is, for the supernatural. A new concept for the supernatural was needed, filled initially by deism and eventually by atheism. The eighteenth century became the first time in Western history when many seemed content to call themselves atheists. Earlier, a few may have wrestled with the possibility, but now it was becoming acceptable, even fashionable.

Many theologians become anti-Trinitarian at this time, leading to the spread of Unitarian views critical not only of Trinitarianism but also of related Christian doctrines such as the incarnation. If Jesus was neither God nor divine, he came to be seen instead as a great teacher of ethics and as a model human. Many intellectuals took satire and ridicule to an exalted literary level, using language that Protestants had previously used of Catholicism, such as superstition and priest-craft, and turning it into criticism of Christianity as a whole. When not criticizing state churches, they also criticized the experiential churches, regarding Quakers, Baptists, Wesleyans, and revivalists in general as fanatical, emotionalists, enthusiasts (a bad word for eighteen-century intellectuals), and deluded, as neglecting reason and misusing passion. Authority in general came under criticism at this time, especially religious authority, particularly when backed by ruling authorities. Reason came to stand for autonomy, freedom, and independence, as something opposed to institutional and religious authority in general. On the other hand, belief became private, and no one was entitled to tell someone else what to believe.

Deists focused attention on the difference between natural and revealed revelation because they advocated natural religion, using it as the criterion with which to judge revealed religions. The content of natural religion, according to Benjamin Franklin, one of its famous adherents, is belief (1) in the existence of God, (2) in providence (that is, in God's governance of the world), (3) in morality as the best way to worship God and live with one's neighbor, and (4) in the afterlife, with punishment or reward based on one's life on earth. By dismissing the relationship between God and morality, the advocates of natural religion had no room for divine intervention; no place for supernatural mystery; no need of priests, dogmatic authority, or incomprehensible dogma; and no need for traditional worship, based on superstitious beliefs and sacraments. Early deists viewed Christianity as transmitter of the universal truths of natural religion and the gospels as vehicles for the religion of reason, correcting the accretions of organized religion. Later deists, however, viewed Christianity as representing the very accretions they despised. By the end of the eighteenth century, Thomas Payne, expressing the views of the "Age of Reason," spoke of Christianity as corrupt and in need of rejection.

Nevertheless, deists tend to admire Jesus, believing that by eliminating the theological and institutional accretions, the figure of Jesus would emerge as a teacher of natural religion. This became the view of Thomas Jefferson, who, while president, took the time to cut and paste what became known as the "Jefferson Bible," which eliminated all miracles and dogmas such as the resurrection and incarnation from the gospels. The result was a thoroughly human Jesus, the proclaimer of natural religion, a view found primarily in the parables and in teachings such as the Sermon on the Mount; gone was Jesus the Savior, the Messiah, and the resurrected Lord.

Enlightenment thought reached a culmination in the work of the German philosopher Immanuel Kant. Denying revelation as a means of attaining certainty, Kant deified reason, an innate way of knowing, as the only epistemological authority. For Kant, scripture should be read and interpreted morally, for, as he argued, "the moral improvement of humanity constitutes the real end of religions of reason." Disagreeing with the Reformers and their biblical predecessors, he argued that moral reason, not the Holy Spirit, should be the interpreter of scripture. God, for Kant, was unknowable, and therefore relegated to the position of a postulate, that is, a useful idea for morality.

Kant spoke of two kinds of knowledge, (a) knowledge of what is, by which he meant scientific knowledge, given to the understanding through sense impressions, and (b) knowledge of what ought to be, by which he meant innate moral knowledge. Kant wanted norms, but he looked within rather than externally to find them. Kant focused on morality, finding within human beings a sense of "oughtness," a universal moral law that he called the "categorical imperative." That people have an inner experience of "ought," said Kant, implies that they possess moral freedom to obey or not to obey that obligation. Arguing that natural reason demands virtue, he found that finite beings, due to their limitations, regularly fall short of the demands of the moral law, since their natural desire for happiness affects their moral will. Because virtue and happiness do not necessarily coincide, humans need help and resolve. For moral progress to be possible, Kant argued that believers should organize and attend church.

Kant articulated his mature religious and ethical ideas in *Religion within the Limits of Reason Alone*, its title succinctly expressing his understanding of Christianity. Kant transformed Christianity from the revelation of God's grace into a completely rational religion. Correct moral behavior replaced worship of God as humanity's primary objective in life. Since only the ethical dimension of religion is universal, Kant made the church into an organization to promote ethical behavior instead of a covenant community of worshipping believers.

Kant is often seen as a bridge to religious subjectivism and existentialism. He did not believe humans could know spiritual reality directly; rather, they could only postulate it by faith, that is, indirectly and subjectively. In Kant, Aquinas's certainty was greatly eroded. Lacking natural revelation, the gulf between the natural and supernatural had become a chasm.

Kant's faith in human rationality and his unstinting confidence in our ability to choose right over wrong supported his view of human autonomy. Consistent with the epistemological subjectivism of modernity, Kant held conscience in high esteem. Many current ethicists attribute to conscience only a minimal role in moral choice because it is susceptible to environmental conditioning. Kant, however, assigned to conscience a primary role in determining and directing morality: "the question is not how conscience ought to be guided [for conscience needs no guide], but how it can serve as a guide in the most perplexing moral decisions."

The climax of a century of progressive European liberal theology was reached in 1900 in a series of lectures titled *What is Christianity?* In these lectures, the learned scholar Adolf von Harnack (1851–1930) argued that the simple gospel preached by Jesus was largely lost when it was translated into a Hellenistic idiom. Harnack thought that the original teaching of Jesus could be summarized as the fatherhood of God, the brotherhood of man, and the infinite value of the human soul. Such views are labeled "liberal" by conservative Christians, for they appear to betray the core biblical values upon which Protestantism was founded.

Liberalism, or modernism, as it is sometimes called, is an attempt to adjust religious ideas to the needs of contemporary society. Harry Emerson Fosdick, minister at the influential Riverside Church in New York City, put it well when he declared that the central aim of liberal theology is to make it possible for a person "to be both an intelligent modern and a serious Christian." Protestant liberalism engaged a problem as old as Christianity itself, attempting to make faith meaningful in a changing world without distorting or destroying the gospel. The apostle Paul tried and succeeded. The early gnostics tried and failed. Gnostic Christians such as Clement of Alexandria, Origen, Evagrius of Pontus, and Denys the Areopagite tried. The jury is still out on liberalism.

Social Ethics

Central to the study of theology, certainly to spirituality and piety, is the topic of morality. Thus far we have focused on private practice, but what about social ethics, that is, the expression of public morality? A danger in religious practice is to focus on the purely private side of morality and not on the larger question of social justice and corporate good and evil. Fortunately, various theologians focused on this topic in the twentieth century, among them the neo-orthodox theologian Reinhold Niebuhr (1892–1971), who addressed this issue comprehensively, both in word and action.

The eighteenth and nineteenth centuries were times of creativity but also of social and economic turbulence. Science made major strides in astronomy, physics, chemistry, biology, and psychiatry. The scientific method profoundly changed the way people viewed their world. Toward the end of the nineteenth century, Protestant liberalism broke from the conservative theology of Reformation orthodoxy. Liberalism sought to develop a reasonable account of Christianity that harmonized with modern science. Deeply tinged with humanism, rationalism, idealism, and Darwinian evolution, Protestant liberals felt compelled to dismiss biblical supernaturalism. Pitting reason against faith, all beliefs had to pass the test of rationality and experience.

The 1800s climaxed a period of worldwide exploration and discovery, culminating in the Industrial Revolution, which forced peasants to abandon the land for work in the industrialized cities. Working conditions helped create urban ghettos, where social problems associated with the exploited poor multiplied. Growing racism and struggle over slavery in America eventually erupted into the American Civil War.

Because of these changes in religion and society, ethics came to occupy a central place for liberal theologians, becoming seen as the very purpose of religion. Liberalism championed the causes of peace, human rights, social justice, racial equality, and economic opportunity. In this regard, liberalism supported the Social Gospel Movement, an attempt by North American and European Christians to solve the social problems growing out of the Industrial Revolution. While building on earlier antislavery and temperance movements, the Social Gospel Movement focused concern on victims of economic and political injustice. A major leader in this phase of the social gospel was the German-American pietist Walter Rauschenbusch (1861–1918), whose writings brought the movement into the mainstream of American Protestant theology and church life. In his *A Theology of the Social Gospel* (1917), we find the beginning of trends that would flower a few years later in the thought of Reinhold Niebuhr.

World War I sounded the death knell for the utopian dreams of the previous century and signaled the beginning of a mood of pessimism. Modernism had been fatally wounded. As previously noted, neo-orthodoxy became a reaction against the theological optimism of liberalism and a protest against the nontheistic humanism that lingered for a decade after the war. The Great Depression in the 1930s, followed by World War II, closed the coffin on the corpse of liberalism, particularly on its confidence in human ability and its expectation of unbridled social progress.

For neo-orthodox thinkers, ethics are vitally important, as we see in the life and works of Richard Niebuhr and Dietrich Bonhoeffer.[1] Niebuhr served as professor of Christian Ethics at Union Theological Seminary in New York from 1928 to 1960. He was primarily interested in applying Christianity to political and social affairs. He graduated from seminary in 1915, filled, like Barth, with the conviction of liberal theology. He believed in the goodness of God and of humans, in the desirability of applying the Sermon on the Mount to the whole of life, and in the optimistic hope that the kingdom of God could be built on earth by competent, well-meaning believers in the near future.

Had he taken a pastorate in a suburban, middle-class environment, he might have become a successful theologian. He went, however, to a small working-class church in Detroit, where he witnessed firsthand the problems of assembly-line workers, the tactics used to suppress union organizations, and the tragic cost in human values that the United States was paying for rapid industrialization. The simple idealism of Niebuhr's traditional faith seemed irrelevant to the complex social issues of the day.

As time passed, he realized that Christian orthodoxy was more realistic and adequate than liberal theology. This did not mean, however, that he turned to fundamentalism. He came to realize that much of the biblical message could be expressed in "myth," such as the Genesis story of the creation and of the fall. In religion, he reasoned, we are dealing with the mystery and depth of life, which elude literal or rational description. Niebuhr compared theology to a painter who, working upon a flat surface, tries to create the illusion of another dimension, depth. Though this is deception, the artist is describing a truth about reality. Similarly, God

---

1. The life and work of Bonhoeffer is discussed in chapter 13.

transcends the categories of the natural world, rendering human thought and language inadequate. Hence, God, like the painter, uses symbols that point to another dimension of reality.

Fundamentalism takes the myths literally, conflicting with science and oversimplifying the relation of God to the world. Liberalism dismisses the myths as folk tales and prescientific speculation. Niebuhr laid a new basis for understanding Christianity and for the meaningful application of Christian ethics to social issues. Labeling his view "Christian Realism," Niebuhr called on Christians to exchange their moral idealism for a more tough-minded approach that paid attention to the dynamics of social change as well as to the ideals of justice and peace.

Niebuhr's point, however, was not simply that Christians needed to be more realistic in their dealings with others, but that they also had to be more realistic about themselves. In this respect, Niebuhr's great contribution was in his doctrine of sin, forcing believers to see that the traditional Christian understanding of human sinfulness was a more realistic analysis of the human condition than any modern alternatives put forward by either liberal theology or secular political thought. For Niebuhr, the basic sin is not any particular deed one performs but the separation from God that precedes the deed. Seeking to share a missional understanding of how the world needs to be changed to reflect the way of life for which God created us and to which God calls us, Christians need to understand how their attitudes, beliefs, and faith are mixed up with their cultural prejudices and with their desire to improve society. They need to hear the gospel not only as it is preached in their own churches, but also as it is read and heard by people who do not share their biases, who live under very different social conditions or in other parts of the world. They need also to understand their resistance to change, and if they are able to change themselves and their communities, they must find ways to make those changes acceptable to those whose desires, needs, and beliefs may be very different from their own.

The chief problem of modernity, according to Niebuhr, is its "easy conscience." Sin clouds our perception, exalting our self-righteousness and pride. This pride manifests itself in three forms: (1) pride of power (pride exalts us, making us feel secure while leading us to misuse power through totalitarianism, racial discrimination, imperialism, and other forms of coercion); (2) pride of knowledge (we claim to possess the truth, even defending fanatically our system of truth, fearing that any admission of the relativity of our knowledge might threaten the quality of our

Ethical Spirituality

lives); and (3) moral pride (we see the speck in another's eye while ignoring or missing the log in our own eye). This hypocrisy expresses itself in religious intolerance, social elitism, and lack of sympathy for "sinners" on the part of "good people."

Along with other realists, Niebuhr stressed the impossibility of realizing social ideals because sin (mainly in the form of self-interest and in the desire to dominate or control others) is present in every person and in every act. The thesis of his first major work, *Moral Man and Immoral Society* (1932) was that society never presents simple moral alternatives. The tragedy of social life is that one must choose the lesser of two evils rather than an abstract absolute good. Those who follow literally and consistently a system of moral absolutes will find that they are making an ineffectual attack upon social evils. Those who fail to see the ambiguity of their own actions regularly fall into self-righteousness or simply give up on society and withdraw, seeking refuge in more secure relationships and situations. For Niebuhr, moral individuals must recognize the tragic necessity of doing their best in social circumstances, recognizing that no action is perfectly good.

Niebuhr acknowledged that while individual morality in face-to-face settings can manifest a high level of goodness, this is contradicted or compromised by the immorality of the larger groups and institutions in which they participate. In view of Niebuhr's concept of sin, this is not to say that individuals can consistently behave morally or sinlessly. However, he did insist that individual acts could be constructed on a higher moral level than social acts. The sin of pride, for example, can express itself more excessively socially rather than individually. Thus, we often claim for our nation, our race, or our political party that which would be outrageous if claimed for oneself.

When dealing with politics, Niebuhr adopted from Barth the interpretation of the Christian ethic as an "impossible possibility." Jesus taught a perfect and therefore an impossible ethic, making no concession to human weakness or to the relativities of the social situation. He demanded the absolute: "Do not resist an evildoer" (Matt 5:39) or "Be perfect" (Matt 5:48). Jesus did not teach rules or laws for conduct, but rather laid down an absolute principle—love, a love so perfect and selfless that no one could attain it in any social setting. For that reason, Niebuhr contrasted love and justice. As selfless regard for the other, love is the purest form of the Christian ethic. However, love cannot be translated into social policy. The best to be hoped for in society is proximate justice, the tolerable but imperfect accommodation of fairness and equity in life, characterized by checks and balances of power. Niebuhr was convinced that without checks and balances, and the moral ideals they reflect, such as liberty and equality, political life in democratically governed nations would quickly deteriorate into a battleground of competing interests, with little to hold them together, except raw power or totalitarian partiality. With this in mind, Niebuhr wrote, "Man's capacity for justice makes democracy possible, but man's inclination to injustice makes democracy necessary."

Despite his strong advocacy for democracy, during his professorship at Union, Niebuhr was prominent in a wide array of public activities, leading in the ecumenical movement, running several times for public office on the Socialist ticket, and later active in the New York Liberal party. Influenced by the doctrine of the incarnation, he no doubt recognized that, like Jesus, he should be at home with common folk, addressing their concerns and needs, even "getting dirty" in partisan politics for the greater good.

Questions for Discussion and Reflection

1. In your own words, define the term "modernity."
2. Explain and assess the medieval Thomistic distinction between "nature" and "grace." How did this distinction prepare the way for the Enlightenment?
3. In your estimation, how did the Enlightenment influence and change the development of Christianity as a religion and as a way of life?
4. In your estimation, how did the Enlightenment influence and change Western society?
5. In your estimation, how did the scientific method influence and change the role of Christianity in society?
6. After reading this chapter, what did you learn about deist spirituality?
7. In your own words, explain the meaning of "liberal" spirituality.
8. Explain and assess Immanuel Kant's understanding of the "categorical imperative," and the influence of Kant's thought on Western epistemology, theology, and morality.
9. Explain and assess the role of Protestant liberalism and neo-orthodoxy on Reinhold Niebuhr's social ethics.

11

Fundamentalist Spirituality
Late Nineteenth- and Twentieth-Century Piety

LIKE MODERNISM, RATIONALISM, AND liberalism, it seems hardly appropriate to speak of fundamentalist spirituality, for fundamentalism is more accurately an ideological movement than a distinct form of spirituality, more religious than spiritual in nature. Nevertheless, as a religious movement, it favors a distinct form of piety and spirituality best characterized as traditional, dogmatic, conservative, and reactionary.

Ideologically, there are currently and have been historically multiple types of fundamentalism in society, some religious, others political, social, and even scientific. Typical of the fundamentalist mindset is the belief that there is only one way of interpreting reality. Viewed as a return to revealed religion, this Western religious ethos is primarily a reactionary approach to modernity. Yet as a product of modernity, this mindset places high value on its own perceived rationality. While Catholic traditionalists often hold fundamentalist values and attitudes, religious fundamentalism technically refers to a Protestant movement that arose in the late nineteenth century, was prominent during the twentieth century, and continues to be attractive to traditional Christians today.

The Modernist–Fundamentalist Controversy

Liberalism and its polar opposite, fundamentalism, were well-defined movements by 1900. Thirty years later, liberals occupied nearly one-third of the pulpits in American Protestantism and controlled at least half of the seminaries. Fundamentalists arose to stem the tide. Even before Nazism, Marxism, and the two World Wars dealt a major blow to belief in progress and the perfectibility of humankind, fundamentalist Christians accused liberals of having destroyed Christianity in their quest for modernity, and prepared to engage them in battle to preserve what they regarded as the essence of the faith.

The term "fundamentalism" derived from a series of pamphlets known as *The Fundamentals*, published between 1910 and 1915 by a group of evangelical Christians. The set of ninety essays focused on five doctrinal affirmations that these evangelicals saw as essential to the Christian faith. The five cardinal theological tenets were the inerrancy of the Bible, the virgin birth of Jesus, substitutionary atonement, the authenticity of miracles, and the resurrection and physical return of Christ. For fundamentalist Christians, these tenets emphasized the difference between the sacred and the secular. Representing the former realm, Christianity was not a cultural artifact but rather embodied divinely revealed truth. Of the five fundamental tenets, the most important was the doctrine of the inerrancy of scripture, a doctrine developed in the nineteenth century by Princeton theologians such as Charles Hodge to combat the threat of liberal theology.

What was new in this mindset was not so much in content as in temper; fundamentalism represented a militant response to threats to its version of the gospel and a willingness to attack all detractors and competitors. Included in that attack were liberal proponents of biological evolution. Liberal theologians, focusing on goals such as truth, coherence, harmony, and unity, believed that Christian theology must come to terms with modern science. Refusing to accept religious beliefs exclusively on authority, they insisted that faith has to pass the tests of reason and experience. Christians, they argued, should keep their minds open to truth from any source. New facts may well change traditional beliefs that rest exclusively on custom and time, but unexamined faith is not worth having.

Liberals viewed the divisions of Protestant denominations as weakening Christianity. Hence, they stressed the underlying unity of the various groups, and worked to achieve denominational unification. Fundamentalists, believing the only way to gain salvation was through Jesus Christ, declared modernism as dangerous as non-Christian religions in leading people to hell.

Fundamentalism advocated literal study of the Bible, for which no part was irrelevant. A close analysis of the prophetic literature of Daniel and Revelation led to an emphasis on millennialism. This included belief in the imminence of the Second Coming of Christ, believed to inaugurate the kingdom of God on earth. Many of the fundamentalists affirmed a version of millennialism termed dispensationalism, which divided history into seven periods. At the end of each of these periods or dispensations, God had tested humanity, found it wanting, and punished it accordingly. Civilization was now in the sixth dispensation, the age of the church. However, due to secularism and liberalism, humanity had failed God's test yet again. Very soon, a new millennial age would begin, with the final battle at Armageddon. The duty of Christians was to proclaim that the end of the world was at hand and to hold fast the entire gospel before Christ returned to begin the final dispensation, an idealist one-thousand-year reign on earth.

Fundamentalism cut across denominational lines. Many adherents came from the Bible Belt, and from holiness and Pentecostal churches. Mainline denominations such as the Baptists and Presbyterians also included modernists, so a struggle began for control of these denominations. Because Baptists followed congregational autonomy, fundamentalists could easily win control of local churches. However, fundamentalists failed when they sought to purge modernists from seminaries and the denominational boards of Northern Baptists and Presbyterians.

World War I delayed the outbreak of the "modernist-fundamentalist" controversy in the Protestant denominations. However, shortly after American soldiers returned from Europe, fundamentalist Christians launched their own war of words over the values and dangers of liberal theology in the church. The debate between liberals and fundamentalists came to a head in the 1920s. Insisting upon the right of localities to control the content of public education, fundamentalists sought to forbid the teaching of evolution in many states. They succeeded in passing such a law in thirteen states, and a science teacher, John Scopes, in a staged case designed to bring money to the small town of Dayton, Tennessee, defied the statute. The 1925 trial pitted two of the most famous Americans against one another, the trial lawyer Clarence Darrow for the defense and an aged William Jennings Bryan for the prosecution. Bryan, a three-time candidate for president of the United States and the secretary of state in the cabinet of President Woodrow Wilson, wished to preserve the authority of the Bible. Clarence Darrow, Chicago's brilliant lawyer, argued that nothing other than intellectual freedom was on trial. When all was over, Scopes was found guilty and fined a token sum. Bryan won in Dayton, but Darrow in the rest of the country. Despite the verdict, no one seemed to notice that the textbook used by Scopes insisted that evolution proved the inferiority of the black race and the superiority of whites. Five days after the trial, Bryan passed away in his sleep; the fundamentalist crusade against the findings of modern science died with him.

Evangelical Fundamentalism

Fundamentalist theology, while outside the mainstream of Christianity, thrived in the United States during the twentieth century. It saw an intellectual revival after World War II, highlighted by the publication in 1947 of Carl F. H. Henry's *The Uneasy Conscience of Modern Fundamentalism*. Henry (1913–2003) affirmed the infallibility of the Bible, the uniqueness of Christ's redeeming work on the cross, and the idea that God's grace is received through a personal act of conversion in which one is "born again." However, Henry was critical of the intolerant, separatist attitude of fundamentalism and argued that it had lost sight of evangelical responsibility for reforming and humanizing society.

Henry's career was characterized by an apologetic effort to engage modernity from the perspective of traditional evangelical Christianity, but also to offer an intellectually viable alternative to theological perspectives he believed had succumbed to the relativism of modernity. This he accomplished in his six-volume *God, Revelation, and Authority* (1976–1983), which set out an extended approach to biblical authority. After embarking on a teaching career, in 1956 he became the editor of the evangelical magazine *Christianity Today*, a position he held for twelve years.

According to Henry, revelation is the source of all truth. Like Barth, Henry argued for an objectivist understanding of God's revelation. However, where Barth focused on Jesus Christ as the revelation, as the sole Word of God, and on the Bible as a witness to this Word, Henry argued that the words of the Bible themselves give us "fixed truths," "moral absolutes," and "a sure and final hope." Thus, unlike Barth, Henry viewed the Bible as absolute truth. The Bible, he believed, comes to humans from without, and consequently serves as an authority to which they must completely submit.

Henry also differed from Barth in that he saw the apologetic task as rational. His task, then, was to counter the arguments of those suspicious of fundamentalist Christianity, demonstrating, in philosophical terms, the rationality of the Bible and of its doctrinal teachings. He did this by adopting a philosophical approach called "presuppositionalism," arguing that all systems of thought are grounded in first principles that cannot be proved with certainty, though they can be rationally defended. His presuppositional starting point was that revelation is the source of all ultimate truth, and that the Bible is the depository of this truth.

From this starting point, Henry argued that rationality is a God-given means to an end of certainty, for it has its basis in the living God. Based on the presupposition that everything in the Bible is literally true, we can arrive at doctrinal certainty. The Bible, therefore, is not primarily metaphorical, nor is its narrative essentially story driven. Rather, it contains God's view of God, the world, and humanity. These cognitive truths had been given by revelation to entrusted spokespersons who recorded the divinely given information in scripture.

Whereas conservative Christians affirm that God inspired the authors of the Bible in such a way that what they wrote is what God intended for humans to know, neo-orthodox theologians disagreed, distinguishing between verbal revelation (that God speaks to humans by means of propositions or statements) and revelation through encounter (that God speaks to humans through existential, spiritual encounter that cannot be fully or even accurately conveyed in words).

Utilizing rationalistic arguments, Henry criticized Barth and others who did not treat the Bible in this verbal, propositional manner. The price Henry was willing to pay for his perspective was a denial of the Bible as literature, arguing instead for a literalist form of interpretation. There was, however, one caveat: for Henry, biblical inerrancy only holds true for the autographs, that is, for the original manuscripts of the Bible, and not for later copies. Unfortunately, later copies are all we have. However, while copies may not be inerrant, they are infallible, meaning that they cannot lead believers astray in their knowledge of God and God's will. What exactly the difference is between infallibility and inerrancy, we cannot always say, but the difference does allow some room to maneuver, for example, in conflicts between science and scripture on the origins of the world and of humanity.

In sum, what Henry wished to give us is a Bible that serves as a handbook of truth, a compendium of information literally reliable and a source of absolute certainty, a view not only at odds with mainstream Catholic and Protestant orthodoxy, but also with modern and postmodern views of revelation.

Biblical Literalism, the "Clarity" of Scripture, and Tradition

If tradition is central to Catholic fundamentalism, Protestant fundamentalism is often defined by biblical literalism. Literalism, in this sense, means either dismissing or setting aside as secondary allegorical readings of scripture. By allegorical interpretation we mean any number of strategies of biblical reading that were developed in the early church and during the Middle Ages that rely in some way on a figurative, symbolic, or nonliteral reading of scripture. Interestingly, there are places already in the Bible where allegory is used to make a theological point. In his letters, Paul frequently used allegory, such as we find, for example, in Galatians 4:21–31, where Abraham has sons by the slave woman Hagar and by his wife Sarah, whom Paul likens to two covenants. Hagar represents Mount Sinai, which corresponds to the earthly Jerusalem, and Sarah represents the heavenly or new Jerusalem (see also Rev 21:2, 10).

In the Bible, allegory has a unique function, appearing mostly in liturgical passages or edificational settings, where temporal things point to spiritual or eternal realities. In using parables as his main form of teaching, however, Jesus was in harmony with the Old Testament tradition, which principally used stories, poetry, proverbs, prophetic symbolism, and liturgical language to convey its deepest message. Allegory also appears regularly in Eastern Orthodox and mystical spirituality, but, for obvious reasons, is not prominent in traditional Protestant settings.

For Luther and Protestants in general, the Bible, unlike church tradition and sacramental theology, is seen as the sole means of certainty, that is, of salvation faith. If what people need is certainty, then what they want is not symbolic discourse or allegory, but a clear literal text that promises forgiveness and salvation. Story theology and metaphorical narrative, while central to the Bible, are not designed to provide certainty, but rather rich diversity of meaning. If one needs certainty, one needs a scripture that can be interpreted literally.

The Protestant notion that literal readings of scripture are possible and desirable probably come from misunderstanding Luther, who spoke of the clarity of scripture. To understand Luther's point, we need to explain several aspects of his thinking. The first was the centrality for Luther of the concept of "conscience," so essential to his stress on biblical authority. Placed in the context of sixteenth-century politics, Luther's appeal to scripture gave him leverage against papal authority. Above all, the scriptures freed Luther's troubled conscience from allegiance to the papacy, for such allegiance was central to late medieval spirituality, which viewed disobedience to religious authorities as disobedience to God. In this respect, conscience involved one's status or standing with God. As Luther came to understand, only scriptural authority determines one's relation to God.

For Luther, scripture alone guides the conscience; scripture alone reveals one's standing before God. In this respect, Luther disagreed with church teaching, such as found in *Unam sanctum*, the famous papal decree issued by Boniface VIII in 1302, which connected salvation with subjection to the Roman pontiff. Luther set such teaching aside as invalid, finding no support in the Bible. In Luther's estimation, the church was free to establish nonbiblical rules, but they should have no effect on our conscience, since they don't affect our salvation. That, for Luther, was the meaning of his guiding principle, "*sola scriptura*." What it came to mean was that only what scripture teaches about salvation could be required; from that point on, neither popes nor church councils could establish articles of faith; only scripture could do so. Popes and councils can err, for they are human traditions, but only scripture is binding. While human traditions can be useful, they are not binding upon our conscience.

However, for Luther, the doctrine of "scripture alone" was not a matter of private interpretation, In that respect, believers are never alone with scripture, meaning that we cannot ignore Christian tradition or church teaching regarding biblical interpretation. While the Holy Spirit helps us in our understanding, the Christian tradition is important, even indispensable for Luther. Such tradition is not independent of scripture, but is an essential part of Christian life.

While disagreeing with many medieval church practices and beliefs, Luther held church tradition in high regard, particularly the creeds, which, for him, were based on scripture, and hence, contained teachings necessary for salvation. When speaking of biblical interpretation, Luther emphasized the importance of learned clergy. While he believed anyone could preach, only ordained clergy should be appointed to public ministry of preaching and teaching. In this regard, they should be well educated, proficient in biblical languages, and familiar with the entire tradition of biblical interpretation. Subject to clerical training and expertise, individual readers of scripture must be informed and compliant with the ways scripture has been read over the years.

At times, church leaders can err, and for that reason, the Reformers spoke of the church as reformed and always being reformed, and hence, forever subject to scriptural correction. Following Luther, Protestants believe that no human institution is infallible, for to be infallible is to be forever locked in the past, unable to compromise or to come under correction. By contrast, Catholics honor tradition, and in so doing, provide depth often overlooked by Protestants. What Catholics lost in the Reformation was this notion of the church as always being reformed, whereas Protestants have trouble affirming authority. Healthy intellectual traditions, by contrast, are both authoritative and self-critical.

In his dispute with papal authority, Luther needed a clear literal text of scripture, clear common ground to support his argumentation. Analogies and symbols work well for prayer and meditation, but for doctrinal proofs, he needed a clear literal text of scripture. It was precisely such a clear Greek text of the New Testament that the humanist scholar Erasmus (1466–1536) provided the church in the early sixteenth century, and this text allowed the emerging Protestant scholarship to present arguments based on a more literal and historical sense of the original meaning of the Bible. Luther deeply appreciated the humanist recovery of the ancient biblical languages, believing that the church once again had the pure and undefiled gospel that he apostles possessed. Such texts enabled Protestant scholars to bypass the medieval biblical text, often obscure in meaning and subject to allegorical distortion. No longer did church theologians have to rely on corrupt medieval commentaries, based on a fifth century Latin Bible, written in a different form of Latin than that used by medieval and Renaissance theologians. In addition, the original Latin text was based on inferior and occasionally on inaccurate Greek and Hebrew manuscripts. Hence, there was much in the medieval biblical text that was unclear, making literal interpretation nearly impossible.

Erasmus published his Greek text in 1516, which included notes and commentary on the meaning of the original Greek syntax and vocabulary, and Luther promptly used it in his university lectures. In Luther's mind, and for later Protestant scholars, a biblical text was finally available that was pure, clear, and undefiled, that said what it meant and meant what it said.

Fundamentalist Spirituality 163

This alliance between Protestantism and cutting-edge biblical scholarship prevailed largely unscathed until the nineteenth century, when a new trend emerged in biblical scholarship called "the historical-critical method" of biblical scholarship. This scholarship produced a new meaning of the historical Bible, based on a new understanding of its setting and authorship, an approach that tended to undermine traditional views of the Bible. It questioned, for example, whether Moses wrote all or even any of the Pentateuch. It also questioned the historical accuracy of many narratives in the Old New Testaments. Such scholarship questioned religious certainty, and it caused a crisis. Of course, something similar had happened during the Reformation, when Protestant scholars had undermined Catholic interpretations of scripture, but now German scholarship was undermining longstanding Protestant interpretation. What scholars came to recognize is that Protestant readings of the Bible are just as dependent on tradition as Catholic readings, and both need to acknowledge their indebtedness to their traditions.

Nineteenth-century scholarship pitted two traditions against one another—cutting-edge academic scholarship and traditional Protestantism—but the long-range effect is that each learned from the other, even while criticizing and arguing with one another. However, if we fail to appreciate these as traditions, then what remains is the pietist notion that reduces spirituality to individual mystical relations with scripture, to cozy relations between individuals and God's Spirit, to interpretations that, while appearing literal, can be disturbingly unliteral. Such private, literalistic, and individualist readings of scripture often lead to conclusions that differ greatly from the conclusions of critical biblical scholarship, assuring conservative Christians that their reading of scripture is pure, accurate, and undefiled, by comparison with the academic study of scripture, viewed as defective and unchristian.

This arrogant, distrusting approach by sincere believers led to Christian fundamentalism, a combination of individualism, rationalism, and biblical literalism. Suddenly, small groups of Christians began arguing that they alone knew the meaning of scripture, and that alternative readings were in error. What they failed to realize, of course, was that there is no such thing as a noninterpretive reading of scripture. Reading passages from the Bible literally, whether Old Testament stories concerning creation, the exodus from Egypt, the giving of the law on Mount Sinai, prophecies, proverbs, and psalms, or New Testament stories concerning the birth, death, and resurrection of Jesus, all involve interpretive decisions equally as much as the decision to read them metaphorically.

The fundamentalist idea that scholars interpret the Bible subjectively while individual believers merely read the Bible literally is clearly erroneous, for whenever individuals read passages of scripture, be they liberal or conservative, literalists or nonliteralists, all approach the text with preconceived notions, making unconscious judgments even before they start reading. In that respect, there is no such thing as a literal or noninterpretive reading of scripture. All literature invites interpretation; important literature demands it. This is particularly true of scripture, its truth claims fraught with meaning and therefore open to investigation. As we now know, all our preconceived judgments and assumptions, particularly those we hold about scripture, come from existing traditions.

When Luther spoke of the clarity of scripture, he meant that the biblical text was now clear and undefiled, as opposed to the obscurity and corruption of older Latin versions. Whenever Luther spoke of the clarity of scripture, he emphasized the principle that scripture interprets itself, by which he meant, not that scripture doesn't require interpretation, but that the biblical storyline consistently points to Christ. For Luther, the clarity of scripture is that scripture always speaks clearly about Christ. If you read the New Testament, and fail to see that it is about Christ, you have misread it. Luther never suggested that to read scripture literally is to read it noninterpretively.

Central to Luther was the idea that it is not possible to read scripture without the help of or apart from some existing tradition. Tradition is what makes something obvious to the reader, what provides clarity or "aha" moments. Tradition provides readers of scripture a lens by which they distinguish good and evil, right and wrong, clarity and confusion.

Biblical scholars, like people in the pew, are part of a tradition, and that tradition provides guidance, clarity, and even, in some cases, certainty. Tradition sharpens our perceptions, teaches us how to understand things, and makes things obvious to amateurs and professionals alike, although to differing degrees. This holds true for any discipline and trade, from car mechanics to brain surgery, and it holds true when we make judgments about different types of literature, particularly biblical literature.

Biblical literalists often appeal to the guidance of the Holy Spirit, and while such guidance should not be discounted, such appeals, like those to reason or authority, often lead to distinct and drastically opposing conclusions. In this sense, the clarity of scripture is always relative to the reader, to his or her brain, needs, assumptions, upbringing, and predilections, and is always related to some form or aspect of the Christian tradition. In this respect, non-Christians cannot be expected to find Christ in the New Testament, only ideas about Jesus, his disciples, and church life, and even these ideas may vary greatly from teachings of the Christian tradition. Even biblical scholars disagree among themselves over how to read and interpret scripture. Their careful study of biblical passages should give pause to those privately figuring out the meaning of scripture for themselves.

Furthermore, Christians often approach scripture with their own set of questions, questions very different from those asked by the original hearers and readers of the New Testament, for whom the Christian scriptures were written. Likewise, few of us can be conversant with the questions Augustine, or Luther, or even other twenty-first-century Christians ask. To a great extent, the questions we ask of scripture determine the answers we find in our reading.

The issues I raise represent only a selection of concerns most fundamentalists ignore in their reading of scripture, issues they avoid at their own peril. In this respect, I remind you that Jesus used parables to subvert our unconscious worldview, unlocking it from within and thereby exposing its illusions. All religions have tried to do the same with riddles and koans and mythic stories. Our entire universe has to be rearranged truthfully before individual teachings can be heard correctly. Unfortunately, what fundamentalist religion has been doing in the West is give people new moral and doctrinal teaching without rearranging their mythic worldview. This approach leads nowhere new. It only creates legalists, specialists, ritualists, minimalists, and literalists, who regularly kill the spirit of a thing.

Reading and Interpreting Scripture

People read the Bible for many reasons: literarily (as great literature), philosophically (as a guide for moral and reflective thought), theologically (as a compendium of truth), or devotionally (as a resource for meditation and a source of comfort). Despite the Bible's widespread scriptural use, most devout people read it only occasionally, and superficially. How people read it is perhaps more important than why they read it. For those who wish to engage with scripture seriously and in depth, I recommend that you find a method of study that works for you, whether individually or with others, and commit to it. Of many valid ways of reading scripture, the following are recommended:

- Reading for *information*—to learn as much as possible about the setting of the authors and their primary audience in order to discover the original meaning of a particular passage of scripture and its potential application.

- Reading for *formation*—to establish one's identity, values, and beliefs in order to live meaningfully, joyously, and securely.

- Reading for *transformation*—to provide resources for developing soulcentrically rather than egocentrically, aligning more deeply with one's powers of nurturing and creating, presence and wonder.

Of course, it is quite possible for these approaches to overlap, due to the complexity of our intellectual, theological, and spiritual needs. It is equally possible that biblical passages convey messages appropriate to our varied abilities and needs. Scripture is multivalent, meaning that it's message allows for multiple interpretations. While one text might strike terror in the heart of an unrepentant person, the same passage might exhort devout believers to greater faithfulness and even greater freedom. When you read any book or section of the Bible, particularly in a group setting, keep in mind the possibility that biblical passages contain multiple messages, depending on one's needs, temperament, and spiritual journey. Scripture, like a good smorgasbord, provides healthy options for different appetites. And you don't always have to eat the same food; sometimes a change of diet can be helpful.

As Paul showed in 1 Corinthians, the important thing is to keep growing spiritually. Paul's concern with the Corinthians was that they were in a state of spiritual immaturity, unable to eat solid food. It takes time—and conscious effort—to grow spiritually, from egocentrism to soulcentrism. How people hear and read scripture (eat spiritually) reflects their spiritual maturity.

While the Hebrew scriptures (the Old Testament) provide codes of behavior and belief that can be systematized into groups of tens or twelves, the canonical writings of Christianity intentionally fail to do so, even for religious matters. To the question, "What does the New Testament teach on X or Y?" the proper answer seems, "What did you read last in the New Testament?" The New Testament is not a collection of books that provides a system of law for personal or public behavior, but rather a way of life based on discernment and wisdom, subjecting morality under fuzzy topics such as "love," "mercy," and "forgiveness."

Christians have always affirmed a close relationship between the Bible and God, just as other religions affirm a close connection between the sacred and their holy scriptures. Foundational to reading the Bible is a decision about how to view its origin. Does it come from God, or is it a human product?

Building on the conviction that divine revelation and man-made religion are fundamentally irreconcilable, fundamentalist Christians believe that the only choice a person can make about the Bible is to view it either as the infallible, inerrant word of God or as a collection of fairy tales with little or no value for modern people. Since the latter is what unbelievers think, fundamentalists believe they must view the Bible as God's very word of truth, defending it in all respects, even on historical and scientific matters. For many, the Bible's reliability is so critical that they will argue, "If I can't believe the Bible when it speaks about creation or history, then how can I believe it about Jesus Christ and salvation?" To frame the question of the inspiration and authority of the Bible in this manner, however, is to do an injustice to the traditional doctrines of the inspiration and authority of scripture.

From the earliest days, Christian leaders formulated theories of biblical interpretation. By the fourth century, clearly defined interpretive theories were already widely accepted by Christian leaders, including that scripture contained four levels of meaning: literal (historical and literal level), allegorical (hidden mystical and spiritual truths), tropological (moral lessons), and anagogical (eschatological level, revealing secrets concerning the afterlife and Christ's future kingdom). While allegorical and other levels of interpretation provided Christian theology with flexibility, giving it the capacity to intertwine written and oral traditions and the ability to adapt to ever-changing situations, in the wrong hands it could be abused, leading to heterodox beliefs and practices. From the fifth through sixteenth centuries, scripture remained firmly in the hands of the church elites who had mastered the accepted exegetical methods. Major controversies were addressed by bishops through synods or councils.

The Protestant Reformers of the sixteenth century declared that the church had become corrupt because it had buried the truths of scripture beneath layers of humanly devised traditions. Claiming to base their reforms on scripture, the reformers encouraged the translation of scripture into the vernacular, a process aided by the invention of the printing press. Martin Luther believed that faith and the Holy Spirit's illumination were prerequisites for an interpreter of the Bible. He laid down the foundational premise of the Reformation, the principle of *sola scriptura* (scripture alone), the primacy of scripture above all other authorities. Asserting that the Bible should be viewed differently from other literature, he downplayed dependence on church authorities to understand the Bible. Luther also challenged the prevailing "rule of faith," maintaining that rather than the church determining what the scriptures teach, scripture should determine what the church teaches. As we noted, he also believed in the clarity or "perspicuity" of scripture, in opposition to medieval dogma that the scriptures are obscure and only the church could uncover their true meaning. He favored a literal understanding of the text, rather than the allegorical method of interpreting scripture, stressing that the interpreter should consider historical conditions, grammar, and context in the process of exegesis.

Probably the greatest exegete of the Reformation was John Calvin (1509–1564), a second-generation reformer. Agreeing in general with the principles articulated by Luther, he too believed that spiritual illumination is necessary and regarded allegorical interpretation as a deceptive device that distorted the clear sense of scripture. Assuming the divine authorship of scripture, he adhered strictly to the principle of harmony, meaning that scripture is its own best interpreter. No passage of scripture should be set up against another; secondary and obscure passages in scripture should always be subject to primary and plain passages. He placed importance on studying the context, grammar, words, and parallel passages, stating that the primary task of an interpreter is to allow the author to speak, rather than to import one's own meaning into the text.

Espousing the priesthood of all believers, the Reformers believed every Christian capable of reading scripture, as guided individually by the Holy Spirit. Rather than leading to unanimity, however, that impetus resulted in further disagreement and fragmentation. Despite their emphasis on scripture as sole authority, the Reformers could not agree with one another on the application of scripture to polity, social issues, and sacramental practices such as baptism or the Eucharist. The unraveling of Christian unity in the sixteenth century led to the emergence of rival communities, each claiming to be the "true" church and to have the correct understanding of scripture.

The Renaissance and the Enlightenment gave rise to ideologies such as humanism, rationalism, skepticism, scientism, and existentialism, each to varying degrees undermined the authority of scripture while simultaneously unleashing a monumental critical effort to ascertain truth in scripture. Searching for truth in scripture, biblical scholars increasingly detected the humanity of the authors who wrote the documents that together constituted the Bible. As Johann Gottfried von Herder argued in the late eighteenth century, the Bible is religious literature, a composite of fact and fiction that must be analyzed as one would study any ancient literature. This approach to the Bible came to be known as higher criticism.

Conclusion

During the nineteenth and twentieth centuries, various patterns of response countered biblical criticism. One response was that of *liberalism*, which stressed morality in religion and gave precedence to reason over supernaturalism. Liberalism attempted to redefine Christian tradition in such a way as to engage modernity directly. Embracing the discoveries of higher criticism, liberals replaced literalistic approaches to scripture with moral ones. A second response was the resurgence of *pietism*, a concerted effort to retreat from the chaos and complexity of modernity to a simpler, less rational approach, where scripture was encountered primarily through one's heart. A third response was that of Protestant *fundamentalism*, which countered modernism by reiterating supernaturalism and the inerrancy of scripture. Fundamentalism was joined by Pentecostalism and evangelicalism, movements that likewise embrace conservative biblicism. A fourth response, that of *Roman Catholicism*, encouraged Catholic laity to engage more directly with scripture, while maintaining that the Catholic Church was the ultimate interpreter of scripture, with the help of the Holy Spirit.

Questions for Discussion and Reflection

1. In a sentence or two, define religious fundamentalism. Do you agree with the author that fundamentalism is a product of modernity? If so, how?

2. Compare and contrast Protestant fundamentalism with the medieval "nature-grace" dualism.
3. Of the five fundamentalist tenets, why is the most important the doctrine of the inerrancy of scripture? In this respect, explain fundamentalism's love affair with biblical literalism.
4. Explain the relationship between religious fundamentalism and modern science? In your estimation, can Christian fundamentalists function as credible modern scientists? Explain your answer.
5. Compare and contrast Protestant liberalism with Protestant fundamentalism.
6. In your estimation, must Protestant evangelicals be fundamentalists? Explain your answer.
7. Explain Carl Henry's concept of "presuppositionalism." How is this approach rationalistic and therefore modernistic?
8. Explain and assess fundamentalism's emphasis on verbal or propositional revelation.
9. How is Protestant fundamentalism's emphasis on biblical literalism based on a misinterpretation of Luther's notion of the clarity of scripture?
10. Do you read the Bible primarily for information, formation, or transformation? Explain your answer.

12

Ecumenical, Pluralist, and Eco-Spirituality

LIKE FUNDAMENTALIST SPIRITUALITY, ONE wonders whether it is possible to speak of ecumenical spirituality, but since ecumenism arose as an essential mindset within twentieth-century Christianity, with distinctive and discernible attitudes and values, ecumenism qualifies as a form of religious sensibility.

Like fundamentalism, ecumenism is a mindset. While both forms of spirituality share conserving and hopeful ideals, they are distinct in goals and methodology. While fundamentalists focus on biblical literalism, doctrinal purity, and ecclesiastical exclusivism, ecumenists focus on sociological concerns, chiefly on collaboration between Christian churches and denominations in a common search for the meaning of obedience to Christ in the modern world. In this respect, the ecumenical movement has two primary concerns. The first and most obvious is the quest for greater and more visible unity. The second, with more far-reaching and lasting consequences, is the need to realize this unity through a concerted commitment to a global mission to which all churches contribute.

Already in biblical times, the apostle Paul and others spoke of the unity of the one Spirit, by which believers are "all baptized into one body ... and all made to drink of one spirit" (1 Cor 12:13). This is not some naïve "everything is one" unity, but the deeper ecumenical unity described by the fourteenth-century mystical visionary Julian of Norwich, who spoke of God's love as a power so great that it creates "such a unity that, when it is seen correctly, nobody can separate himself from anybody else" (*Revelations*, 65).[1]

The letter to the Ephesians, written by a devoted admirer of Paul during the last two decades of the first century, is influenced by a dominant concern, namely, the unity of the church under the headship of Christ. The church at this time had become predominantly Gentile and was in danger of losing its sense of continuity with Israel. The author of Ephesians, desiring to underscore the larger history and tradition that defined Christianity, as well as the mystical unity of believers in Christ, portrays that oneness in three predominant images: the church is (1) the body of Christ (1:22–23), (2) the building or temple of God (2:20–22), and (3) the bride of Christ (5:23–32). The church's solidarity, Paul makes clear in Galatians 3:28, has social implications, namely, challenging racial, social, and sexual barriers. Because Christ is one, church members are united. Because Christ is one, church members are equal. Because Christ is one, church members are free to serve one another. In Ephesians, love is not a commandment but a new reality in human relationships that has been initiated by God's prior love through Jesus Christ. The church is a fellowship of love, the highest endowment of God's Spirit (see 1 Cor. 13:13; 1 John 4:7–21).

The theme of the unity and faithfulness of the church in the world is elaborated in John 17, Jesus' so-called "high-priestly prayer." In his final prayer, two prepositions are important: "out of" and "into." God has summoned a people for Christ "out of" the world (John 17: 6). Indeed, the New Testament word for church (*ekklēsia*) literally means "called out" and suggests the idea of God calling people out of the world into a new and unique fellowship. However, the church is not taken out of the world into a detached life, but rather is sent "into" the world (John 17:15, 18).

During the second and third centuries of the Common Era (up to 313), Christianity was threatened by conflict within (orthodoxy versus heterodoxy) and without (conflict with other elements of society, such as pagan philosophers, and imperial persecution by the Roman state). At its inception, the period was characterized by great diversity of beliefs and practices, some Jewish, some pagan, and others uniquely Christian, but by the end of the period, Christianity was searching for agreement and unity. Unity demanded a universal version of the church and over time there developed a term of great resonance for Christianity, the word

---

1. Armstrong, *Visions of God*, 216.

"catholic," from an ordinary Greek adjective for "general," "whole," or "universal." Bishop Ignatius of Antioch provides the first known use of the term in his letter written to the Christians of Smyrna, in the early second century. Since he did not bother to explain exactly what he meant by the "catholic church," he evidently expected his readers to be familiar with the expression. This was a momentous development, for Christians have never abandoned their hope for unity, despite their general inability to sustain it at any stage in their history.

The church is aware of living in an interim, "between the ages." Because it cannot bring in the expected kingdom of God, it can only testify to its reality, living by the spiritual and ethical principles established by Jesus. Because the citizens of the kingdom belong to a community of believers and are not isolated individuals, they are responsible to maintain the four "notes" or marks of the church, that is, its four defining characteristics as noted in the creeds of Christendom: (1) retaining faithfulness to its founding principles, (2) maintaining its holiness or purity, that is, its sense of calling to service in the world, (3) affirming its inclusivity and universality, and (4) embodying its oneness or unity in Christ.

As Christians of all denominations, cultures, and races are discovering, unity is better than discord, and cooperation more beneficial than isolation. Learning from history, modern Christians are setting aside ecclesiastical and sociological differences, affirming the trajectories that provide forward momentum to the faith.

A fragmented world awaits this unified church, its members working together for the healing of the nations. This cannot take place unless believers join hands, informed by their varied traditions and beliefs and empowered by the larger Christian narrative. What transpired during the canonical process—one Bible representing multiple voices and perspectives—needs to occur yet again, one church representing many voices, cultures, and traditions. Such unity in mission and service does not occur automatically, but only through an informed appreciation of a mutual heritage, a common scripture, and a shared story.

Since the Reformation, Christianity has been divided into Orthodox, Roman Catholic, and Protestant branches, with further divisions within Orthodoxy and Protestantism. Although the divisions among the three main branches of Christianity seem unlikely to be healed, certain elements within Protestantism seek cooperation. Such cooperation between ecclesiastical bodies began in the late eighteenth and early nineteenth centuries, primarily around missionary and evangelistic efforts.

Among the first was the London Missionary Society, formed in 1795, the Religious Tract Society, begun in 1799, the British and Foreign Bible Society, founded in 1804, and the American Bible Society, organized in 1916. The Sunday School movement was a similar effort.

The nineteenth century witnessed a series of missionary conferences to discuss common issues such as Bible translation, education, and social change. The missionary movement became the leading area of ecumenical cooperation, primarily because the futility of denominational differences was most obvious on the mission field, where millions of non-Christians outnumbered a handful of believers. During the nineteenth century, a number of nondenominational, multinational Protestant organizations emerged to deal with specialized ministries, including the Young Men's Christian Association (YMCA), founded in 1844, and the Young Women's Christian Association (1854). Such groups focused on reaching urban workers and college students with varied forms of spiritual and material assistance such as job training, recreational outlets, and Bible studies.

A decisive moment in the ecumenical movement occurred in Edinburgh, Scotland, at the World Missionary Conference held in 1910. Inspired by that groundbreaking conference, Protestant leaders from around the world joined forces in the belief that full church cooperation might occur in the twentieth century. From this conference came a Continuation Committee to organize meetings approximately every ten years and to provide communication among mission agencies regarding social issues, relations with emerging churches, and mission during wartime. Out of this commitment arose the desire to organize councils of missions and, where possible, councils of churches.

Following World War I, the greatest challenges faced by the ecumenical movement were to restore Christian trust and understanding across national lines and to care for the millions of refugees in Europe and Asia. Missionaries ran soup kitchens, clinics, and employment programs for refugees across Europe and even in Asia.

During the 1920s, movements toward church union gained momentum. The founding of the League of Nations inspired Orthodox churches, having suffered horribly during the world war, to participate in ecumenical events. By the late 1930s, various ecumenical groups formulated a constitution for the World Council of Churches. As missions gave way to the formation of churches in Asia, Africa, and Latin America, the young churches could become members of the global fellowship on an equal basis. Delayed by World War II, the World Council of Churches formally began in 1948. Some 147 churches from 44 nations joined during the First Assembly meeting in Amsterdam. Only the Roman Catholic Church and fundamentalist Christian denominations remained aloof from the World Council. By the time of the Second Assembly, gathered in Evanston Illinois, in 1954, 163 distinct church groups were present. When the Third Assembly gathered in New Delhi, in 1961, the member churches numbered 197.

Significantly, at a time when the Cold War was beginning, the Council called on all churches to reject both Communism and liberal capitalism, and to oppose the mistaken notions that these two systems exhaust all possible alternatives. As could be expected, this declaration, and similar later ones, were not always well received. By the Sixth Assembly, gathered at Vancouver in 1983, the delegates insisted on relating issues of peace and justice. By then, in response to the new openness of the Catholic Church connected with the work of Pope John XXIII and the Second Vatican Council, the World Council had also established constructive conversations with the Catholic Church, leading to collaboration in various projects and studies.

Another impulse toward church unity was the attempt to merge mission-founded churches in the non-Western world. Non-Western Christians felt little need for separate Lutheran, Anglican, Presbyterian, Methodist, and Baptist churches. Mergers of various Protestant denominations resulted in such union churches as the Church of Christ in China (1927), the Church of Christ in Japan (1941), the Church of South India (1947), and the United Church of Christ in the Philippines (1948). Ecumenical church conferences began meeting in Latin America as early as 1916; in 1958, Christians from across Africa met to form the All Africa Conference of Churches. By the 1950s, Asian churches began sending cross-cultural missionaries to other parts of Asia or to other ethnic groups within their national borders. In the United States, the Consultation of Church Union (COCU) proposed to its participating denominations a plan for a "Church of Christ Uniting," a vision that led to cooperation in social ventures and shared pulpits, but not to the anticipated union.

Despite Protestant and Orthodox participation in the ecumenical movement, the separation of Christians was most marked in the Roman Catholic Church. Since the sixteenth century, Rome taught that it alone was the church; non-Roman Christians could only belong if their baptism was Catholic, and the denominations to which they belonged were not churches. In the nineteenth century, when Catholicism centralized itself ever more in Rome, Pope Pius IX admitted that individuals might be saved outside the church, but only by reason of ignorance of the true faith. This concession, however, made no difference to the strict feeling that the Catholic Church could not cooperate in any way with other churches, lest it mislead them into thinking that they also were recognized as such. When the ecumenical movement gained ground in the 1920s, Pope Pius XI formally refused to take part, lest participation imply recognition that the Roman Catholic Church was but one of a number of denominations. Pope Pius's 1928 encyclical prohibited Roman Catholics from participating in conferences with non-Roman Christians.

While changes took place after World War II, the accession of Pope John XXIII in 1958 began to transform the atmosphere. Part of his object in summoning Vatican Two was to heal the separation between Christians. As a result, Catholics recognized Protestants as separated brothers. The doctrine that Roman Catholics could not share in worship with other Christians was eventually annulled by the Polish Pope John Paul II in 1982, when he attended Canterbury Cathedral ceremoniously with Anglican Archbishop Runcie. They were not, however, able to receive the sacrament together. Serious disagreements remain between Catholics, Orthodox, and Protestants, including issues of contraception, abortion, church authority, sacraments, social justice, the ministry of women in the church, and the ways of being religious.

Religious Pluralism

Is there only one way to God? we ask. If God exists, why hasn't he revealed himself in the same way to all nations and cultures? Alternatively, has God already revealed himself, only through different faiths, symbols, and interpretations? Are all religions simply different paths to the same ultimate reality? In the past several decades, the question of religious pluralism has become a burning issue not only among theologians and philosophers of religion, but also among monotheists.

In the twentieth century, ecumenical mindsets led some to particularism, others to inclusivism, and yet others to pluralistic perspectives. These three broad approaches have not so much to do with the relation between Christians but with the relation between Christians and other religious traditions. It must be stressed, however, that these approaches are concerned with Christian theology and hence, with evaluating other religions traditions from the perspective of Christianity itself. While not intended to gain approval from non-Christians, these approaches can be distinguished as follows:

1. *Particularism.* Also known as exclusivism, this view holds that only those who hear and respond to the Christian gospel may be saved.[2] Most exclusivists adopt the position that knowledge of God is only available in Christ.

2. *Inclusivism.* While affirming Christianity as the normative revelation of God, this view maintains that salvation is possible for non-Christians. Some inclusivists argue for the validity of other religions, while others envision other religions as valid only insofar as they point toward their fulfillment in Christianity. A third option is that of Jesuit theologian Karl Rahner, which regards faithful adherents of non-Christian religions as "anonymous Christians." Inclusivists are unified by the notion that whereas salvation might be available in principle to all human beings, however and wherever it occurs, it is the work of Christ.

3. *Pluralism.* This view holds that all religious traditions are equally valid paths to the same ultimate religious reality.

In this segment we focus on the third option. The basic feature of the pluralist approach to the relation of Christianity to other faiths is that each religion is understood to represent a distinctive, yet equally valid, grasp of the ultimate spiritual reality Christians call "God." Since some religions are nontheistic, pluralist thinkers tend to refer to the spiritual reality that they believe to lie behind all religions as "ultimate reality" or "the Real," thus avoiding the monotheistic term "God."

The most significant recent exponent of the pluralist approach to religious traditions is John Hick, the British philosopher of religion who argues for a need to move away from a Christ-centered to a God-centered approach. Viewing God at the center of Christianity and other world religions as revolving around the same divine reality, Hick suggests that the aspect of God's nature of central importance to the question of other faiths is his universal saving will. If God wishes everyone to be saved, that is, to be properly related to the Real, it would be inconceivable for such a

---

2. Salvation, in this sense, is understood to include forgiveness of sins, restoration of proper relationship to God, and assurance of eternal life.

reality to will to save only a small portion of humanity. From this, Hick draws the conclusion that it is necessary to recognize that all religions lead to the same God. Thus, Christians have no special access to God, for God is universally available through all religious traditions.

To understand Hick's view, it helps to know his personal story. In his writings, he tells us that he became a Christian by conversion as a first year law student, influenced and encouraged by friends who were fundamentalist in their beliefs, packaging their Christianity in an extremely conservative form of Calvinist orthodoxy. After a year, he left school to serve in an ambulance unit during World War II. When he returned to school, it was to study philosophy in preparation for the Presbyterian ministry. For twenty years, he maintained fairly conservative views of Christianity. However, in 1967, while lecturing in philosophy at Birmingham University, a British city of many immigrants, he began participating in ecumenical and interfaith activities, in active fellowship with Jews, Hindus, Sikhs, Marxists, and humanists. As he writes, "it was not so much new thoughts as new experiences that drew me, as a philosopher, into the issues of religious pluralism, and as a Christian into interfaith dialogue."[3] Encounters with remarkable individuals in these faiths reinforced the realization that very different religious traditions constitute genuine human response to the one ultimate divine Reality. As he worked with representatives of these groups, he came to see that there were no attempts to convert others, but rather only the desire to join with one another in respect and service to people in need. As Christians joined in these efforts, they found themselves transformed by a broader understanding of religious purpose and identity, unifying yet pluralistic.

Participating in interfaith dialogue led Hick to confront and later to dismiss the assumptions of the religious superiority of his own tradition. Doing so enabled him to explore, often with genuine fascination and profit, ways by which people of other faiths know and serve God. Because religious traditions conceive, experience, and respond to God in specific and therefore in limited ways, pluralism can offer new and insightful ways to reflect on the meaning and possibilities of our human existence. As the noted Sufi poet Jalaluddin Rumi noted, "The lamps are different, but the Light is the same; it comes from Beyond."

In his book of essays titled *Disputed Questions*, Hick admits that there was a time in Christendom when religious disputations concerned

---

3. Hick, *Disputed Questions*, 141.

relatively minor topics, since the most basic and important matters were agreed upon. Today, he notes, the situation has changed dramatically, to the point where Christians debate most theological issues. Furthermore, he writes, "Christian discourse itself is now part of the wider universe of discourse that includes all the great religious and philosophical traditions of the world."[4] By this he implies that a contemporary Christian can no longer be content to look inward, at his or her own tradition, for to do so is to be less than Christian. To be a true Christian, Jew, or Muslim, according to Hick, means to look and live beyond one's comfort zone, to be curious about other faith traditions and cultures and to be in dialogue with them, particularly if one believes, as do Christians, that all humans are made "in the image of God."

In his essays on religious pluralism, Hick asks the question, "Do adherents of the world's monotheistic religions all worship the same God?" Recognizing the historical particularities of Judaism, Christianity, and Islam, one possible answer is to say that they worship the same God, but call that God by different names. In so doing, each tradition is thus focusing on that aspect of the divine nature that is most relevant to its needs and understanding.

The difficulty facing this suggestion is that it is not only the names but also the descriptions and the messages that go with them that are different. Since these doctrines and conceptions cannot successfully be harmonized, Hick proposes a compromise, namely, by suggesting a distinction between God as Ultimate or as the Real and personifications of God. Terms such as the Real, the Ultimate, or Ultimate Reality are thus ways of speaking of God "*an sich*," that is, of God's divine essence, which humans cannot know. Conversely, terms such as Yahweh, Adonai, Elohim, Allah, and the Christian Trinity are the joint product of the universal divine presence and historically formed modes of constructive religious imagination.

Hick believes that individual religious traditions are limited in their discussion of the Real because they only use concepts that have meaning to that tradition. He then attempts to transcend plural descriptors by thinking philosophically, envisioning a concept that is universal rather than limited to the data, culture, and experience of any one tradition. Consequently, he suggests that what the various religious traditions

---

4. Hick, *Disputed Questions*, vii.

describe as the Ultimate is not the Ultimate as it is in itself (*an sich*), but only the Ultimate as conceived by particular traditions and cultures.

Using arguments from philosophy of religion, Hick discovers various religious personifications of authentic religious traditions and deduces two possible options concerning their validity, namely, whether they are authentic or spurious manifestations of the Real *an sich*. If they are authentic, at best they are no more that human metaphors, conditioned by varying streams of historical and cultural consciousness.

Having established that the Real might become manifest personally in theistic traditions (*personae*), Hick posits a second possibility, namely, that this paradigm might also apply impersonally to nontheistic religious traditions (*impersonae*). Of course, such a proposal is not suitable to all religious possibilities, since it requires the rejection of atheism, religious exclusivism, and polytheism. However, to affirm the Real is to affirm that religious belief and experience in its plurality of forms is not simple delusion, but constitutes a human, and therefore an imperfect, partial, and distorted range of ways of being affected by the universal "presence" of the Real. Ultimately, we cannot say whether the Ultimate is personal or impersonal. All that we can say is that these concepts, which have their use in relation to human experience, do not apply, even analogically, to the Real *an sich*.

Thus, the Real *an sich* cannot be the object of a religious cult. As Hick notes, humans cannot worship or achieve union with the Real. We can only worship one or another of its personae, or we can only seek union with one or more of its impersonae. For pluralists, a deity or an absolute is an authentic manifestation of the Real when it promotes the transformation of human existence from self-centeredness to Reality-centeredness. Only then does the form of worship or of meditation focused upon this personification constitute "true religion." In principle, humans are free to choose between personae and impersonae, that is, between personal and non-personal manifestations of the Real to worship or upon which to meditate.

Pluralism, for Hick, satisfies the human intuition that each of the great world faiths has such intrinsic value that it would be false and harmful to regard any one of them alone as true or authentic and the others as false or inauthentic. At the same time, pluralism removes any temptation to think of the different traditions as the same or alike, and can free us to notice and be fascinated by all the difference that the phenomenology of religion reveals.

Hick's proposal, while attractive, is not without its problems. For example, it is clear that the religious traditions of the world are radically different in their beliefs and practices. Hick deals with this point by suggesting that such differences must be understood as complementary, rather than contradictory, insights into the one divine reality, a reality that lies at the heart of all the religions. This idea strikes many scholars as similar to that propounded by deist writers, who spoke of an original universal natural religion that had become corrupted through time.

Furthermore, to accept Hick's thesis, Christians must be willing to set aside cherished beliefs such as evangelism, the doctrines of salvation, heaven, and hell, the uniqueness of Jesus Christ, and the authority of scripture. Affirming beliefs all religions have in common also makes it difficult to accept that they are speaking of the same God. To do so, we must depersonalize God, meaning God has no biases, no favorites, no truths peculiar to specific cultures and nations, and above all, no speech, for this God must remain silent. Is Hick actually talking about the Christian God at all, we wonder. The implications for traditional Christians are particularly drastic, for gone is the idea of divine revelation, since, according to Hick, all scriptures are but human wisdom.

Ultimately, however, pluralistic possibilities might not be all bad, for they require due diligence on the part of believers. If one believes that the Bible is the Word of God, as fundamentalists and biblical literalists maintain, one must have a God who is fluent in ancient Hebrew and in Koine Greek, while capable of speaking colloquially at times and even ungrammatically on occasion. Furthermore, if God is fluent in ancient human languages, is God also fluent in old Latin, medieval Latin, old German, old English, King James English, and modern English, among the many languages and dialects into which the Bible has been translated? After all, what is the sense of reading and trusting in the Bible if it has been translated by fallible human beings into modern languages, with modern meanings? Can such Bibles be authoritative or inerrant?

Ecospirituality

Whether you are an ecumenist or a pluralist, ultimately, if you love God, yourself, and others, you will love the earth and all its creatures. "The heavens are telling the glory of God," says the psalmist, "and the firmament proclaims his handiwork" (Ps 19:1). From its inception, the

Christian tradition viewed nature (creation) as a means of revelation. The concept of Two Books, the Book of Nature and the Book of Scripture, was first articulated by Tertullian (c. 160–c. 230), an early Christian theologian. Nature and scripture proceed alike from the creative Word of God, and, when properly interpreted, reveal truth that is not contradictory.

Francis of Assisi (1181–1226), founder of the Franciscan Order, had a great love for everything God had made. He is well known for preaching to the birds, but he loved everything in nature that was beautiful as belonging to God. Moreover, he saw everything natural as symbolic of God—sheep and lambs, surely, but also trees, rocks, and light. His *Canticle to the Sun*, written late in life, shows his love of the natural world. Bonaventure (1217–1274), known for writing deeply mystical works, joined the Franciscans in 1243 and took Francis's practical life orientation to the level of theology. He wrote, "unless we are able to view things in terms of . . . how God shines forth in them, we will not be able to understand."

Unlike most theologians of his time, Bonaventure paid little attention to sin, merit, justification, or atonement. His vision was mystical, cosmic, and intimately relational. He focused attention on perception and intuition, believing that a positive theology resulted in the enjoyment of life. Bonaventure's theology was not about fearing or placating a distant or angry God, but about delighting in God's all-pervasive plan. For Bonaventure, God is not an offended monarch throwing down mighty thunderbolts, but a fountain of fullness that flows and fills all things to overflowing.

Bonaventure's positive, coherent, and meaning-filled view of reality is at odds with the reward/punishment view that predominates when people merely uphold dogmatic propositions without experiencing God's presence. If modern Christians were able to recover Bonaventure's perspective of life, nature, and God, it could provide the framework society lacks in our age of cynicism and despair. In *The Soul's Journey into God*, Bonaventure expressed the Franciscan awareness of the presence of God in nature. Bonaventure envisioned nature in terms of cosmic connectedness. Quite simply, nature (creation), like Christ, is the mirror and image of the holy, God's "fingerprint" and "footprint." The physical universe, like the human soul, reflects God; each is a rung in the ladder leading to God. Theologians in this tradition give us confidence to believe that "everything belongs" in the circle of life. From this perspective, God "is the intelligible sphere whose center is everywhere and whose circumference is nowhere."

In his seminal work *Original Blessing*, former Dominican scholar Matthew Fox[5] calls for a paradigm shift in religious thinking about human origins and the nature and destiny of human beings, from the fall/redemption paradigm to creation spirituality. The reasons for his appeal are compelling, intellectually and spiritually.

Fox argues that the fall/redemption paradigm, based upon the doctrine of original sin, developed during medieval times and is essentially foreign to scripture. This paradigm, dualistic and patriarchal, considers all nature "fallen" and does not seek God in nature. This tradition does not teach believers about creativity, justice-making, and social transformation, or about the God of play, pleasure, and delight. Unfortunately, this perspective has proven unfriendly to artists, prophets, science, and women. Creation spirituality, on the other hand, begins with original blessing, embodying the biblical emphasis on the goodness of creation.

Whereas fall/redemption theology begins with original sin and ends with redemption, creation theology begins with original blessing and flows to all subsequent blessings, including those we share with our loved ones and those we affirm in creativity, compassion, birthing, and justice-making; all are prefigured in the grace of creation. Creation spirituality does not ignore sin, but views it differently. Boredom, depression, arrogance, violence, addictive behavior—these occur when we are cut off from the sense of grace and blessing. In this respect, original sin is not "original" or primary in time or in biblical theology but derived. Evil, in creation theology, is conceived as neither original nor eternal, but rather as something good gone bad.

Hope for humanity and the future of our planet must be based on a proper understanding of the doctrine of creation, one that is not antithetical to science but rather is the subject of the scientist's search, the source of the prophet's vision, and the subject of the mystic's commitment. According to Fox, the universe loves us every day, and the Creator loves us through creation. The following quotation captures his perspective beautifully:

> Creation is the source, the matrix, and the goal of all things—the beginning and the end, the alpha and the omega. Creation is our common parent, when "our" stands for all things. Creation is the mother of all beings and the father of all beings, the birther and the begetter. It is all-holy; it is awe-filled . . . Creation is never

---

5. Joining the Episcopal Church following his expulsion from the Dominican Order, in 1993 Fox became an Episcopal priest.

finished, never satisfied, never bored, never passive. Creation is always newly born, always making new. . . . How can such a drama be jeopardized as it is today? Only because our species, with its religions, education, moralities, governments, and economics, has lost the sense of creation. When that happens, nothing is holy; nothing seems worth the struggle for justice that is necessary to preserve it. Community dies, and relations no longer exist.[6]

In his writings on creation spirituality, Fox describes spirituality as a way of life characterized by four paths: (1) The Via Positiva: Befriending Creation; (2) The Via Negative: Befriending Darkness; (3) The Via Creativa: Befriending Creativity; and (4) The Via Transformativa: Befriending New Creation. For each path he provides a signpost or commandment (italicized below):

- Via Positiva: *Thou shalt fall in love at least three times a day.* This applies to human beings, to nature in all its magnificence, and also to activities such as music, poetry, and dance. Creation has much to do with falling in love. This first commandment, one of praise, flows from the awe of being alive.

- Via Negativa: *Thou shalt dare the dark.* Every spiritual journey moves from the surface to the depths, and there is no moving from superficiality to depth without entering the dark. "Daring the dark" means entering nothingness and letting it be nothingness while it works its mystery on us. "Daring the dark" also means allowing pain to be pain and learning from it. Being at home in the dark involves relinquishing control—letting go and letting be.

- Via Creativa: *Do not be reluctant to give birth.* Spiritual discipline in the creation tradition is focused on the development of the aesthetic. Beauty, and our role in co-creating it, lies at the heart of the spiritual journey. Such creativity wrestles with the demons and angels in the depths of our psyches, embracing our "shadow" side as well as our visions and dreams. "To give birth" is to enter the Creator's realm. The work of co-creation engages the image of God (*imago dei*) that is in every person, essential for assisting nature and history in carrying on the creativity of the universe.

---

6. Fox, *Creation Spirituality*, 10–11.

Ecumenical, Pluralist, and Eco-Spirituality

- Via Transformativa: *Be compassionate, as your Creator is compassionate.* This commandment, the summation of Jesus' ethical teaching (Luke 6:36), corresponds in meaning to Matthew's passage from the Sermon on the Mount, translated "Be perfect, as your heavenly Father is perfect" (Matt 5:48). A better rendition of Matthew's Greek word *teleios* is: "Be mature" or "Be complete." As Luke's version makes clear, for humans to be perfect or complete is for them to be compassionate to all creatures (Luke 6:36). In this understanding, compassion is not about the actions that flow from a superior to an inferior, but as a result of our interdependence. True compassion, therefore, involves a deep respect for other cultures and traditions and the willingness to work together in our need for mutual wisdom.

If spirituality can be defined as "meeting with God in history," as Leonardo Boff defined it, and if a new spiritual era is emerging, then a new meeting with God is also upon us, providing a self-disclosure of God that is less warlike, less patriarchal, and more concerned with compassion, justice, celebration, beauty, and creativity.[7]

Questions for Discussion and Reflection

1. In a sentence or two, define "ecumenism" and "ecumenical."
2. How do ecumenists differ from fundamentalists?
3. The epistle to the Ephesians uses three images to portray the unity of believers. In your estimation, which of these best epitomizes the solidarity of believers? Explain your answer.
4. What is the meaning of the term "catholic," and when and why did the expression "catholic church" arise?
5. After reading this chapter, what did you learn about the origin of the modern ecumenical movement? Do you consider yourself an ecumenical Christian? Why or why not?
6. In your estimation, should Christians work together toward the ideal of one visible church on earth? If so, what differences must they downplay or eliminate?

---

7. Fox, *Creation Spirituality*, 18–23, 31.

7. Explain and assess the differences between ecumenism and pluralism.

8. Do you consider yourself a particularist, an inclusivist, or a pluralist? Explain your answer.

9. Compare and contrast the fall/redemption paradigm with Matthew Fox's creation spirituality. Which approach do you find most compelling? Explain your answer.

10. In your own words, briefly explain Matthew Fox's four paths of spirituality. Which path most resembles your own? Explain your answer.

13

Secular Spirituality
Late Twentieth- and Twenty-First-Century Piety

THE MIDDLE AGES AND the Reformation were centuries of faith in the sense that reason served faith and the mind obeyed authority. To Catholics it was church authority, to Protestants biblical authority, but in either case, faith came first, not reason. The Enlightenment changed that orientation; reason replaced faith, and concerns for this life replaced preparation for the next. Science, prosperity, and reason became the best guides to happiness, not emotions, myths, or superstition. The spirit of that age was nothing less than an intellectual revolution, a new way of looking at God, the world, and oneself. The Enlightenment gave birth to modernism and its twin, secularism. If hatred of religious bigotry, coupled with a devotion to religious pluralism, has a familiar ring, it is because the modern ethos is not outdated. It lives today in the values of the Western world.

When barbarians destroyed the Western Roman empire in the fifth century, the Christian church put together a new order called the Holy Roman Empire. The underlying concept was Christendom, which united empire and church. Inspired by Old Testament theocratic society (a covenantal community under the rule of God) but likely also by centuries of Roman imperial rule, Latin Christendom began under Charlemagne in the eight century. The crowning of Charlemagne as emperor by Pope Leo III signaled an event that shaped Christian life in the West for the next seven or eight centuries. For the next 800 years and more, the politics, learning, social organization, art, music, economics, and law of Europe would be Christian, at least in name if not always in practice.

The Protestant Reformation resulted in the division of Christendom, but not in its abandonment. The idea of Christendom survived the sixteenth century Reformation practically unscathed. One group, later called Anabaptists or Radical Reformers, protested and established new ecclesiastical and political options, but mainline Protestant Reformers established territorial and state churches, holding to the idea of Christendom as firmly as the Catholics. What they sought was a reformed Christendom, not the possibility of opting out.

Bloody religious conflict between Catholics and Protestants followed the Reformation. The period between 1550 and 1650 witnessed such struggles as the English Civil War, the persecution of French Huguenots, the Spanish Inquisition, and the Thirty Years' War (1618–1648), the deadliest religious war and one of the most destructive conflicts in human history.

While one root of modernity lies in Renaissance humanism, a movement that also gave birth to the Reformation, another root emerged from the state-sponsored religious warfare in the sixteenth and seventeenth centuries. This resulted in the birth of the Enlightenment, an era characterized by a thirst for tolerance and a search for truths common to all people. The architects of this optimistic era soon discovered that a way to achieve peace was to secularize non-religious institutions. Secularity, then, is based on neutral space, and a division of society into sacred and secular realms. In this arrangement, priests would serve God, while princes would serve the people. A distinction of modernity would be this notion that public institutions should be secular and that religion should be private activity. Ironically, two of the chief legacies of the Reformation for the modern world were political secularization and religious privatization, a modern achievement largely unintended by Luther and the mainline Reformers. In this respect, one can define Western modernity as secularized Christendom, its culture Christian in origin and in much of its intellectual resources, and yet, while opposed to religious fanaticism, self-consciously determined to be neutral with respect to religion.

After a rise in religious observance immediately after World War II, during the 1960s, the Western world, starting in Europe, experienced a sudden loss of faith. As young people rebelled against religious, civic, and even parental authority, many adults stopped going to church. In both Europe and the United States, sociologists proclaimed the triumph of secularism. In 1965, Harvard theologian Harvey Cox published *The Secular City*, a best seller that claimed God to be dead and urged religion to focus on humanity rather than on a transcendent deity. If Christianity failed to absorb these new values, churches would disappear. Cox saw the decline of organized religion as a sign of major cultural change, when many of the institutional structures of modernity came into question. Young people called for a just and more equitable society, creating a far-reaching counter-cultural movement.

Despite its rejection of authoritarian religious institutions, the youth culture of the 1960s demanded a more spiritual way of life. Instead of going to church, young people turned to Eastern spirituality, while dabbling in cultic groups, some religious and others primarily psychological. This quest for spirituality, though short-lived, was often wild, self-indulgent, and unbalanced. It was, however, premature to speak of the death of God or even of the death of organized religion.

While modernity's dominance over Western society continues to this day, eventually a new mindset emerged, vying for the allegiance of artists, intellectuals, and visionaries, if not yet the general populace. If philosophy, theology, and mythology can be said to respond to the views of the day, a philosophical movement developed in the 1960s that embraced the optimism of the rationalists, the skepticism of the empiricists, the pessimism of Nietzsche, and the indeterminacy of Einsteinian physics. It is called postmodernism, a way of thinking that builds on the assumption that what we call reality is constructed by the mind, and that human understanding is interpretation rather than acquisition of accurate, objective information. From this it follows that knowledge is relative, subjective, and fallible rather than certain and absolute, and that truth is inherently ambiguous.

While some observers decry this movement as iconoclastic and relativistic, that is, as deconstructive of certainty, truth, and assurance, postmodernism has an upside, for in arguing that humans can never arrive at a wholly accurate version of truth, it opens the door to faith and to polyvalent approaches to questions of truth and meaning. Fundamental to postmodern thought is the conviction that sense data cannot force humans to adopt a particular worldview, whether philosophical, scientific, or religious. Thus, humans have a choice in what they affirm—as well as immense responsibility.

While postmodernism has not meant the death of modernity, it recognizes modernity as a tradition with a specific past and with its own authorities. Due to its complex and ambiguous nature, postmodernism can be divided into two camps, (1) "left-wing" or skeptical forms of thinking, and (2) "right-wing" or self-critical forms. Giving up the quest for certainty, "left-wing" postmodernists deny ultimate authority and overarching truths, thereby abandoning tradition altogether. "Right-wing" postmodernists, likewise, disavow the possibility of certainty, but they affirm the ubiquity of tradition, arguing that all traditions are called to be self-critical of themselves, their rationality, and their claims to certainty and authority. Like science, itself a tradition, "right-wing" postmodernists distinguish between truth and certainty. While traditions such as science and religion enable truth for "right-wing" postmodernists, they exist as "ongoing arguments" rather than as conclusions, remaining open to newness and change, their strength and attractiveness exemplified when advocating debate among themselves and conversation with competing traditions.

The Masters of Suspicion

One early example of this critical "right-wing" mindset is found in French philosopher Paul Ricoeur's (1913–2005) 1973 essay "The Critique of Religion," in which he calls Marx, Nietzsche, and Freud the "masters of suspicion." Unlike medieval and Reformation theologians, who placed great trust in the Bible and Christian theology, and unlike modern philosophers, who placed great trust in the clarity and transparency of human consciousness, the masters of suspicion questioned human consciousness altogether, rejecting the autonomy and transparency of consciousness and, thus, the ability of consciousness to clarify and correct itself. Ricoeur summarized Marx, Nietzsche, and Freud as follows:

1. For Karl Marx (1818–1883), consciousness, including religious ideology, conceals the social origins of alienation and domination.

2. For Friedrich Nietzsche (1844–1900), consciousness, including religious ideology, conceals struggles for power over self, others, and life itself.

3. For Sigmund Freud (1856–1939), consciousness, including religious ideology, is shaped by conflicts at the heart of psychic life, particularly repressed desire and wish fulfillment.

Each of these thinkers saw religion as a product of false consciousness. Rooting the phenomenon of religion in the human psyche, they felt it was not enough to dismiss religion as a mistake. Instead, it is necessary to diagnose religion, to understand it and thus interpret it as a symptom of fundamental conflicts and conditions human beings cannot face.

While these three thinkers employed the hermeneutics of suspicion[1] from an atheistic perspective, Ricoeur wished to employ their tactics as a form of "purification" of religion. In other words, mature faith cannot be based on fantasy and the desire to escape from reality. Such faith must incorporate in some way a hermeneutic of suspicion. The masters of suspicion show us the importance of confronting our "will to power," our economic exploitation, and the reality of our hidden desires, demonstrating how these can work to distort our religious lives. So mature faith must help us confront and defeat our "religious atheism," that is, our overt and covert idols, in order to create space where we can hear a more primal language, which, though addressed to us, we no longer hear.

Influenced by the twentieth century theologians Karl Barth (1886–1968) and Rudolf Bultmann (1884–1976), Ricoeur focused on ways by which we might enhance spiritual receptivity to God's Word. He used the concept of demythologization, finding ways to set aside historical and cultural concerns about the historical Jesus and about what is factual in the Bible, in order to encounter the living Christ through scripture and church worship. For Ricoeur, demythologization meant translating the Bible into ways that make sense today, and thus, to encounter the timeless or core teachings of the Bible rather than its superficial cultural overlay.

This task, however, requires that we direct the hermeneutic of suspicion toward ourselves and our personal values, asking why it is that things make sense to us today. In this regard, we need to be suspicious of our own culture, Ricoeur argued, with its distinct values, including modern and postmodern assertions of human autonomy. Why, for instance, do modern people place hope in material possessions or economic success, and trust in cultural supremacy or on reason? Why are we driven by dominance and control over others, ourselves, and our planet? In this regard, Ricoeur calls us to explore our imagination, using this facility to experience the world in new ways. For example, literature such as poetry, myth, and epic can be revelatory, helping us to see ourselves in new ways. Thus, we must learn to apply poetic creativity to our reading of scripture and to our theological thought. This, for Ricoeur, is the power of

---

1. The term "hermeneutic" refers to a system or methodology of interpreting a concept, a perspective, or a text. The key feature of a hermeneutic of suspicion is that it takes the meaning of religion to be hidden from the consciousness of individual believers.

revelation, that it opens our imagination to the new world of the gospel, to that reality we call the "kingdom of God." This task of opening believers to what Ricoeur calls "the grace of imagination" in revelation is what distinguishes the theistic from the atheistic masters of suspicion. While Ricouer focused on special revelation (through scripture), he remained open to the possibility of general revelation (through history and in nature) as well, for, like an effective Lover, God uses any and all means to connect with the Beloved.

Other scholars, including "liberation theologians," "Black theologians," and "feminist theologians," direct the "hermeneutics of suspicion" against both secular and religious sources of domination and oppression, applying their concerns not only to dominant theological perspectives and religious institutions, but also to the church's complicity in oppressive systems of sexism, racism, and economic exploitation. The Latin American version of liberation theology is shaped by the long history of colonization in that region and by the wide gap between the rich and the poor that it produced. It criticizes the complicity of the church in the oppression. For example, El Salvador's martyred Catholic archbishop, Oscar Romero, spoke of the "beautiful but harsh truth that the Christian faith does not cut Christians off from the world but immerses them in it" as a key for thinking about the way liberation theologians seek to reimagine the task of religious thought.

In his analysis of the masters of suspicion, Ricoeur sought to decode "false consciousness," looking for thinkers that could destroy idols in order to create space where human beings might hear God's Word and engage with God's Will in ways undiluted by human activity. In so doing, he showed how such an approach to religion could deepen "the language of faith" by understanding it as symbolic language that opens up new possibilities for human existence.

Nietzsche's Dance with Nihilism

Postmodernism is not a rejection of modernity but refers to a complex and ambivalent attitude toward modernity grounded in a hermeneutics of suspicion directed at some of modernity's foundational ideas. In *The Gay Science*, sometimes translated as *The Joyful Wisdom* or *The Joyous Science*, published in 1882, Nietzsche criticized religion by arguing that God had died and was no longer relevant.

Let's be clear. For Nietzsche, God had not died literally. Saying that "God is dead" meant that the Christian God was no longer believable. The death of God, however, was not Nietzsche's main point. The real news is that "we have killed him," meaning that modernity had made God irrelevant. The challenge is, are we ready to live with what we have done, that is, to remove all traces of Christian piety from society? In place of religious "slave morality"—timid, anxious, ascetic, and pessimistic—Nietzsche was interested in the possibility of a "gay science," by which he meant ways of living and thinking that were bold, dancelike, experimental, expansive, and daring; self-affirming rather than self-denying, life affirming rather than life-denying.

Closely connecting the death of God with a loss of meaning, the question of how we live after the death of God became crucial for him. His critique of religion also made him suspicious of modernity, including almost everything human beings find valuable and meaningful, including truth and morality. Like Kierkegaard, Nietzsche criticized modernity from an "existentialist" perspective that, unlike the traditionalists or fundamentalists, looked ahead to something beyond modernity.

Nietzsche claimed that for life to have meaning, our wills must have a goal. Affirming the death of God, Nietzsche wonders whether it is possible to find another meaning, another ideal or goal for the will. Nietzsche never directly answers the question of the alternative to religion. He suggests that we may not be in a position yet to answer the question of meaning, but acknowledges that the only real meaning to be found in life is precisely through immersion in our human predicament. In *The Gay Science*, Nietzsche goes into more detail about the ways in which immersion in the problem of truth might be meaningful. He introduces the idea of the "free spirit," contrasting one kind of faith, the "wish for certainty," with another, a faith that allows him to dance near, without plunging into, the abyss of nihilism. This is faith not in another life, not in progress toward a utopia, but in the affirmation of life in all its strange, confusing, and painful reality.

Unlike Platonic and theistic solutions, the goal of life is not to escape this world, this Platonic "cave," with all its suffering and delusion. All humans have is the "cave," and we must learn to embrace it and make the best of it, motivated by what Nietzsche calls the "will to power"—in this case, the will to overcome our sick or guilty conscience. Two approaches, he suggests, enable us to embrace life fully; first, by exploring life with a suspicious eye toward all denials of life, and then by pursuing a kind of creative, artistic effort to make life beautiful. For Nietzsche, the death of God is not primarily about the end of religion but about the beginning of nihilism, a state in which one's life has no overarching goal, orientation, or direction. Nietzsche distinguished two forms of nihilism, the state in which our will wills nothing, and the state of traditional religion, in which people aim at God and goodness, which ultimately are delusions, what Nietzsche called forms of "willing nothingness" and theists call idolatry, meaning false worship or adoration.[2]

Martin Heidegger (1889–1976), the German philosopher widely regarded as one of the most important philosophers of the twentieth century, is most readily associated with phenomenology and existentialism. Exploring the meaning of Nietzsche's death of God, Heidegger argued that it should be understood, not as an actual death of a being that was once alive but has died due to age or neglect, but as the death of metaphysics, the death of a certain way of thinking and doing philosophy.

Bonhoeffer's Call for "Religionless Christianity"

Following the challenges of modern thinkers, including the radical critiques of the "masters of suspicion," the growing secularization of the "first world" in the latter half of the twentieth century further challenged religious thought. The "death of God" movement responded to secular suspicions of religious other-worldliness by embracing secularization. A major influence on these theologies was the German theologian Dietrich Bonhoeffer's call for a "religionless Christianity."

Bonhoeffer (1906–1945), a pastor and theologian who studied under Barth and Bultmann, was arrested and executed by the Nazis for participating in plots against Hitler. Unlike Barth, who stressed the "otherness" of God, Bonhoeffer focused on the unity of God and humanity through Jesus Christ in the church. This idea was explored in his early writings, but it took a sharp turn in his letters from prison. In these writings, Bonhoeffer focuses less on the church as the place of encounter with God and more on how this union is to be found in the secular world.

---

2. In his letters from prison, Dietrich Bonhoeffer notes his disagreement with the usual interpretation of idolatry as "wealth, sensuality, and pride," finding such emphasis unbiblical and merely moralizing. "Idols are things we worship, and idolatry implies that people still worship something." However, according to Bonhoeffer, people nowadays don't worship anything, not even idols. "In that regard," he adds, agreeing with Nietzsche, "we're truly nihilists." *Letters & Papers*, 336.

Disdaining religiosity as something superficial and unchristian, Bonhoeffer writes to his friend Eberhard Bethge,

> You would be surprised, and perhaps even worried, by my theological thoughts and [to] the conclusions that they lead . . . What is bothering me incessantly is the question what Christianity really is, or indeed who Christ really is, for us today . . . We are moving towards a completely religionless time; people as they are now simply cannot be religious any more. Even those who honestly describe themselves as "religious" do not in the least act up to it, and so they presumably mean something quite different by "religious". . . What do a church, a community, a sermon, a liturgy, a Christian life mean in a religionless world? . . . How do we speak in a "secular" way about "God"?[3]

Later he writes, "To be a Christian does not mean to be religious in a particular way . . . It is not the religious act that makes the Christian, but participation in the sufferings of God in the secular world."[4] Bonhoeffer felt that seeking Christ privately, apart from the world, or exclusively through the church were both ways of avoiding the cost of discipleship.

He wrote about modernity as a "world come of age," in which "before God and with God we live without God." In other words, we should come to see modernity not as threatening our unity with God, but as a new, more mature stage of this unity. For Bonhoeffer, "The world that has come of age is more godless, and perhaps for that very reason nearer to God, than the world before its coming of age."[5] This meant that the criticisms of religion found in Marx, Nietzsche, and Freud should be taken seriously, not as blanket condemnations of Christianity, but as ways of understanding that organized religion represents a kind of immature stage of the relation between God and humans.

What became crucial for Bonhoeffer was not the religious form of faith in God and Christ, but faith as discipleship, as following Christ in his work in the world. From this perspective, the point is not to develop theories of God, or cultivate inner spirituality, but to engage others and the world in a Christlike way. At least in some way, this meant, for Bonhoeffer, that we should learn "before and with God to live without God." By so doing, we meet God at the cross, meaning through vulnerability and suffering, rather than in the comfort and convenience of "life as usual." In

---

3. Bonhoeffer, *Letters & Papers*, 279–80.
4. Bonhoeffer, *Letters & Papers*, 361.
5. Bonhoeffer, *Letters & Papers*, 362.

this respect, it is no surprise that Bonhoeffer has had a powerful effect on liberation theology as well as the "death of God" and "secular theology" movement. His death as a martyr prevented him from conceptualizing further the implications of his hypothesis, but a religionless—perhaps even a nontheistic or godless—Christianity appeared on the horizon of his thinking.

Bonhoeffer's writings gained fame and credibility because of his remarkable life. Despite a short life, ended tragically and prematurely at age thirty-nine, Bonhoeffer remains an influential thinker today, inspiring theologians and Christians of widely different persuasions. To a great extent, the influence of Bonhoeffer is based on his life. Active in the ecumenical life of global Christianity, he was one of the first Germans to detect the evil of Nazism. Because of his outspoken criticism of Hitler's regime, he often had to work underground. For a time he was in charge of an illegal seminary, speaking of the strength he gathered from worship in *Life Together*. He left Germany for brief periods, including a time when he was pastor of an English congregation. In 1939, just prior to World War II, he was visiting in the United States. His friends urged him to stay, but he felt he could only participate in the postwar rebuilding of Germany if he had been there through the dark years, so he returned home. While there, he became involved in the underground resistance movement against Nazism, even joining a group that plotted Hitler's death. He was arrested in 1943 and spent two years in prison before his execution on April 9, 1945, just weeks before American troops arrived to liberate his area.

While in prison, Bonhoeffer won the respect of his inmates and guards. The latter allowed him to smuggle out letters to Bethge, published eventually under the title *Letters & Papers from Prison*. He died as he lived, witnessing to his faith. As guards came to take him to his death, he said quietly to an inmate, "This is the end. For me the beginning of life."

A major problem in interpreting Bonhoeffer is deciding what is significant in his letters. Personal in nature, they were never intended for publication. Do they indicate a new direction in his thinking, or should they be understood as extensions of his earlier ideas? Based on such striking phrases as "the world has come of age" and has grown "beyond religion," some scholars argue that Bonhoeffer was moving away from Christianity. Others argue that he had come to see that in order for Christianity to survive in the modern world, it must be restructured. Of course, we will never know precisely what he felt or envisioned about his faith. Perhaps the most we can say is that he was "a creative and dynamic thinker who was continually developing his thought."[6]

Bonhoeffer focused on ethics in his last major work, left incomplete and published posthumously. In *Ethics* (1949) we find many of the themes in the prison letters, often more fully developed than in his letters. Bonhoeffer had a gift for putting his thought into striking phrases, such as "cheap grace" and "costly grace." These concepts, developed in his classic work, *The Cost of Discipleship* (1937), challenged Protestant churches in general and his own Lutheran church in particular with the costly price tag of grace, costly for God and for Jesus and his followers. His book was a call for a radical discipleship that confronts not only secular culture but all forms of Christianity that fail to challenge Christians with the true meaning of discipleship: "When Christ calls a man," he wrote, "He bids him come and die." For Bonhoeffer, the cross is the true measure of discipleship and ethics, for to hear the call of Jesus is to hear the command to follow the crucified and risen Christ in suffering, rejection, and even in death. At the height of World War II, Bonhoeffer was already looking ahead to the postwar world, where he saw that people would need new ways of thinking about their society.

In speaking of society "come of age" and of "religionless Christianity," Bonhoeffer was combatting the popular assumption that humans are religious by nature, or that the religious aspirations of humanity find their most adequate fulfillment in Christianity. This is what Schleiermacher had done by beginning with the universal religious feeling within humans, and arguing from this to the superiority of Christianity. Bonhoeffer also singled out Paul Tillich as an example of approaching unbelievers on the assumption that they are already religious.

If we are to understand Bonhoeffer's call for religionless Christianity, we need to understand what he meant by "religion." Bonhoeffer disdained the word "religion" because of its inherent dualism, that is, as a perspective that divides life and the world into competing spheres, sacred and secular, or holy and profane. Life, for a "religious" person, is the place of tension and conflict between the demands of the sacred and the profane. Religions see certain individuals, professions, acts, and books as sacred and the rest as profane. Religion values the sacred and devalues the profane. Like Luther, Bonhoeffer fought this division, arguing for a unitive consciousness. In speaking of costly grace, Bonhoeffer

---

6. Hordern, *Layman's Guide to Protestant Theology*, 213.

had in mind serving Christ in the world. Rather than separating from society, Christians must be in the world, working in all phases of society to remind humanity that God loves the word, not a world fractured by religion, but united and loved by grace.

Religion has disappeared, Bonhoeffer argued, because humanity has "come of age." The modern world answers all questions and solves all problems without reference to God. It seems, Bonhoeffer states, that God has willfully accepted being edged out of the world and on to a cross because it is not through omnipotence that God saves the world, but rather through weakness. Thus the world, come of age, has cleared the decks for the incarnated, crucified God of the Bible. Jesus offers the opposite of what "religious" humans expect. The biblical God is not calling disciples away from the world and into purely sacred realms and endeavors, but rather is calling us to plunge into the religionless world and share the sufferings of God. In denying the sacred-secular distinctions of religion, Bonhoeffer is also rejecting the inward-outward and individual-social dichotomies of religion. The Old Testament, Bonhoeffer argued, shows no interest in personal or individual salvation and, properly understood, neither does the New Testament.

By "religionless Christianity," Bonhoeffer did not mean to imply that Christians should abandon the church or quit praying and worshiping. However, through his life, he attacked the idea that there are any spheres that do not belong to God. As Christ cannot be confined to the "sacred" society of the church, so Christians should not confine themselves to "sacred" activities or to "inner" spirituality as though it were the sole source and repository of their spiritual talents or resources. The Bible sees humans as a totality, and it is our wholeness that is claimed by God. Thus, the place for the church is not on a hill far away, but at the center of society, not on the borders of life but in the factories, laboratories, and marketplaces of life.

We do not know how Bonhoeffer would have developed his thought had he lived a longer life, but one concept we must examine is his reference to God as being not on the boundaries of life but as "the Beyond in the midst of life." While reaffirming the traditional view that God is both immanent and transcendent, Bonhoeffer emphasized that God is to be found in what we know, not in what we do not know. Often we relegate God to the "gaps" of life, to the realm of mystery or the unknown. However, when we do this, we reduce God, making God too small rather than too large, limiting God to the level of things we already known, only greater. We call God the First Cause because everything needs a cause. However, despite our references to "bigger and better," God has simply become another cog in the wheel, another number in a series. As such, God is no longer the "Beyond."

Nevertheless, if God is the Beyond "in the midst of life," we acknowledge that God is in the processes we know, working through them, yet in a manner and dimension different from them. In Bonhoeffer's sense, God is to be found, "not in a few exotic experiences or situations, but as a dimension in the whole of life."[7] Therefore, Christians are called to plunge fully into the life of this world, not to fall into the shallows of life, the kind of worldliness characterized by the convenient, the busy, the comfortable, or the salacious, and there remain. Faith requires far more, including acquaintance with death and resurrection. To be "in Christ," for Bonhoeffer, is to live fully in the moment, for it is only by living fully in the world that we learn to believe.

Vattimo's "Secular Theology"

The term "secular theology" might sound like an oxymoron, but it has been a significant movement in European and North American Christian theological circles since the middle of the twentieth century. Secular means "worldly," and many see the process called secularization—a process in which religion plays a diminishing role in society—as central to what we are calling modernity. This transformation has occurred in various ways, including in the separation of church and state, and more recently, in the significant decrease in the number of people who consider themselves religious or who regularly attend church worship. We also see the privatization and individualization of religion and note that these trends mean less influence of organized religion on public life.

Bonhoeffer's thought led in various directions, but one such direction was that taken up by the Italian philosopher Gianni Vattimo (born 1936), who describes his book *Belief* as an effort to treat secularization as "the constitutive trait of an authentic religious experience." Vattimo and other contemporary theologians have been influenced by philosophical postmodernism, particularly by Nietzsche and Heidegger. Vattimo appropriates the postmodernism that comes out of Nietzsche and Heidegger by describing secularization as a "purification" of Christianity.

---

7. Hordern, *Layman's Guide to Protestant Theology*, 229.

God's revelation, according to Vattimo, is a revelation of love that Christians are to embody in the world. Vattimo views secularization not as a threat to religion but as the end of the otherworldly "metaphysics" that characterizes traditional religion. Echoing Hegel, he reads the incarnation of Christ as marking the end of such otherworldliness, and understands divine transcendence as the emptying of divine love into the world.

Vattimo argues that from the beginning religion was an essentially interpretive discourse, proceeding by endlessly deconstructing its own sacred texts, so that from the start it had the potential to liberate itself from metaphysical orthodoxy. In opposition to the Enlightenment view, which envisioned freedom as lying in the perfect knowledge of and conformity to the structure of reality, Vattimo substitutes an appreciation of multiple discourses and the contingency and finitude of all religious, ethical, and political values—including our own. He wants to bring down "walls," including the walls that separate theists and atheists; the ideal society should be based on charity rather than truth.

Religion, as described by postmodern philosophers, may sound alien to much "modern" religion, but it evokes many of the insights of the past. Vattimo's claim that religion is essentially interpretive recalls the maxim of the rabbis: "What is Torah? It is the interpretation of Torah." When Vattimo affirms the primacy of charity and the communal nature of religious truth, we recall the rabbis' insistence that "when two or three study Torah together, the Shekinah [the immanence of God] is in their midst." This is also the story of Emmaus and the communal experience of liturgy.

Like Vattimo, the American philosopher John D. Caputo stresses the importance of the apophatic, arguing that atheists and theists alike should abandon the modern appetite for certainty. Such perceptions, once central to religion, tended to be submerged during modernity, and the fact that they have surfaced again in a different form suggests that this type of unknowing is inherent in our humanity. The distinctively modern yearning for absolute and empirically proven truth is most likely an aberration. Noting that atheism is always a rejection of a particular conception of the divine, Caputo concludes: "If modern atheism is the rejection of a modern God, then the delimitation of modernity opens up another possibility, less the resuscitation of premodern theism than the chance of something beyond both the theism and the atheism of modernity."[8]

---

8. Caputo, "Atheism, A/theology," 283.

This raises a tantalizing possibility. If, as Caputo argues, we are entering a "postmodern" phase, is it possible that modern atheism will, like modern theism, become obsolete? Will the growing appreciation of the limitations of human knowledge—which is just as much a part of the contemporary intellectual scene as atheistic certainty—give rise to a new kind of apophatic understanding of theology?

A common criticism of postmodernism is that it is a destructive relativism that only takes things apart, deconstructive of tradition rather than reconstructive. This criticism has made room for what we might call postmodern traditionalism, an approach found in the work of the Jewish thinker Emmanuel Levinas, a philosopher who was born in Lithuania but spent most of his life teaching in Paris. Influenced by Heidegger, Levinas argues that ethics should not be subordinated to metaphysics or epistemology, but rather should be based on the "experience of obligation" for "the other," a transcendent imperative central to all human relationship. For Levinas, it is in the ethical relationship with "the other" and with "otherness," particularly with the suffering of "the other," that we are freed from our human narcissism. This is the way of self-surrender, of divine kenosis;[9] through "surrender to divine justice," we find ourselves related to God. Ultimately, it is faith that allows us to live, make decisions, find meaning, and act morally. Levinas helps us to find a faith freed from the modern distinction between the secular and the religious, a faith freed, you might say, both from metaphysics and from dogma.

Postmodernism as a Way of Unknowing

Philosophy and theology have always responded to the science of the day, and postmodernism is both a philosophical and a theological movement that embraces the indeterminacy of the new physics. Postmodernism is a way of thinking that builds on the assumption that what we call reality is constructed by the mind, and that human understanding is interpretation rather than acquisition of accurate, objective information. From this it follows that our knowledge is relative, subjective, and fallible rather than certain and absolute, and that truth is inherently ambiguous.

Postmodernism is iconoclastic. Inherited ideas are the products of a particular historical and cultural milieu, including the modern emphasis

---

9. The kenosis of Jesus (that is, his self-emptying) is found in Paul's "kenotic hymn" in Philippians 2:6–11.

on reason and science as paths to peace, certainty, and a better future, and therefore are to be deconstructed. Since this analysis is not based on any absolute principle, there is no assurance that we can ever arrive at a wholly accurate version of truth. Fundamental to postmodern thought is the conviction that sense data cannot force us to adopt a particular worldview, so we have a choice in what we affirm—as well as an immense responsibility.

While postmodernism is suspicious of Big Stories—whether theological, scientific, economic, ideological, or political—it is also averse to an atheism that makes absolute, totalistic claims. As Jacques Derrida (1930–2004) cautioned, we must be alert to "theological prejudices," not only in religious contexts, where they are overt, but in all metaphysics—even those that profess to be atheist. Derrida, a secularized Jew, had a messianic hope for a better world and inclined to the view that, since no absolute certainty is within our grasp, for the sake of peace, we should hesitate to make declarative statements of either belief or unbelief. While some religious believers are repelled by such unabashed relativism, there are aspects of Derrida's thought that recall earlier theological attitudes. His theory of deconstruction, which denies the possibility of finding a single, secure meaning in any text, is rabbinical. He has also been called a "negative" theologian, for he was greatly interested in Meister Eckhart, the medieval apophatic mystic.

While today we still find many defenders of the secularization thesis, who view secularization either as inevitable or at least as an ideal toward which America must strive, others argue that secularization is faulty or invalid, and that the resurgence of public religion indicates that modernity is over and that we have entered a postmodern phase of American history, a time of new thinking about the role of religion in public and private life. The spectrum of possibilities is extensive, ranging from "death of God" thinking to increased emphasis on faith and the validity of divine revelation.

For some postmodern thinkers, there really is no such thing as pluralism, whereby one "truth" fits all, and even what we call pluralism is a form of disguised exclusivism. For other postmodern thinkers, the best answer to religious diversity is neither exclusivism, inclusivism, or pluralism, but rather one or another form of secularism. Accepting the general framework of modernity, the state, they argue, should remain separate from religion, and the secular state should guarantee the politics of liberation, that is, a politics of liberty and the pursuit of happiness. Secularism is the ideal for modernists and postmodernists alike, for it seeks to create a context in which people from all faiths and even with no religious faith can debate and engage on a level playing field.

Questions for Discussion and Reflection

1. The author calls the birth of social secularism during the age of Enlightenment "nothing less than an intellectual revolution, a new way of looking at God, the world, and oneself." In your own words, explain the origin and the causes of the phenomenon we label "secular."
2. According to Harvey Cox, the 1960s generated an equally social secular revolution in American society. Did it last? Why or why not?
3. In a sentence or two, define "postmodernism." Is this mindset or movement primarily secular, religious, both secular and religious, or neither?
4. How would you distinguish the hermeneutics of suspicion from Enlightenment questions about religion? How does Ricoeur seek to integrate suspicion into the theological task?
5. What did Nietzsche mean by "nihilism"?
6. In your estimation, what did Nietzsche mean by the "death of God"?
7. Explain why Bonhoeffer's writings have influenced Christian thinkers across the theological spectrum, from modern to postmodern, conservative to liberal.
8. Explain and assess Gianni Vattimo's understanding of the relation of secularization and Christianity?
9. Explain and assess Emmanuel Levinas's notion of postmodern traditionalism.
10. In your estimation, is postmodernism primarily a way of knowing or unknowing? Explain your answer.
11. After completing this book (or class or seminar), has your reflection changed the way you relate to God, to yourself, and to others? If so, how?

Epilogue

SPIRITUALITY IS FOR EVERYONE and in everyone. It is not something human beings acquire during a crisis or at some distinct phase of life. Spirituality—like personality—is in our lives all along. For some, personality and spirituality are ill formed; for others, a strong foundation creates personal and spiritual equanimity, purpose, and vision. The goal of spirituality is not monolithic or one-dimensional. While the goal is always to love and honor God and others, the means of this goal remain open and diverse. As we have seen in our historical survey of spirituality, these twelve phases of spirituality are personal and yet inclusive, multi-faceted and multi-cultural. In mature spiritual thinking and living, personality and individual interests and concerns, led by God and shaped by elements in people's personal stories, determine the focus. Ultimately, it is not what we are or what we have been that counts, but what we want and need to be.

An enormous breakthrough occurs when we honor and accept the divine image within ourselves, for we cannot help but see it in others as well, knowing it is just as undeserved in others as it is in us. That is when we stop judging and how we start loving unconditionally.

In my estimation, all human love has its source and its ultimate object in God. I use the adjective "all" intentionally, having in mind not only the love of a spouse for another or the love of a parent for a child, but also self-love, friendship, attachment to pets, and even desire for material possessions. All love is ultimately rooted in our separation from God and in our goal to return to the God who created us.

Epilogue

I am not the first to utter this claim, for it is certainly biblical. This claim underlies the doctrine of creation, with its emphasis on the universality of the image of God. This claim is central to biblical covenant language, where one faith group is called into existence in order that God's blessing might be extended to all humanity, and it is affirmed in Jesus' declaration that the familial relationship he has with God is intended for all humanity.

The claim that God and humans are inextricably intertwined and eternally interrelated is also affirmed by Augustine in his famous prayer found at the start of his *Confessions*, in which he declares that "to praise you is the desire of humans, this small part of your creation. You motivate humanity to delight in praising you, because you have made us for yourself, and our heart is restless until it rests in you." It is expressed most sublimely by the medieval anchoress Julian of Norwich, who declared in her visionary work, *Revelations of Divine Love*, that despite the messiness of life, God intends to make everything right, for "all will be well, and every conceivable thing will be well" (*Revelations*, 27).[1]

According to Julian, when God created us, "he united us to himself, and this union keeps us as pure and noble as when we were first created" (*Revelations*, 58).[2] Why, then, did God create? she asks. "For love. Hold fast to this and you will learn and understand more and more. But you will never learn or know anything else throughout eternity." God created in love and for love, and in this love, she concludes, "we will live forever. We began when we were created, but the love in which (God) created us had no beginning. Our beginning is in this love, and we shall see all this in God forever and ever" (*Revelations*, 86).[3]

You may have heard the expression, "What you see is what you get." That axiom is as true spiritually as it is in other realms of life. The image of God in you calls forth the image of love in others. Wholeness sees and calls forth wholeness in others. Unconditional love in you calls forth unconditional love in others. Another axiom holds equally true; "What you seek is what you get." If we want others to be more loving, we must choose to love first; if we seek peace in the outer world, we must create it inside first; if we seek a just world, we must start being just ourselves.

---

1. Armstrong, *Visions of God*, 193.
2. Armstrong, *Visions of God*, 207.
3. Armstrong, *Visions of God*, 221.

As the popular contemplative and ecumenically minded theologian Richard Rohr exhorts: "If you want to find God, then honor God within you, and you will always see God beyond you. For it is only God in you who knows where and how to look for God."[4]

---

4. Rohr, *Naked Now*, 161.

Bibliography

Allison, Jr., Dale C. *Constructing Jesus.* Grand Rapids, MI: Baker, 2010.
———. *The Historical Christ and the Theological Jesus.* Grand Rapids, MI: Eerdmans, 2009.
———. *Jesus of Nazareth: Millenarian Prophet.* Minneapolis, MN: Fortress, 1998.
Althaus, Paul. *The Theology of Martin Luther.* Philadelphia: Fortress, 1966.
Anderson, Bernhard W. *Contours of Old Testament Theology.* Minneapolis: Fortress, 1999.
———. *Creation versus Chaos.* New York: Association Press, 1967.
———. *Rediscovering the Bible.* New York: Association Press, 1951.
———. *Understanding the Old Testament.* 5th ed. Upper Saddle River, NJ: Pearson Prentice Hall, 2007.
Armstrong, Karen. *The Case for God.* New York: Anchor, 2010.
———. *A Short History of Myth.* New York: Canongate, 2005.
———. *Visions of God: Four Medieval Mystics and Their Writings.* New York: Bantam, 1994.
Bass, Diana Butler. *Christianity After Religion; The End of Church and the Birth of a New Spiritual Awakening.* New York: HarperOne, 2012.
Bauckham, Richard. *The Theology of the Book of Revelation.* Cambridge: Cambridge University Press, 1993.
Bonhoeffer, Dietrich. *Letters & Papers from Prison.* Edited by Eberhard Bethge. Enlarged ed. New York: Touchstone, 1997.
Borg, Marcus J. *The God We Never Knew.* San Francisco: HarperSanFrancisco, 1998.
———. *The Heart of Christianity: Rediscovering a Life of Faith.* San Francisco: HarperSanFrancisco, 2003.
———. *Meeting Jesus Again for the First Time.* San Francisco: HarperSanFrancisco, 1995.
———. *Reading the Bible Again for the First Time.* San Francisco: HarperSanFrancisco, 2002.
Borg, Marcus, and N. T. Wright. *The Meaning of Jesus: Two Visions.* San Francisco: HarperSanFrancisco, 2000.

Boring, M. Eugene. *Revelation*. Interpretation: A Bible Commentary for Teaching and Preaching. Louisville: John Knox, 1989.

Brown, Raymond E. *The New Jerome Biblical Commentary*. Upper Saddle River, NJ: Prentice Hall, 1990.

Brueggemann, Walter. *Theology of the Old Testament*. Minneapolis: Fortress, 1997.

Caputo, John D. "Atheism, A/theology and the Postmodern Condition." In *The Cambridge Companion to Atheism*, edited by Michael Martin, 267–83. Cambridge: Cambridge University Press, 2007.

Cary, Phillip. *Augustine: Invention of the Inner Self: The Legacy of a Christian Platonist*. New York: Oxford University Press, 2000.

———. *The History of Christian Theology*. The Great Courses Guidebook. Chantilly, VA: Teaching Company, 2008.

———. *Luther: Gospel, Law, and Reformation*. The Great Courses Guidebook. Chantilly, VA: Teaching Company, 2004.

Chopra, Deepak. *The Seven Spiritual Laws of Success*. San Rafael, CA: Amber–Allen, 1994.

Clement, Keith W. *Friedrich Schleiermacher: Pioneer of Modern Theology*. Minneapolis: Fortress, 1991.

Clifford, Richard J. *The Wisdom Literature*. Nashville: Abingdon, 1998.

Cox, Harvey. *The Secular City: Secularization and Urbanization in Theological Perspective*. New York: Macmillan, 1965.

Crenshaw, James L. *Old Testament Wisdom: An Introduction*. Atlanta: John Knox, 1981.

Crossan, John Dominic. *Jesus: A Revolutionary Biography*. San Francisco: HarperSanFrancisco, 1994.

Crossan, John Dominic, and Richard G. Watts. *Who is Jesus?* Louisville, KY: Westminster John Knox, 1996.

Ehrman, Bart D. *A Brief Introduction to the New Testament*. 3rd ed. New York: Oxford University Press, 2013.

———. *The Historical Jesus*. The Great Courses Guidebook. Chantilly, VA: Teaching Company, 2000.

———. *Jesus: Apocalyptic Prophet of the New Millennium*. New York: Oxford University Press, 1999.

———. *The New Testament: A Historical Introduction to the Early Christian Writings*. 7th ed. New York: Oxford University Press, 2020.

———. *The New Testament*. The Great Courses Guidebook. Chantilly, Virginia: Teaching Company, 2000.

Eichrodt, Walther. *Theology of the Old Testament*. Vol. 1. Philadelphia: Westminster, 1961.

Fox, Matthew. *Creation Spirituality*. San Francisco: HarperSanFrancisco, 1991.

———. *Original Blessing*. Santa Fe, NM: Bear & Co., 1983.

Gonzalez, Justo L. *The Story of Christianity*. 2 vols. San Francisco: Harper & Row, 1984.

Gordis, Robert. *The Book of God and Man: A Study of Job*. Chicago: The University of Chicago Press, 1965.

———. *Koheleth—The Man and His World: A Study of Ecclesiastes*. 3rd ed. New York: Schocken, 1968.

Grenz, Stanley J., and Roger E. Olson. *20th-Century Theology: God & the Word in a Transitional Age*. Downers Grove, IL: InterVarsity, 1992.

Bibliography

Henry, Carl F. H. *The Uneasy Conscience of Modern Fundamentalism*. Grand Rapids, MI: Eerdmans, 2003.
Hick, John. *Disputed Questions in Theology and the Philosophy of Religion*. New Haven, Yale University Press, 1993.
———. *God and the Universe of Faiths*. New York: Macmillan, 1973.
Hillers, Delbert R. *Covenant: The History of a Biblical Idea*. Baltimore: Johns Hopkins Press, 1969.
Hoffecker, W. Andrew, and Gary Scott Smith. *Building a Christian World View*. 2 vols. Phillipsburg, NJ: Presbyterian and Reformed, 1986, 1988.
Holmes, Urban T. *The History of Christian Spirituality*. New York: Seabury, 1980.
Hordern, William E. *A Layman's Guide to Protestant Theology*. Rev. ed. New York: Macmillan, 1968.
Jenkins, Philip. *The Next Christendom: The Coming of Global Christianity*. Rev. ed. New York: Oxford University Press, 2007.
Johnson, Luke Timothy. *The History of Christianity: From the Disciples to the Dawn of the Reformation*. 2 vols. Chantilly, VA: Great Courses, 2012.
Jones, Cheslyn, et al. *The Study of Spirituality*. New York: Oxford University Press, 1986.
Kee, Howard Clark. *Community of the New Age: Studies in Mark's Gospel*. Philadelphia: Westminster, 1977.
Kee, Howard Clark, et al. *Christianity: A Social and Cultural History*. 2nd ed. Upper Saddle River, NJ: Prentice Hall, 1998.
Koterski, Joseph W. *Biblical Wisdom Literature*. Lecture Transcript of 36 Lectures. Chantilly, VA: Great Courses. 2009.
Latourette, Kenneth Scott. *A History of Christianity*. New York: Harper & Brothers, 1953.
Levinas, Emmanuel. *Otherwise than Being, or, Beyond Essence*. Pittsburgh, PA: Duquesne University Press, 2002.
Lewis, C. S. *The Abolition of Man*. New York: Macmillan, 1947.
Lindbeck, George. *The Nature of Doctrine*. Philadelphia: Westminster, 1984.
Lull, Timothy. *Martin Luther's Basic Theological Writings*. Minneapolis: Fortress, 1989.
MacCulloch, Diarmaid. *Christianity: The First Three Thousand Years*. New York: Viking, 2009.
———. *The Reformation: A History*. New York: Viking, 2003.
Marsden, George W. *Fundamentalism and American Culture: The Shaping of Twentieth-Century Evangelicalism, 1870–1925*. New York: Oxford University Press, 2006.
McGinn, Bernard M. *The Presence of God: A History of Western Christian Mysticism*. Vol. 1. New York: Crossroad, 1991.
McGrath, Alister E. *Christian Theology: An Introduction*. 5th ed. Malden, MA: Wiley-Blackwell 2011.
McManners, John. *The Oxford Illustrated History of Christianity*. New York: Oxford University Press, 1990.
Murphy, Roland F. *The Tree of Life: An Exploration of Biblical Wisdom Literature*. 3rd ed. Grand Rapids, MI: Eerdmans, 2002.
Noll, Mark A. *Turning Points: Decisive Moments in the History of Christianity*. 3rd ed. Grand Rapids, MI: Baker Academic, 2012.
O'Connor, Kathleen M. *The Wisdom Literature*. Collegeville, MN: Liturgical, 1990.
Pelikan, Jaroslav. *Luther's Works*. St. Louis: Concordia, and Philadelphia: Fortress, 1955–1976.

Plantinga, Alvin, and Nicholas Wolterstorff. *Faith and Rationality: Reason and Belief in God*. Notre Dame, IN: University of Notre Dame Press, 2004.

Reagan, Charles E., and David Stewart. *The Philosophy of Paul Ricoeur: An Anthology of His Work*. Boston: Beacon, 1978.

Rist, J. M. *Augustine: Ancient Thought Baptized*. New York: Cambridge University Press, 2003.

Roberts, Tyler. *Skeptics and Believers: Religious Debate in the Western Intellectual Tradition*. Course Guidebook. Chantilly, VA: Teaching Company, 2009.

Rohr, Richard. *Falling Upward: A Spirituality for the Two Halves of Life*. San Francisco: Jossey-Bass, 2011.

———. *Immortal Diamond: The Search for Our True Self*. San Francisco: Jossey-Bass, 2013.

———. *The Naked Now: Learning to See as the Mystics See*. New York: Crossroad, 2009.

———. *The Universal Christ*. New York: Convergent, 2019.

———. *What the Mystics Know*. New York: Crossroad, 2015.

Sanders, E. P. *Jesus and Judaism*. Minneapolis: Fortress, 1985.

———. "Jesus: His Religious Type." *Reflections* 87 (1992) 4–12.

———. Paul, the Law, and the Jewish People. Minneapolis, Fortress, 1983.

Schweitzer, Albert. *The Quest of the Historical Jesus*. New York: Macmillan, 1968.

Shelley, Bruce L., and R. L. Hatchett. *Church History in Plain Language*. 4th ed. Nashville: Thomas Nelson, 2013.

Spong, John Shelby. *Eternal Life: A New Vision*. New York: HarperOne, 2009.

———. *Liberating the Gospels: Reading the Bible with Jewish Eyes*. San Francisco: HarperSanFrancisco, 1996.

———. *A New Kind of Christianity for a New World*. New York: HarperOne, 2001.

———. *Rescuing the Bible from Fundamentalism*. San Francisco: HarperSanFrancisco, 1991.

———. *The Sins of Scripture*. New York: HarperOne, 2006.

———. *Why Christianity Must Change or Die*. New York: HarperOne, 1999.

Stark, Rodney. *The Rise of Christianity*. Princeton, NJ: Princeton University Press, 1996.

Starr, Mirabai. *The Showings of Julian of Norwich*. Charlottesville, VA: Hampton Roads, 2013.

Taylor, Charles. *A Secular Age*. Cambridge, MA: Belknap Press of Harvard University Press, 2003.

Urban, Linwood. *A Short History of Christian Thought*. Rev. ed. New York: Oxford University Press, 1995.

Vande Kappelle, Robert P. *Adventures in Spirituality: A Journey from Belief to Faith*. Eugene, OR: Wipf & Stock, 2020.

———. *Beyond Belief: Faith, Science, and the Value of Unknowing*. Eugene, OR: Wipf & Stock, 2012.

———. *The Church Alumni Association: A Handbook for Believers in Exile*. Eugene, OR: Wipf & Stock, 2021.

———. *Dark Splendor: Spiritual Fitness for the Second Half of Life*. Eugene, OR: Resource, 2015.

———. *Hope Revealed: The Message of the Book of Revelation–Then and Now*. Eugene: OR: Wipf & Stock, 2013.

———. *The New Creation: Church History Made Accessible, Relevant, and Personal*. Eugene, OR: Wipf & Stock, 2018.

———. *Refined by Fire: Essential Teachings in Scripture.* Eugene, OR: Wipf & Stock, 2018.
———. *The Second Journey: Visions and Voices on First- and Second-Half-of-Life-Spirituality.* Eugene, OR: Wipf & Stock, 2020.
———. *Securing Life: The Enduring Message of the Bible.* Eugene, OR: Wipf & Stock, 2016.
———. *Wisdom Revealed: The Message of Biblical Wisdom Literature–Then and Now.* Eugene, OR: Wipf & Stock, 2014.
Vattimo, Gianni. *Belief.* Stanford, CA: Stanford University Press, 1999.
Walker, Williston. *A History of the Christian Church.* 4th ed. New York: Scribner, 1985.
Williams, Rowan. *On Christian Theology.* Oxford: Blackwell, 2003.
Worthen, Molly. *The History of Christianity II: From the Reformation to the Modern Megachurch.* 2 vols. Chantilly, VA: Great Courses, 2017.
Wright, Robert. *The Evolution of God.* New York: Little, Brown, 2009.

Index

Abraham (patriarch), 12–13, 14, 16, 23, 125, 126, 127, 137, 160
afterlife, doctrine of, 37, 67, 93, 94, 147
Alexander the Great, 44
Amos (prophet), 20, 40
Anabaptists, 90, 101, 106, 107, 110, 188
Anselm of Canterbury, 69–70, 85
apocalyptic(ism)
    and Christian theology, 56–58
    as ideology, 46
    literature, 52
apophatic, 63, 133, 200, 201
Apostles Creed, 96, 98
Aquinas, Thomas (Thomism), 64, 66, 72, 73, 133, 142, 149
Arndt, Johann, 110, 111
atheism, 140, 147, 180, 200, 201
    religious, 191
Augustine, 62–71, 72, 103, 117, 131, 133, 136, 142, 165, 205
    and authority, 65–66
    church and politics, 78–79
    and evil, 70–71
    and faith, 64–65
    and free will, 66–67, 68–69
    and grace, 66–69, 70, 71
    and happiness, 62, 63
    and knowledge, 65
    and love, 62–63, 66–67, 68–69, 70, 71
    and merit, 66, 89
    and spirituality, 62–69, 85, 87, 92, 103
    and truth, 63, 65
Ávila, Teresa, 74

Babylonian exile, 28, 32, 53
Bacon, Francis, 144
Baptists, 106, 107, 108, 109, 147, 157
Barth, Karl, 129–37, 151, 153, 158, 159, 191, 194
Bass, Diana, 2
Beard, Charles A., 33
benefice, 78, 81, 84
Bernard of Clairvaux, 72, 91
Bible, 117, 130, 132, 157, 173, 181, 191
    authority of, 43, 74, 101, 105, 106, 109, 157, 158, 159–60, 161, 167, 181, 187
    as fallible, 133
    as inerrant, 156, 167, 181
    as infallible, 158, 159, 167
    inspiration of, 132
    interpretation of, 160–69
    spirituality of, 11–58
    study of, 43, 112
    theology of, 43
Black Death, 85
Boff, Leonardo, 185
Bonaventure, 73, 182
Bonhoeffer, Dietrich, 151, 194–99

Buddhism, 4
   Zen, 121
Bultmann, Rudolph, 191, 194

Calvin, John, 67, 71, 85, 101, 105, 136, 142, 168
Camus, Albert, 121, 122, 123
Caputo, John D., 200, 201
Cary, Phillip, 62
Chopra, Deepak, 7
Christendom, 81, 82, 89, 105, 123, 125, 173, 178, 187, 188
Christianity, 56, 82, 107, 114, 117, 119, 123, 125, 137, 141–42, 148, 172, 173, 176–77, 189, 196
   and apocalypticism, 56–58
   emergence of, 44–45
   evangelical, 156, 158–60
   purification of, 199
   religionless, 194–99
church, 89, 90, 106
   catholic, 173
   images of, 172
   marks of, 173
   as reformed, 162
   and society, 78–82, 90, 106, 107–8, 198, 199
Cloud of Unknowing, The, 64, 73
conscience, 85–87, 91, 96, 114, 149, 161
Constantine (emperor), 44, 61, 71
conversion, religious, 111, 158, 178
corporate personality, 11, 19
covenant
   definition of, 15
   lawsuit, 19–22
   theology, 13–22, 41
Cox, Harvey, 189
creation, doctrine of, 13–14, 53–54, 183–84, 205
creation spirituality, 183, 184

Daniel, book of, 31, 40, 52–53, 56
deism, 141–48, 181
Denys the Areopagite, 63, 64, 149
Derrida, Jacques, 202
Descartes, René, 140, 144, 145
Deuteronomy, book of, 18, 40
dualism, dualistic, 3–5, 14, 38, 52, 197

Duns Scotus, John, 73

Ecclesiastes, book of, 31, 33, 35, 39
Eckhart, Meister, 73, 202
ecospirituality, 181–85
ecumenical movement, 154, 173–76, 196
Eichrodt, Walter, 14, 15
election, doctrine of, 12–13, 135, 136–37
Elijah (prophet), 25, 26
Enlightenment, 15, 113, 139, 140, 142, 143, 145, 146, 148, 169, 187, 188, 200
Erasmus, Desiderius, 162
eschatology, biblical, 51, 56–58
ethics. *See* morality
evil, 31, 46, 47, 48, 52, 54, 55, 58, 92, 112, 183
exclusivism, 171, 177, 180, 202
excommunication, 81, 82, 96
existentialism, 121–29, 130, 149, 169, 193, 194
exodus, the, 17, 23

faith, 13, 62, 69, 89, 101, 103, 106, 109, 110, 123, 126, 131, 134, 140, 149, 189, 193, 195, 199, 201, 202
   justification by, 91, 95, 96, 97, 98, 100
   leap of, 128
   mature, 191
   paradox of, 128
   and reason, 156, 187
Fosdick, Harry Emerson, 149
Fox, George, 107
Fox, Matthew, 3, 183–85
Francis of Assisi, 72, 73, 182
Francke, August Hermann, 111
Franklin, Benjamin, 147
free will, 66, 68, 69
Freud, Sigmund, 190, 195
fundamentalism. *See* religious, fundamentalism

God, 8, 87, 132–34, 143, 181, 182, 185, 194, 195, 198, 199, 204, 205, 206
   becoming like, 69

Index

as covenant partner, 11–26
as Creator, 127, 205
and death, 87
death of, 189, 192–93, 194, 196, 202
as the Eternal, 129
eternal purpose of, 137
existence of, 139, 140, 141
experience of, seeing, 60, 61, 62, 63, 64, 67, 70, 103, 108, 114, 115, 128, 133–34
immanence of, 200
incomprehensibility of, 63, 64
as the Infinite, 114, 115
judgment of, 85, 86, 91, 92, 99
knowing, 62, 63, 64, 67, 69, 70, 131, 134, 148
love of, 68, 99, 172, 192
loving, 66–67, 68, 69, 70, 71, 91–92
name of, 24
presence with humanity, 22–26
reconciliation with, 118
as righteous, 18, 98, 103
as Savior, 137
as Self, 7
transcendence of, 132
trusting, 87, 103, 126
as ultimate Reality, 5, 6, 177, 178, 179–80
gospel, 13, 87, 92, 124, 137, 152
and law, 87
grace, 8, 13, 17, 41, 63, 68, 69, 70, 71, 86, 92, 109, 118, 134, 137, 142, 158, 197, 198
assisting, 67
cooperative, 66, 67, 142
and death, 87, 90
and free will, 66, 68
operative, 66, 67, 142
supernatural, 64
See also Augustine, and grace
See also Luther, and grace
Gutenberg, Johannes, 84

happiness, 62, 64, 66
Harnack, Adolf von, 149
heaven, 62, 68, 76, 181
Hegel, G. W. F., 124, 126, 146, 200
Heidegger, Martin, 121, 194, 199, 201

hell, 70, 76, 81, 82, 86, 93, 99, 156, 181
Henry, Carl F. H., 158–60
Herder, Johann G. von, 169
Hick, John, 177–81
Hildegard of Bingen, 72
Hinduism, 4
Hobbes, Thomas, 144–45
Hodge, Charles, 156
holistic, 4, 5, 6, 41
Holy Spirit, 6, 7, 60, 69, 101, 108, 109, 111, 133, 135, 148, 161, 163, 164, 168, 169, 171, 172
Hosea (prophet), 21
humanism, humanist, 14, 113, 126, 143, 150, 162, 169, 188

inclusivism, 176, 177, 202
indulgences, 93, 94, 95
interdict, 81, 82
Isaiah (prophet), 21, 22, 26, 33, 40, 52, 53–55
Islam, 4, 146, 179
Israel, Israelites, 11, 12, 14, 15, 16, 17, 19, 24, 26, 32
postexilic (Restoration) period, 28, 29, 32, 33
sages, 14, 31, 33, 34–38
wisdom literature of, 31–41
themes of, 31, 36–37

James, book of, 37
Jefferson, Thomas, 148
Jeremiah (prophet), 20–21, 22, 26
Jerome, 65, 72
Jesus Christ, 7, 26, 37, 43, 61, 86–87, 92, 94, 97, 98, 106, 119, 128, 134, 135, 136–37, 148, 153, 154, 165, 172, 173, 205
as apocalyptic Jew, 45–51
crucifixion of, 45, 57, 58
as divine teacher, 128
as ethical teacher, 147
ethical teaching of, 49–50. 185
historical, 45, 46, 191
as King of the Jews, 51, 56
as Logos, 5, 34
as Messiah, 50, 51, 148
resurrection of, 56–57, 58

Jesus Christ (*cont.*)
  as Son of Man, 48, 56
  uniqueness of, 181
  as wisdom of God, 37
  and wisdom spirituality, 37–38
  as Word of God, 133, 158
Jewish, Judaism, 4, 5, 32, 146, 179
Job, book of, 31, 33, 35, 37, 39
John of the Cross, 74
John the Baptist, 46, 48
Judas Iscariot, 50–51
Julian of Norwich, 74, 171–72, 205
justification. *See* faith, justification by

Kant, Immanuel, 112, 115–16, 121, 140, 146, 148–49
Kempe, Margery, 86
Kierkegaard, Søren, 121, 122–29, 130
kingdom of God, 46, 47, 48, 49, 50, 51, 52, 53, 56, 57, 58, 130, 151, 173, 192

lay investiture, 79–80
Levinas, Emmanuel, 201
Lewis, C. S., 5
Lex Talionis, 18
liberalism, 155
  theological, 6, 117, 130, 131, 132, 149, 150, 151, 152, 155, 156, 157, 169
literalism, biblical, 160–65, 171, 181
liturgy, liturgical, 11, 29, 61, 108
love, 62–63, 87, 91–92, 106, 128, 133, 153, 172, 204, 205
  See also Augustine, and love
  See also Luther, and love
Loyola, Ignatius, 5, 74
Luther, Martin, 66, 67, 68, 69, 71, 84, 85, 87, 111, 123, 142, 168, 188, 197
  and belief, 103
  and the church, 105
  and "clarity" of scripture, 160–65, 168
  and divine judgment, 85
  and faith spirituality, 89–103
  and gospel, 92, 94, 96–99, 101, 102
  and grace, 92, 93, 94, 95, 97
  and law, 92, 97, 98, 100–103
  and love, 91–92
  and merit, 95, 98, 101, 103
  and promise, 97–98, 98–99, 102, 103
  and scripture, 95
  and sin, 102

Machiavelli, Niccolò, 84
Marx, Karl, 121, 190, 195
Mass, 76, 77, 78, 86, 108
masters of suspicion, 190–92, 194
merit, 69, 85, 103, 142
  See also Augustine, and merit
  See also Luther, and merit
Micah (prophet), 21–22, 40
millennialism, 157
missionary movement, 173–74
modernism, modernity, 109, 121, 139, 140, 141, 149, 151, 152, 155, 156, 157, 158, 187, 188, 189, 192, 195, 199, 200, 202
  definition of, 139, 140
monasticism, 61, 71–74, 77, 80
monism, 5
morality, 62, 69, 114, 125, 126, 143, 147, 148, 201
  social, 150–54
Moravians, 116
Moses, 14, 15, 16, 17, 20, 23–25, 26, 134, 163
Murphy, Roland, 39
mystic/al, 5, 6, 60

nature-grace dualism, 142
neo-orthodoxy, 129, 130, 137, 151, 159
Newton, Isaac, 143
Niebuhr, Reinhold, 150, 151–54
Nietzsche, Friedrich, 121, 189, 190, 192–94, 199
nihilism, 193
nondualistic. *See* holistic

O'Connor, Kathleen, 38

papacy, 78, 79, 80, 81, 82, 83, 85, 94, 95
  Babylonian captivity of, 83
  Renaissance, 84, 93
particularism, 177

Index

Paul (apostle), 48, 56, 58, 61, 69, 90, 91, 100, 101, 117, 130, 132, 134, 160, 166, 171, 172
   letters of, 37
Pax Romana, 45–46
penance, 86, 91, 92, 94
Penn, William, 108
Philo, 34
pietism, pietist, 6, 105–12, 163, 169
   definition of, 112
piety, 1, 5
pluralism. *See* religious, pluralism
Poe, Edgar Allan, 124
poetry, 29
polarity, polarities, 1, 3, 4
postexilic. *See* Israel, postexilic (Restoration) period
postmodern(ism), 129, 189, 192, 199, 201, 202
predestination, 136
Presbyterian(s), 157, 178
presuppositionalism, 159
prophets, prophetic, 13, 14, 17, 32, 41
   and eschatology/apocalyptic, 51–55
   task of, 19–22
Protestant, 66, 74, 77, 90, 105, 109, 113, 129, 144, 155, 156, 160, 162, 173, 187, 188
   liberalism. *See* liberalism, theological
   Reformation, Reformers, 68, 69, 71, 74, 77, 83, 84, 89–103, 105, 106, 108, 117, 140, 148, 162, 163, 168, 173, 187–88
   Scholasticism, 110
proverb, 39
Proverbs, book of, 31, 33, 34, 35, 36, 39
psalms, 23, 28–31, 40
purgatory, 76, 86, 93, 94
Puritanism, 105, 107, 109

Quakers, 106, 108, 109, 147

Rahner, Karl, 177
Rauschenbusch, Walter, 150
reason, rationalism, 112, 114, 115, 140, 142, 143, 144, 147, 148, 187
Reformers, Reformation. *See* Protestant, Reformation

religion, 1–3, 5, 8, 60, 117, 131, 139, 140, 141, 146, 151, 180, 190–91, 192, 193, 200
   decline of, 188–89
   natural, 147, 148, 181
   and politics, 78–82, 202
   purification of, 191
religious, 1, 5, 6, 23, 119, 131, 140, 179–80, 190, 195, 197
   fundamentalism, 137, 151, 152, 155–60, 163–65, 169, 171, 178, 181, 193
   pluralism, 176–81, 187, 202
   and spiritual, 1–3
religiousness, 126
Renaissance, the, 72, 144, 162, 169, 188
revelation, 131–34, 142, 143, 147, 158, 191, 192, 202
   existential, 132, 159
   general, 131–32, 192
   natural, 143, 147, 149
   special, 131–32, 192
   verbal, propositional, 132, 159
Revelation, book of, 44, 55, 58
Ricoeur, Paul, 190–92
Rohr, Richard, 206
Roman Catholicism, 66, 68, 74, 76, 89, 90, 91, 95, 105, 108, 113, 160, 162, 169, 175, 176, 187, 188
Rumi, Jalaluddin, 178

sages. *See* Israel, sages
salvation, 66, 68, 69, 81, 86, 89, 91, 97, 101, 103, 109, 120, 128, 134, 135, 136, 137, 142, 156, 177, 178, 181, 198
Sartre, Jean-Paul, 121, 122, 123
Satan, 4, 52, 55
Schleiermacher, Friedrich, 112–20, 129, 131, 135, 197
Schweitzer, Albert, 46
Scopes Trial, 157–58
secular, secularization, 9, 39, 78, 108, 130, 187–89, 194, 199–200, 202
self, 7
Self. *See* God, as Self
Septuagint, 32

Sermon on the Mount, 44, 49, 148, 151, 185
sin, 66, 86, 92, 99, 102, 117–18, 120, 128, 137, 142, 152, 153, 183
Sirach, book of, 31, 32, 35, 36, 41
Smith, Cantwell, 4
Son of Man, 47, 48, 49, 50, 51, 56
Spener, Jacob Philip, 110, 111
Spirit. *See* Holy Spirit
spiritual, 1–3, 5, 6
spirituality, 1–3, 5, 6–7, 8, 9, 11, 184–85, 204
   apocalyptic, 43–58
   and conscience, 85–87
   and corporate worship, 28–31
   covenant, 11–26
   definition of, 5, 6–7, 8, 185, 199
   deist, 145–49
   ecological, 181–85
   ecumenical, 171–76
   ethical, 139, 141–42, 147, 148–49, 150–54
   existential, 121–29
   fundamentalist, 155–60, 163–65
   goal of, 9, 62, 204
   medieval, 61–71, 76–78, 85–87, 93, 161
   monastic, 71–74
   and morality, 39
   mystic, 60–74
   penitential, 76–87
   and personality, 204
   phases of, 9
   pietist, 105–20
   pluralist, 176–81
   Reformation, 89–103
   Romantic, 112–20
   secular, 187, 188–89, 194–95, 199, 201, 202–3
   stages of, 8
   task of, 8
   wisdom, 31–41
      See also Israel, wisdom literature, themes of
suffering, 37

Tao, Taoism, 4, 5
Ten Commandments, 17, 21, 25, 86
Tertullian, 182
theology, 131, 134, 140, 142, 146, 151
   dialectical, 131, 134, 135–36
   liberal. *See* liberalism, theological
   liberation, 192, 196
   secular, 196, 199
Tillich, Paul, 197
Torah, 5, 22, 26, 30, 31, 32, 33, 34, 40, 146, 200
tradition, 161, 163, 164, 189–90, 201
Trinity, the, 133, 135, 179
Troeltsch, Ernst, 89
truth, religious, 128, 129, 132, 140, 143, 156, 189, 200
Tyndale, William, 84

Unitarian, 147
universalism, 137

Vatican Two, 175, 176
Vattimo, Gianni, 199–200
Voltaire, 145
Vulgate, 65, 84

wisdom
   sources of, 36
   and spirituality, 38–41
   See also Israel, wisdom literature; sages
Wisdom, book of, 31, 32, 40–41
wisdom literature. See Israel, wisdom literature
worship, 68–69
   corporate, 28–31
   individual, 31, 32
Wycliffe, John, 84

yang, 4
yin, 4

Zwingli, Ulrich, 101, 105

www.ingramcontent.com/pod-product-compliance
Lightning Source LLC
Chambersburg PA
CBHW070316230426
43663CB00011B/2146